IMAGES
of America

LAKEWOOD

LAKEWOOD INSTITUTIONS

The institutions of Lakewood are many and diverse. They have been organized and are maintained in perfect condition to meet the needs of residents and guests. Spiritual, mental and physical demands are anticipated by these institutions.

Georgian Court College for young ladies, under the guidance of the Sisters of Mercy, is a liberal arts college.

St. Mary's Academy, a parochial school for young children.

The Paul Kimball Hospital, affiliated with the American Hospital Association is designated a Class A Hospital by the American College of Surgeons.

Several nursing homes cater exclusively to convalescents.

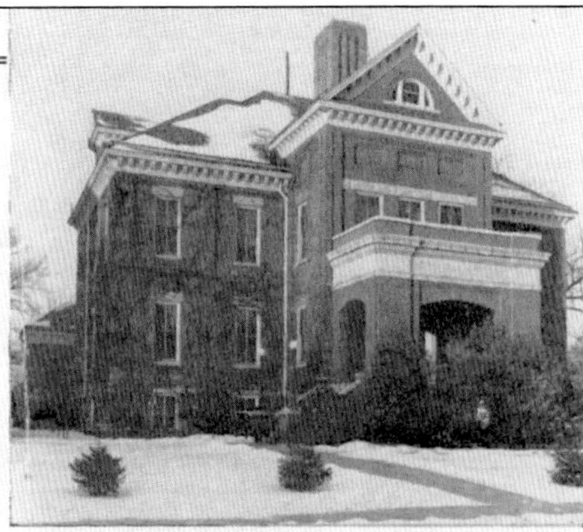

Municipal Building

Third Street, between Clifton and Lexington Aves.

OFFICES IN BUILDING

Township Clerk
Board of Health
Police Department
Tax Collector
Building Inspector
Welfare Officer and Overseer of Poor
Treasurer
Selective Service Board No. 1
O.P.A. Rationing Board
Municipal Court Room
License Bureau
Board of Assessors
Visiting Nurse
Chamber of Commerce

LAKEWOOD INSTITUTIONS

A high school and two grade schools, with 58 class rooms, provide for approximately 2,000 pupils. The school faculty includes 61 teachers, four principals and a supervising principal. The system is one of the most modern in the state.

There are ten churches, one synagogue, a Jewish Center, and four churches for Negroes.

Lakewood Talmud Torah, conducts classes throughout the year for the teaching of the Jewish religion. YMCA and YWCA buildings open daily. Reading and recreation rooms, gyms. Bowling alleys and swimming pool at YMCA. Red Cross headquarters at YWCA.

Public Library open daily. Department for children.

FOR FURTHER INFORMATION
PUBLICITY DEPARTMENT
LAKEWOOD, NEW JERSEY

A Pictorial Guide to the Township of Lakewood, created by John Edward Bedell, was published by the Lakewood Chamber of Commerce *c.* 1942. John Edward Bedell was one of three sons of John Allison Bedell and Lillian S. Havens Bedell. John Allison Bedell once operated a successful and popular sheet metal business in town, and Lillian S. Havens Bedell served for a period of time as the treasurer of Lakewood Township.

Cover Image: Pictured on the cover is John Davison Rockefeller posing with a group of local Boy Scouts as he prepares to hand out his 10¢ trophies. Known for his charity, Rockefeller handed out a lot of shiny new dimes over the years.

IMAGES
of America

LAKEWOOD

Scott M. Kozelnik

ARCADIA
PUBLISHING

ISBN 978-0-7385-0458-2

Published by Arcadia Publishing
Charleston, South Carolina

Printed in the United States of America

Library of Congress Catalog Card Number: 00104060

For all general information contact Arcadia Publishing at:
Telephone 843-853-2070
Fax 843-853-0044
E-mail sales@arcadiapublishing.com
For customer service and orders:
Toll-Free 1-888-313-2665

Visit us on the Internet at www.arcadiapublishing.com

Contents

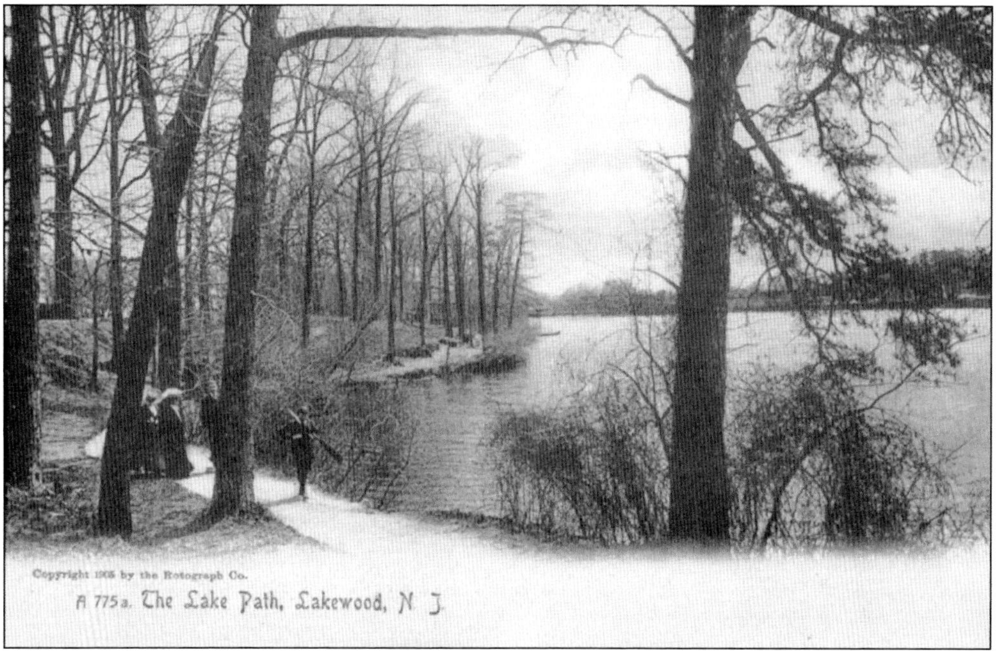

Close nestled in the Pines,
With moss and laurel dressed,
Fair Lakewood offers many charms,
To those in search of rest;
Her air is like a breath of dawn,
Kindling anew the spirit worn...

—Selection from an advertising pamphlet for the prestigious Laurel-in-the-Pines Hotel.

This book is dedicated to my mother, Irene Kozelnik, and my late father, Daniel G. Kozelnik. Both of them, in different ways, instilled in me the strong work ethic with which this book was written.

INTRODUCTION

The city of Lakewood is located in south central New Jersey in Ocean County. It is centered equally between New York City and Philadelphia, and its eastern border is about 6 miles from the Atlantic Ocean. The area of Lakewood covers about 25 square miles.

The Township of Lakewood was incorporated in 1892 after separating from Brick Township. The area we now know as Lakewood had four different prior names. The territory was first designated Three Partners' Mill and then Washington's Furnace, followed by the Bergen Iron Works, Bricksburg, and then finally Lakewood in 1892. The first industry in the area consisted of a lumber mill, bog iron mining, and a blast iron furnace. During the late 1800s and early 1900s, Lakewood became one of the most successful and frequented winter resorts in the United States. Lakewood was promoted as having a warmer climate than New York and other northern cities during the winter. Lakewood's hotel industry included the Laurel House, the Lakewood Hotel, and the Laurel-in-the-Pines, which were considered to be some of grandest structures in the world at that time.

The vacation season in Lakewood was from October to May; during these months visitors enjoyed numerous activities including polo, golf, carriage and sleigh rides, ice-skating, hunting, dances, teas, and much more. The infrastructure around town quickly developed to address the entertainment needs of the numerous vacationers. A boardwalk, boathouse, and casino were constructed on the north side of Lake Carasaljo, which added to the ambiance of the already impressive pine-laden lakeshore. Some of the vacationers became so impressed with the charm of the area that they purchased real estate in town and called Lakewood their home. Some of these visitors-turned-residents included such famous figures as John Davison Rockefeller, George Jay Gould, and Charles Pack.

Lakewood has gone through incredible metamorphoses from sleepy mill town, to grand resort and entertainment center, to industrial competitor. This book should not be misconstrued as a complete history of the Township of Lakewood. It should be used as a vehicle, allowing you to touch upon some of the people and places that made Lakewood's past so memorable. I hope you enjoy the outstanding array of historical photographs and documents that have been used to complete this work. Thank you.

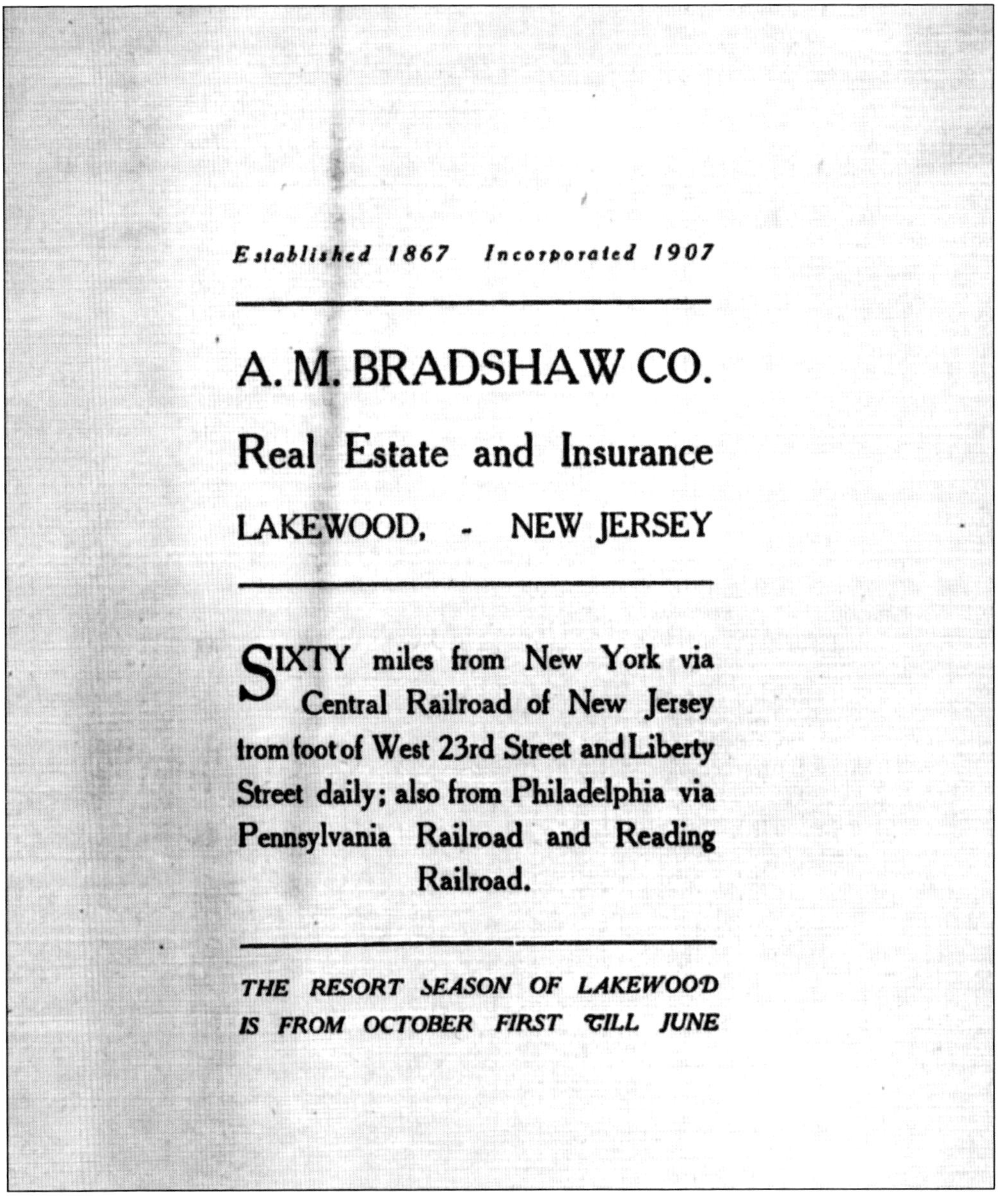

Albert M. Bradshaw served as captain and army quartermaster during the Civil War. After the war he settled in the area and became interested in real estate. He established the A.M. Bradshaw Company in 1867. He took on as a partner Walter C. O'Leary and incorporated the company in 1907. Bradshaw had a very influential role in the incorporation and of Lakewood in 1892.

One

AROUND TOWN

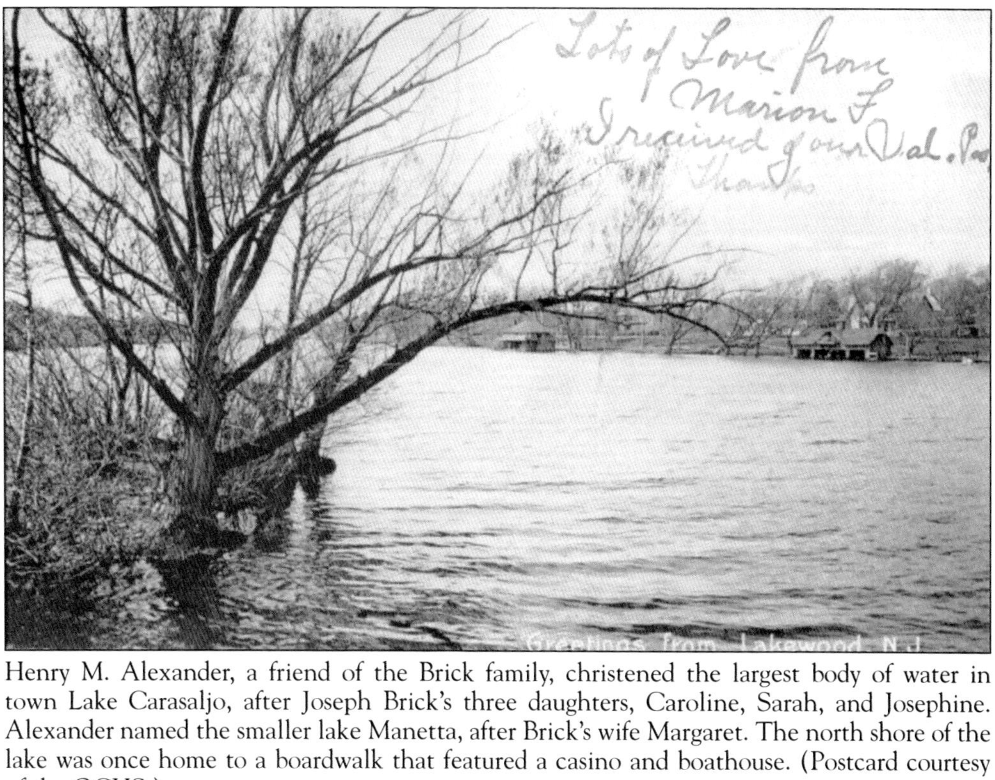

Henry M. Alexander, a friend of the Brick family, christened the largest body of water in town Lake Carasaljo, after Joseph Brick's three daughters, Caroline, Sarah, and Josephine. Alexander named the smaller lake Manetta, after Brick's wife Margaret. The north shore of the lake was once home to a boardwalk that featured a casino and boathouse. (Postcard courtesy of the OCHS.)

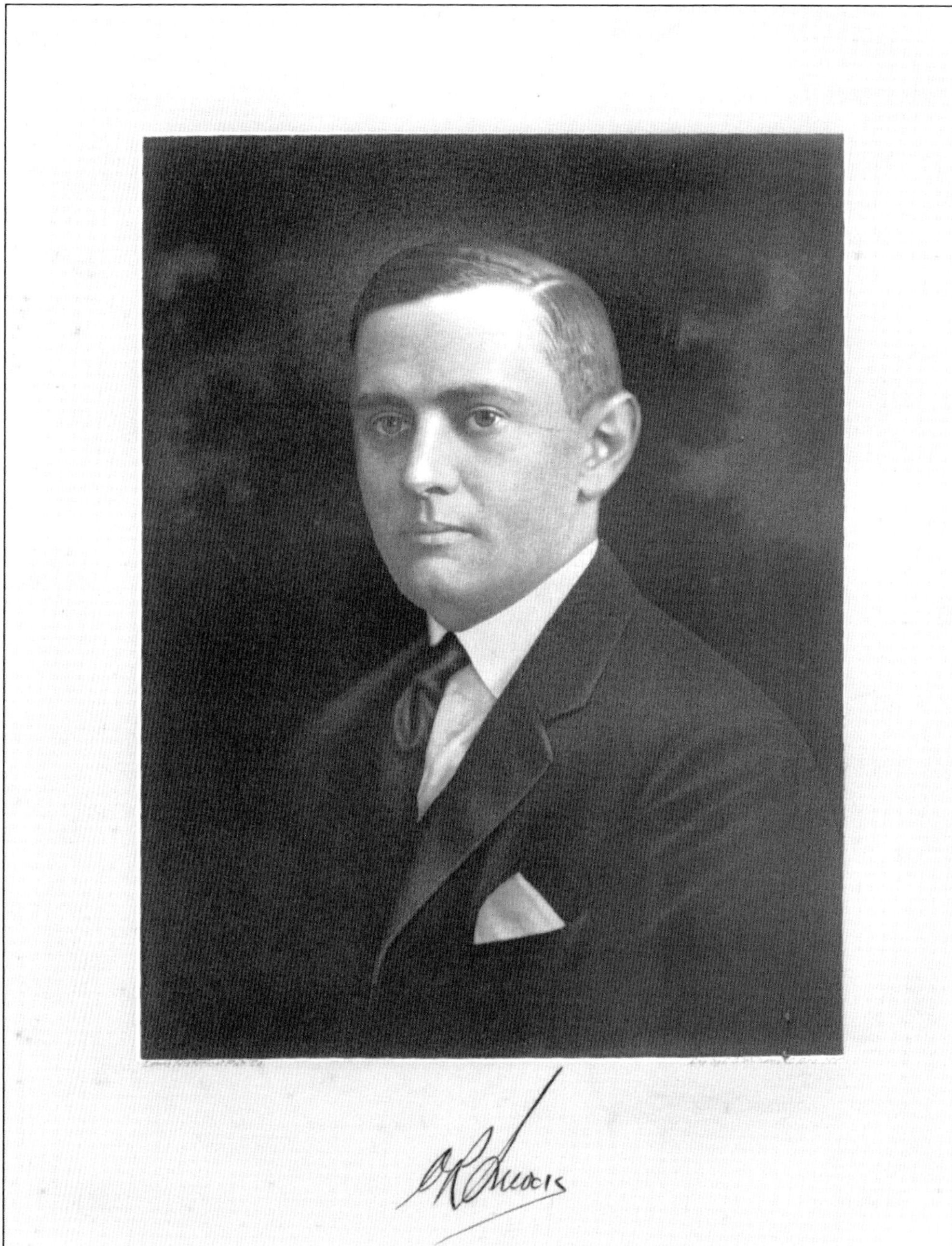

Arthur R. Smock graduated from Lakewood High School with the Class of 1903. One of his first jobs was at the Lakewood Post Office, where he served under then postmaster Albert M. Bradshaw. Smock left the post office to pursue a career in the real estate profession. In 1911, he was hired by Bradshaw to manage the A.M. Bradshaw Company and in 1917, he founded the Smock Real Estate Agency. (Photograph courtesy of the OCHS.)

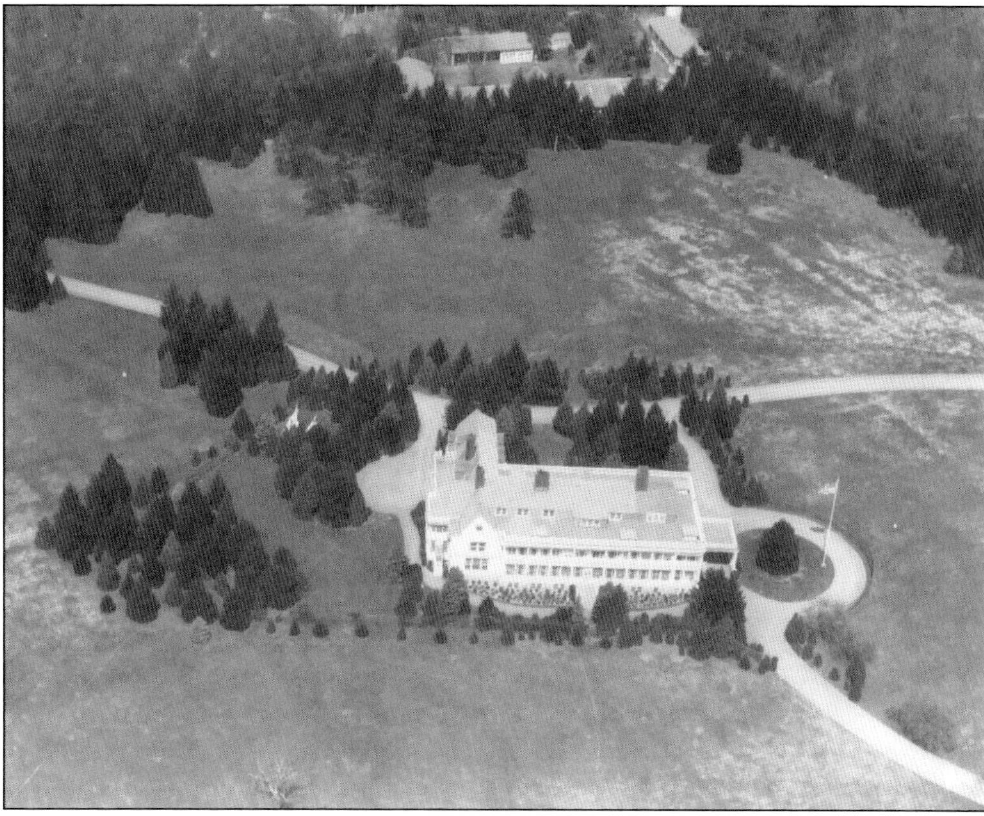

An aerial view of John Davison Rockefeller's estate, which was located in what is now Ocean County Park. After his death, the trustees of his estate offered the property to Ocean County. In 1966, the remnants of Rockefeller's mansion were demolished and cleared from the property. (Photograph courtesy of the OCHS.)

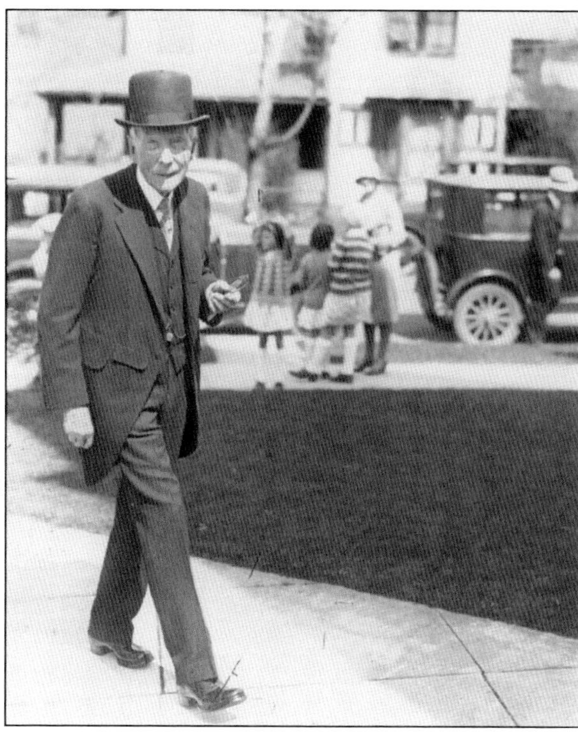

John D. Rockefeller, president of the Standard Oil Company and one of America's wealthiest businessmen, started purchasing real estate in Lakewood in the early 1900s. It is said that Rockefeller paid about $13,000 for the Ocean County Hunt and Country Club. He renovated some of the buildings on the property and used the estate as a midway rest stop from his travels to New York and Florida. (Photograph by F.W. Tupper, courtesy of the OCHS.)

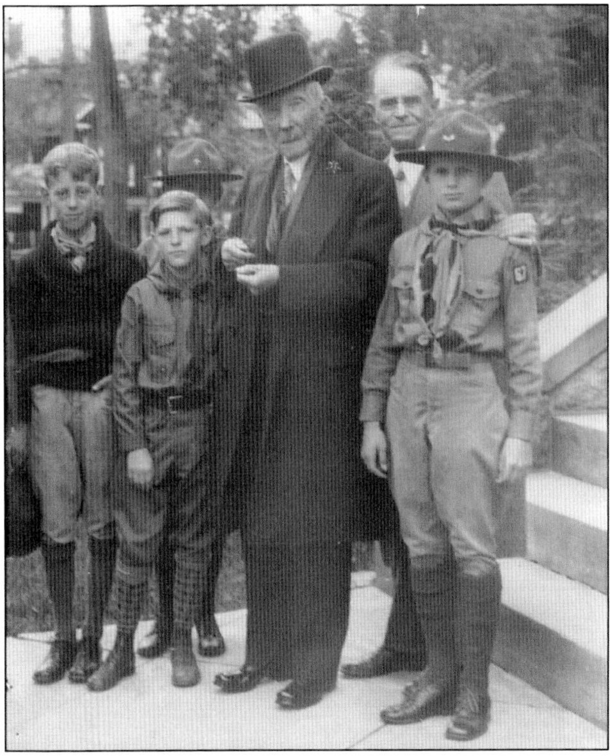

When in Lakewood, John D. Rockefeller would share his fortune with the local children by handing out dimes. Rockefeller's charitable ways can be seen as he hands out gifts to a group of local Boy Scouts, left. Below, local children share a moment with Rockefeller. The young boy in the white shirt is H. George Buckwald. (Photographs by F.W. Tupper, courtesy of the OCHS.)

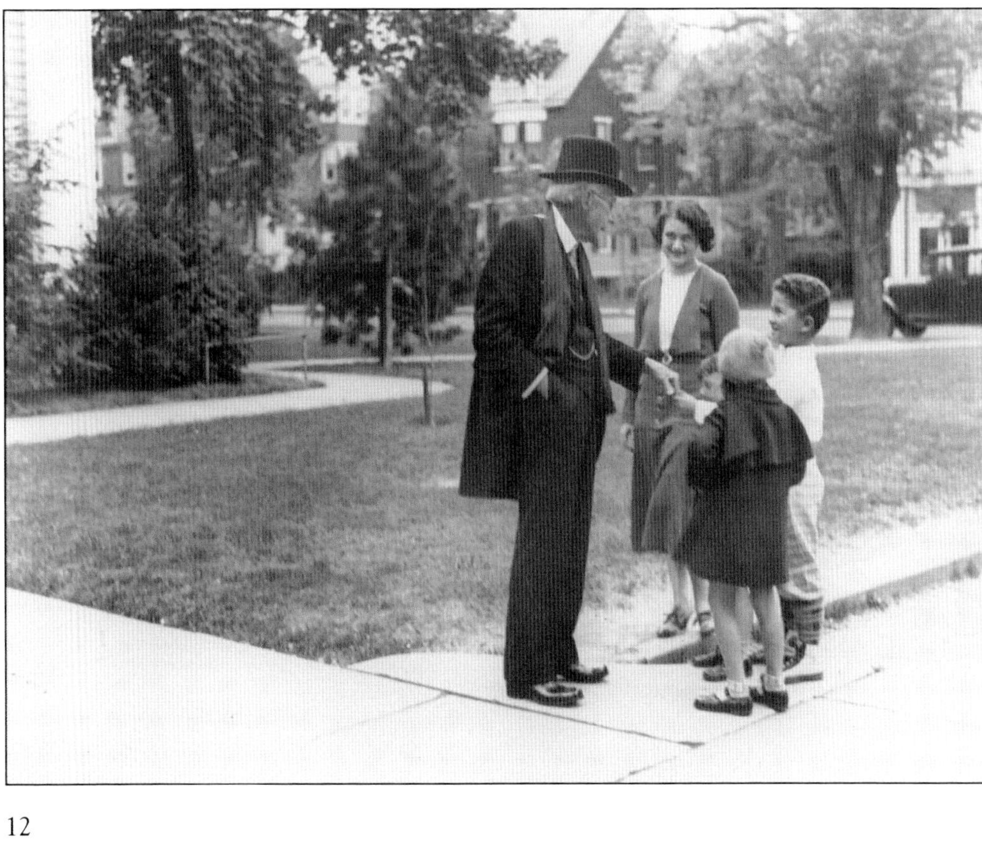

John D. Rockefeller stands outside the steps of the First Baptist Church on Clifton Avenue. A newspaper article on page 2 of the *Lakewood Item* dated January 31, 1903, addressed the adoration Rockefeller had for the First Baptist Church. The article read, "A short time ago, John D. Rockefeller offered to donate $2500 toward paying off the mortgage of $5000 of the church, providing the congregation raised the other half." (Photograph by F.W. Tupper, courtesy of the OCHS.)

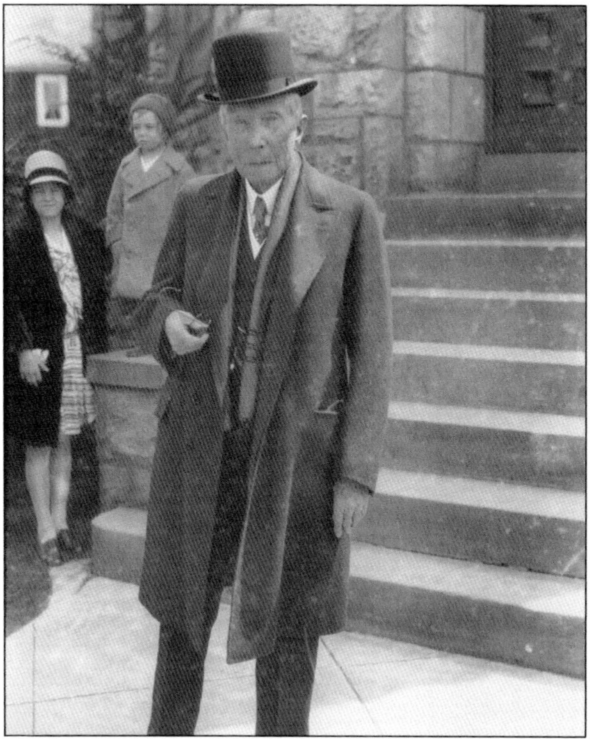

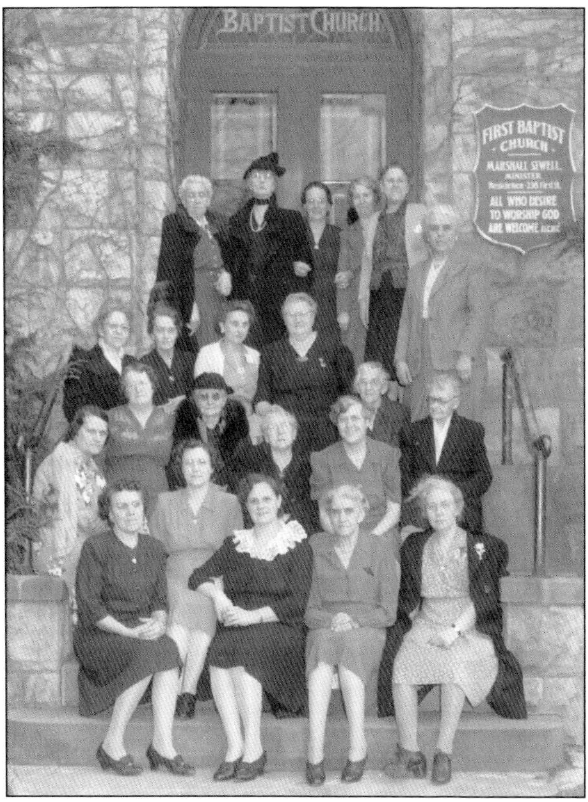

The Baptist Mission Circle is shown c. 1930. Pictured, from left to right, are the following: (first row) Mrs. E.L. Linke, Mrs. W. Wilson, Mrs. H. Manley, Mrs. G. Gunther, and Mrs. C. Foster; (second row) Mrs. C. Bennet, Mrs. E. Robertson, Mrs. D. Cook, Mrs. H. Thomas, and Miss L. Helbling; (third row) Mrs. Garon, Mrs. E. Frye, Mrs. E., Mrs. Whitmore, and Miss. F. Helbling; (fourth row) Miss S. Parker, Mrs. A.D. Davis, Mrs. R. Dix, Mrs. Sewell, Mrs. Muller, and Mrs. A.B. Pettet. (Photograph by F.W. Tupper, courtesy of the OCHS.)

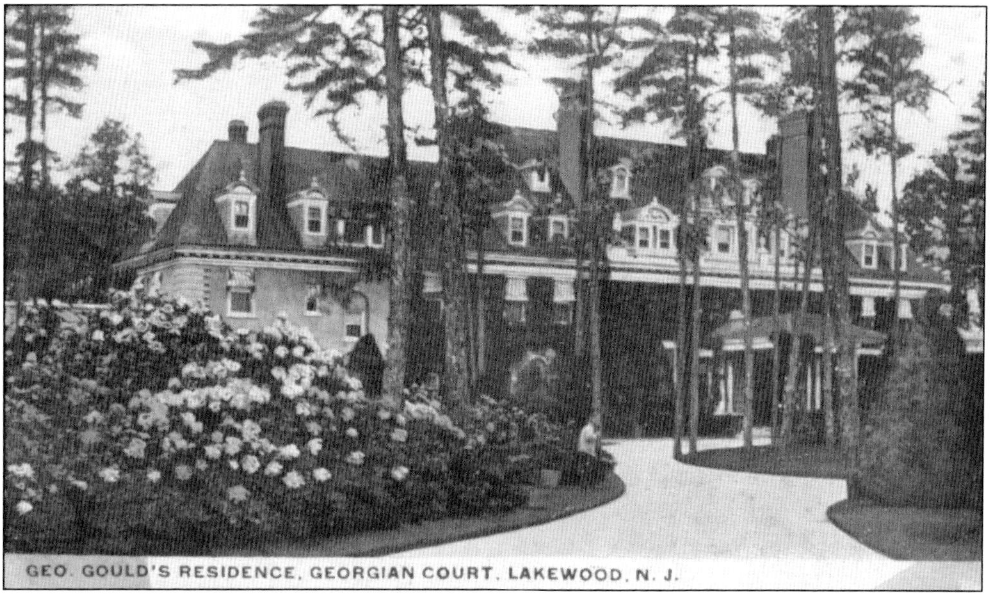

In 1896, George Jay Gould met with Albert M. Bradshaw of the Bricksburg Land and Improvement Company and decided to purchase a large plot of land that was situated on the north side of Lake Carasaljo. Over the next few years, Gould accumulated nearly 200 acres upon which his lavish estate Georgian Court was built. After Gould's death, the estate was sold to the Sisters of Mercy. Today, the property is home to Georgian Court College. (Postcard courtesy of the OCHS.)

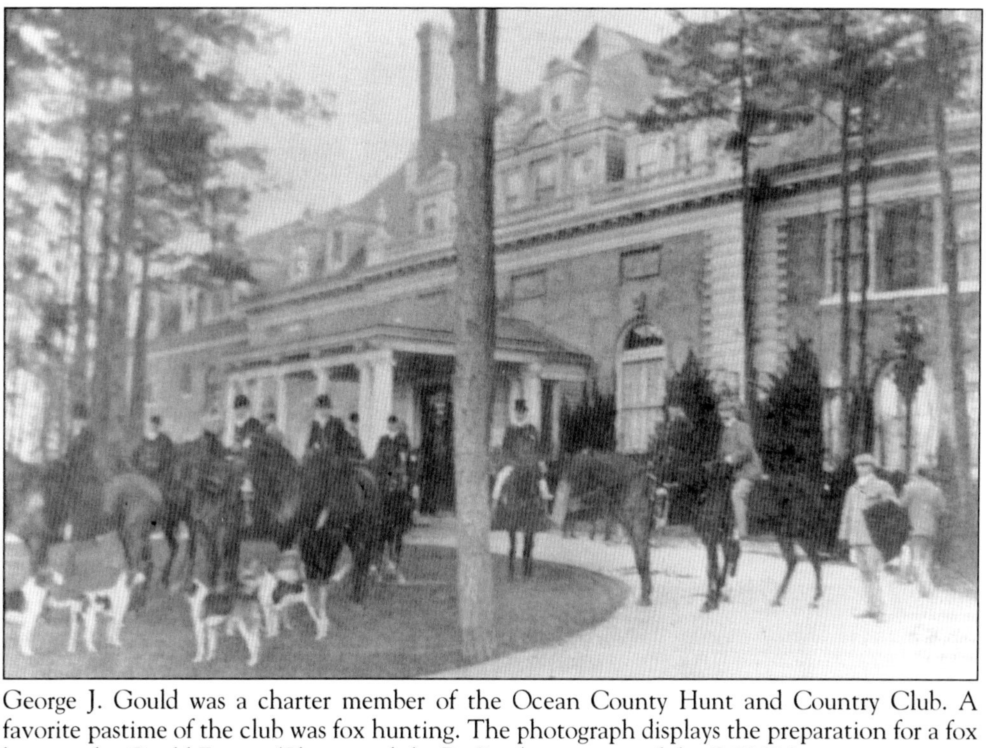

George J. Gould was a charter member of the Ocean County Hunt and Country Club. A favorite pastime of the club was fox hunting. The photograph displays the preparation for a fox hunt at the Gould Estate. (Photograph by R. Steele, courtesy of the OCHS.)

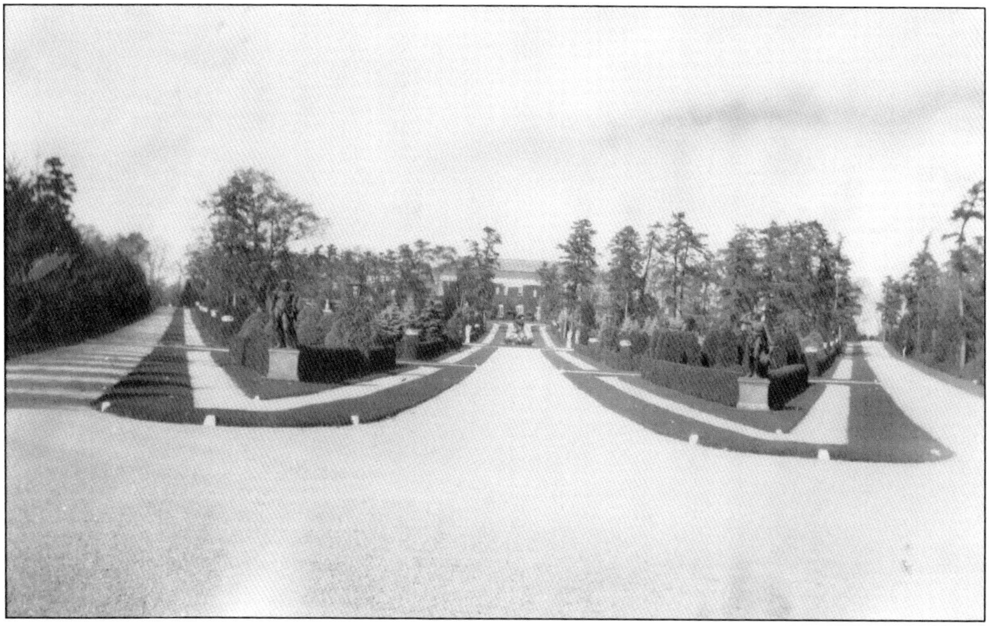

In this view from Georgian Court, three roads lead further into the lavish European-style gardens of the estate. (Photograph courtesy of the OCHS.)

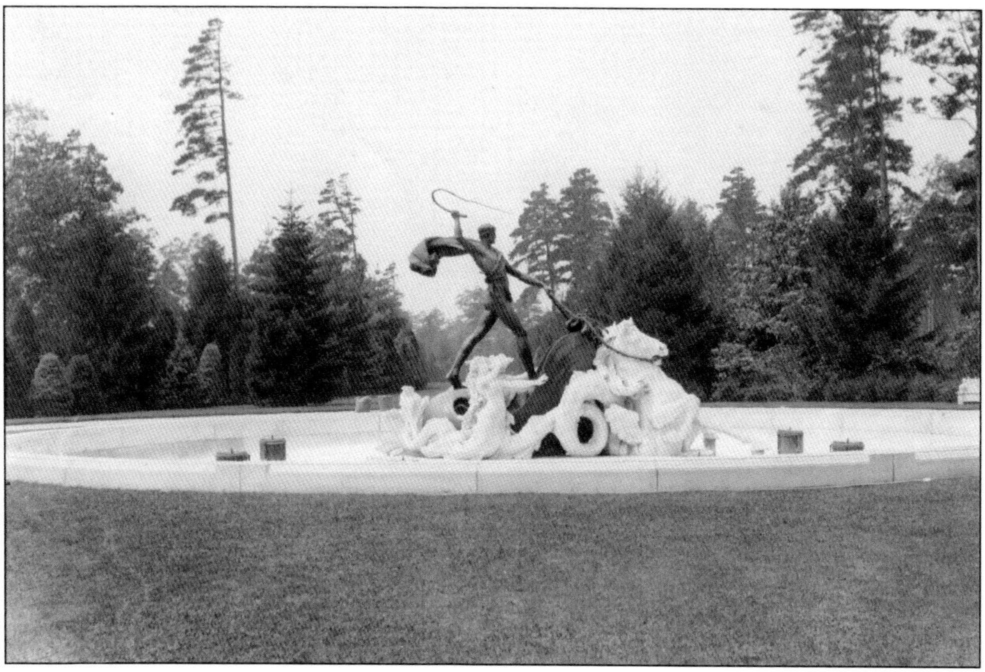

The Apollo fountain at Georgian Court was a birthday present from George J. Gould to his wife, Edith Gould. It was unveiled during her birthday celebration in 1902. The fountain uses nearly 25,000 gallons of water per hour. (Photograph courtesy of the OCHS.)

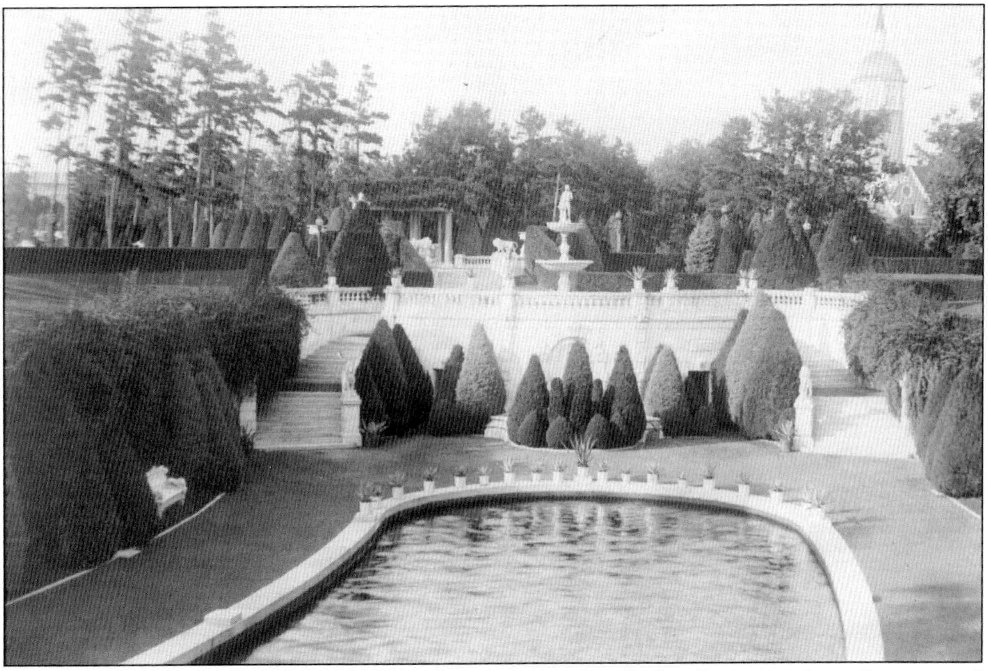

The sunken gardens at Georgian Court are connected to Lake Carasaljo through a natural inlet. It is here where the water for the Apollo fountain is obtained. The sunken gardens take on the character of some of the most famous European and Italian formal gardens. (Photograph courtesy of the OCHS.)

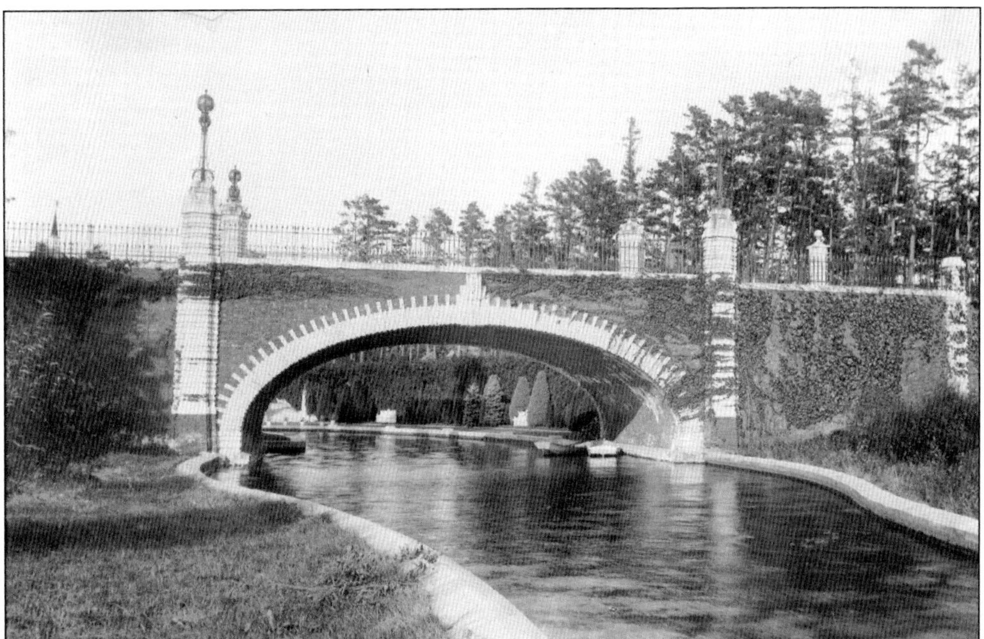

The Georgian Court Bridge is located on North Lake Drive. It not only provides passage over the sunken gardens, but also allows a glimpse of the beautiful architecture and gardens located on the property below. (Photograph courtesy of the OCHS.)

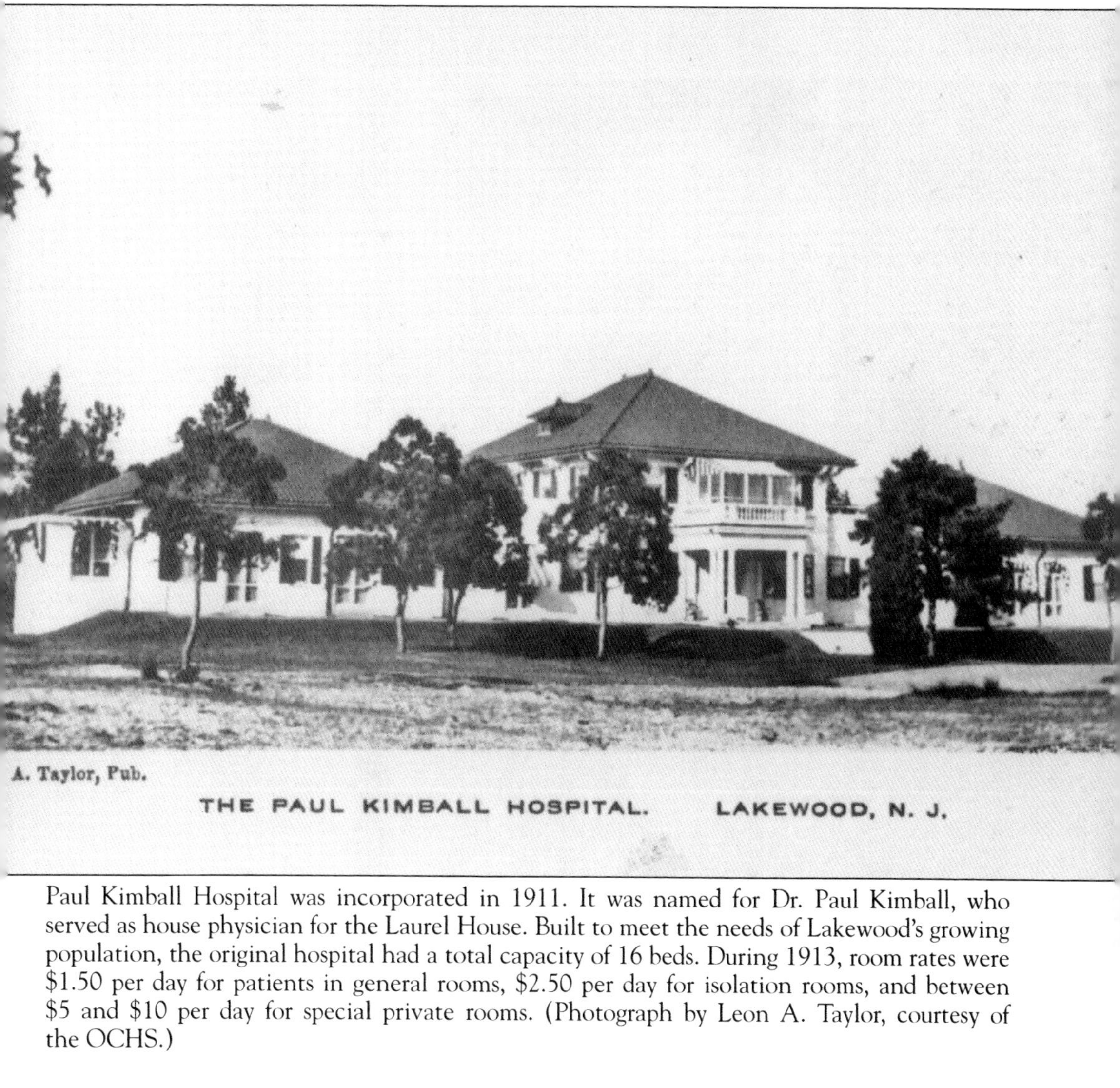

Paul Kimball Hospital was incorporated in 1911. It was named for Dr. Paul Kimball, who served as house physician for the Laurel House. Built to meet the needs of Lakewood's growing population, the original hospital had a total capacity of 16 beds. During 1913, room rates were \$1.50 per day for patients in general rooms, \$2.50 per day for isolation rooms, and between \$5 and \$10 per day for special private rooms. (Photograph by Leon A. Taylor, courtesy of the OCHS.)

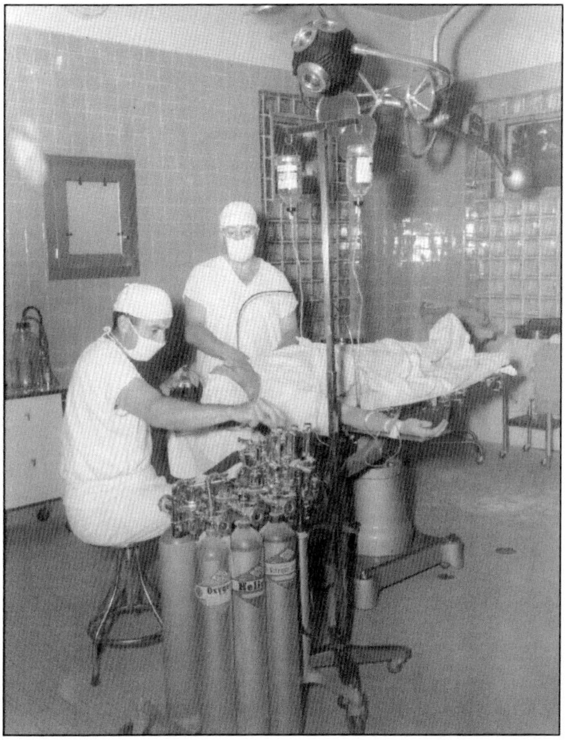

This scene is from the operating room at Paul Kimball Hospital, c. the 1940s. Dr. Raymond Taylor (standing) prepares for surgery while Dr. Bernard Gartlan (seated) is ready to administer the anesthesia to the patient. (Photograph by F.W. Tupper, courtesy of the OCHS.)

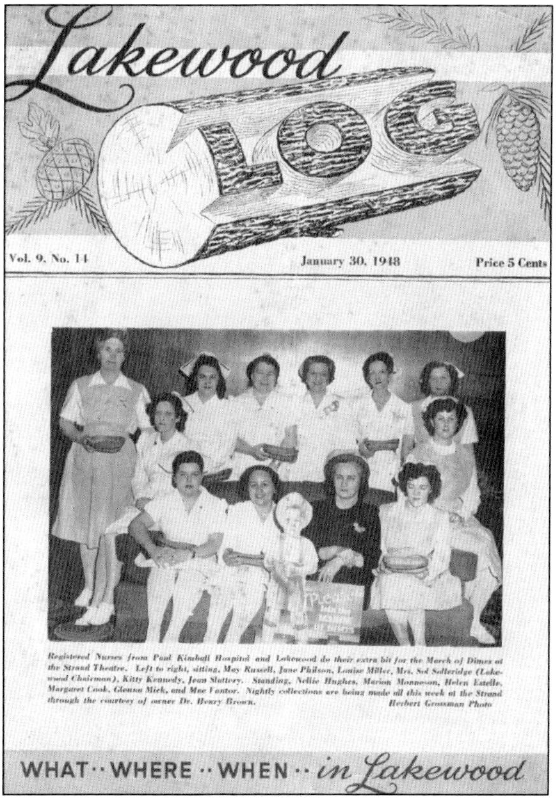

Lakewood LOG

Vol. 9, No. 14 January 30, 1948 Price 5 Cents

Registered Nurses from Paul Kimball Hospital and Lakewood do their extra bit for the March of Dimes at the Strand Theatre. Left to right, sitting, May Russell, Jane Philson, Louise Miller, Mrs. Sol Selleridge (Lakewood Chairman), Kitty Kennedy, Jean Slattery. Standing, Nellie Hughes, Marion Monneson, Helen Estelle, Margaret Cook, Glenna Mick, and Mae Fantor. Nightly collections are being made all this week at the Strand through the courtesy of owner Dr. Henry Brown. *Herbert Grossman Photo*

WHAT · · WHERE · · WHEN · · *in Lakewood*

The cover of the *Lakewood Log,* issued on January 30, 1948, featured nurses from Paul Kimball Hospital and the rest of Lakewood who participated in a fund-raising event for the March of Dimes at the Strand Theater.

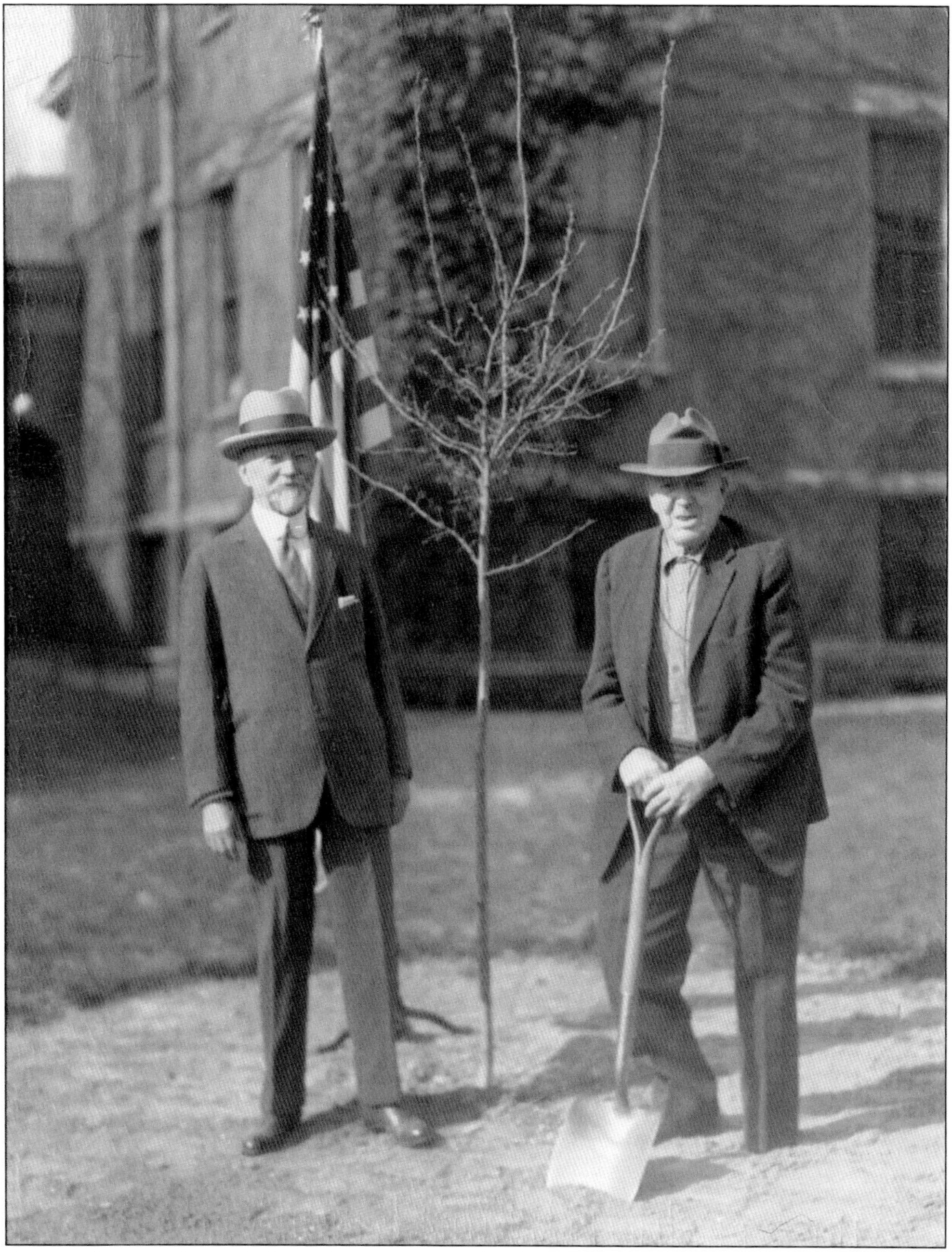

Charles Lathrop Pack (left) and a veteran of the Civil War pose for a picture during a tree-planting ceremony at the old municipal building in 1926. Pack made his fortune in the forestry and banking industries. Among the first Americans to be educated abroad in the field of forestry, he was one of the country's leading conservationists and tree experts. Pres. Theodore Roosevelt personally appointed Pack to serve on the National Conservation Commission. (Photograph by F.W. Tupper, courtesy of the OCHS.)

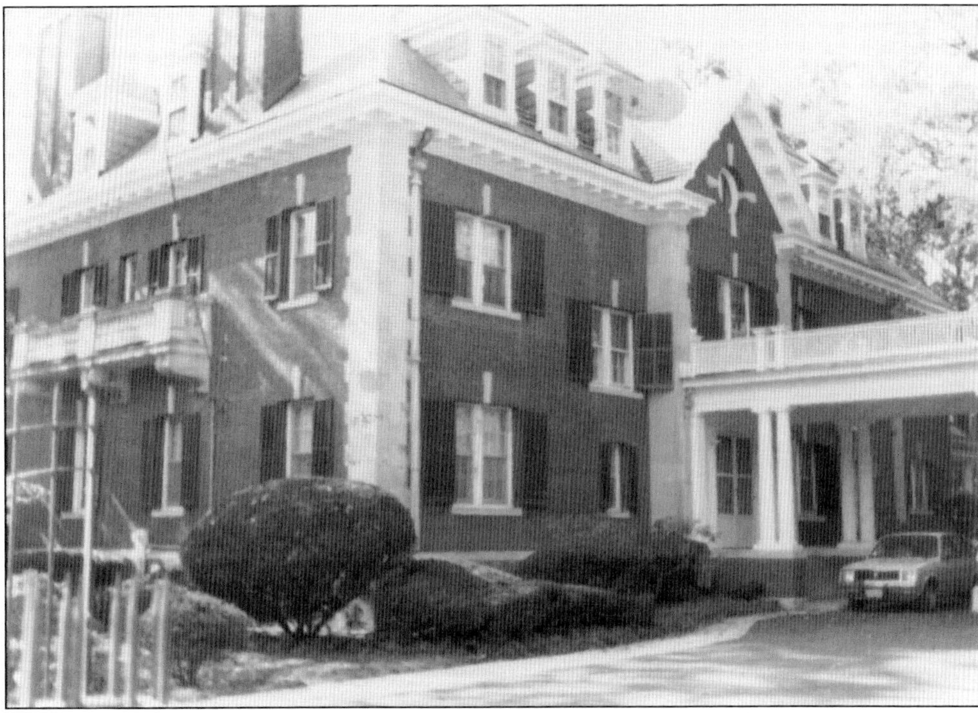

Lathrop Hall, the residence of Charles Lathrop Pack, was located at 250 Forest Avenue. Pack lived in Lakewood for nearly 40 years until his death in 1937. He used his knowledge of forestry to decorate his estate with exquisite landscaped gardens of flowers and trees. (Photograph courtesy of the OCHS.)

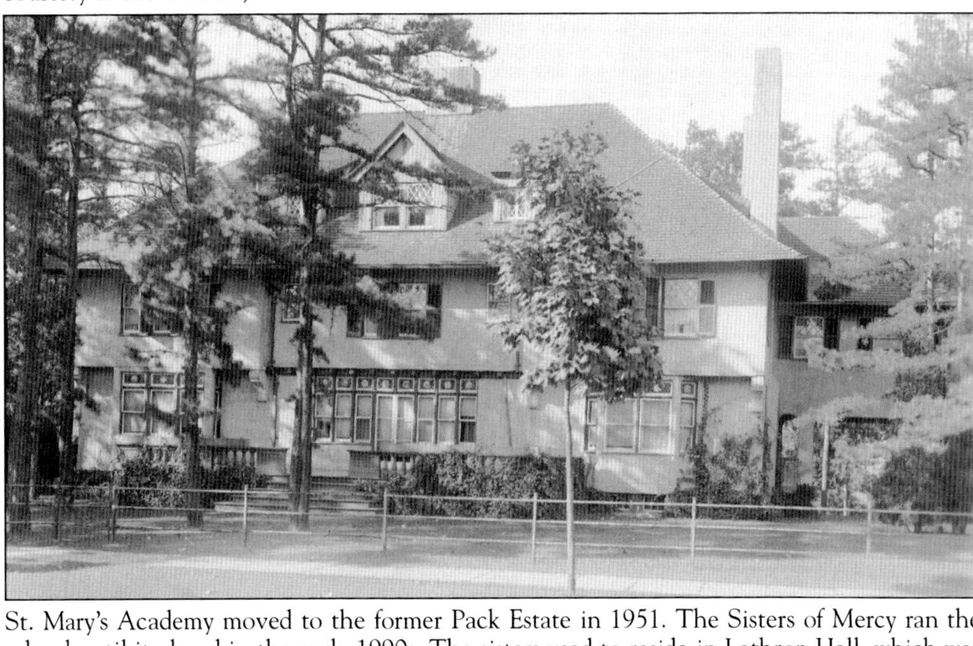

St. Mary's Academy moved to the former Pack Estate in 1951. The Sisters of Mercy ran the school until it closed in the early 1990s. The sisters used to reside in Lathrop Hall, which was the main house on the Pack Estate. The classes were conducted in other buildings around the estate grounds. (Photograph courtesy of the OCHS.)

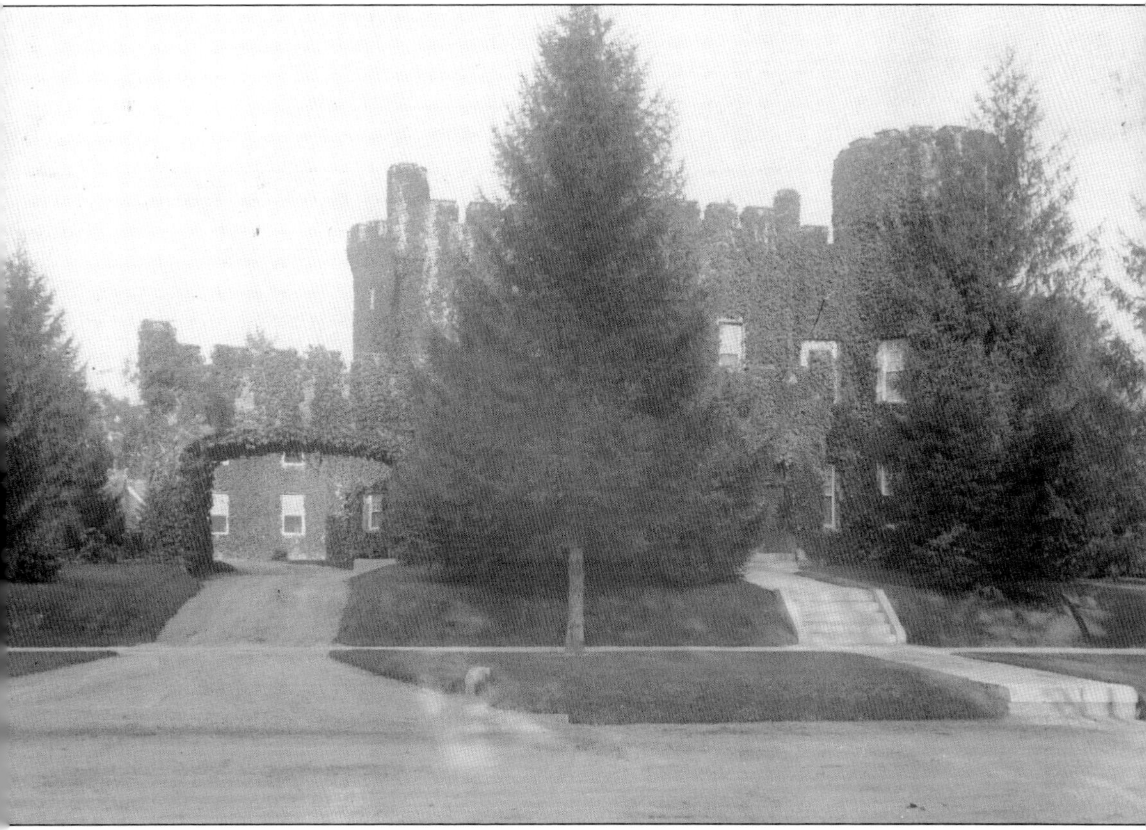

Lynx Hall was located on Forest Avenue and First Street. It was built by Jasper and Rachel Lynch. Jasper Lynch made his fortune in real estate and was an established golfer and a charter member of the Ocean County Hunt and Country Club. Rachel Lynch was a prominent figure in the Lakewood Society for the prevention of Cruelty to Animals. She hosted extravagant fund-raisers, concerts, and recitals at Lynx Hall to benefit her crusade against cruelty to animals. (Photograph courtesy of the OCHS.)

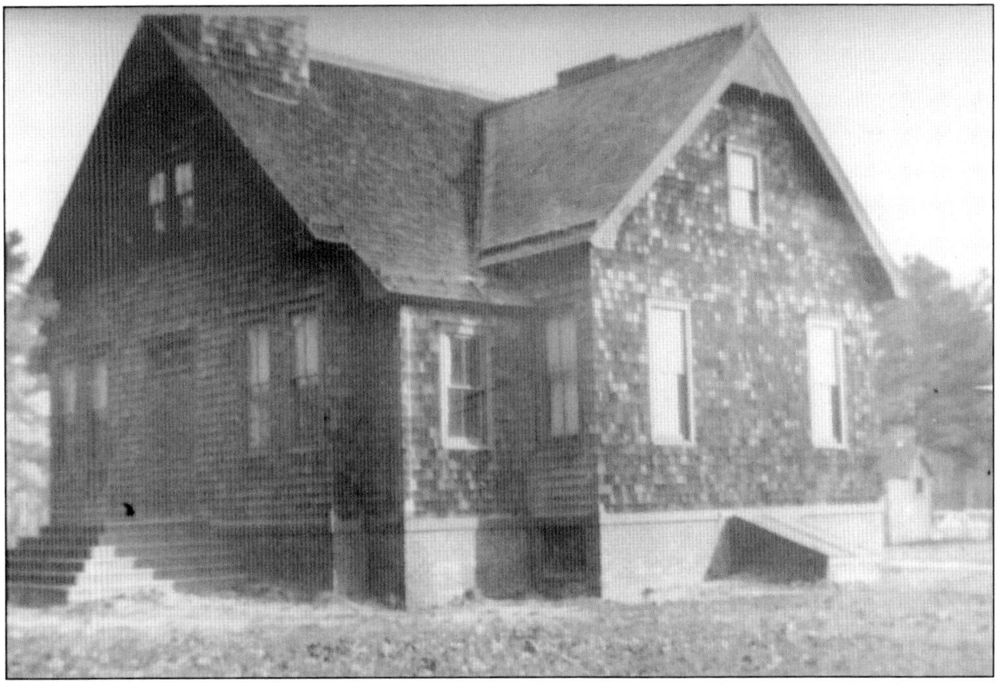

The Runyon's School was located on the corner of County Line and Hope Roads. The school dates from as early as 1857 and was closed in 1896. (Photograph courtesy of the OCHS.)

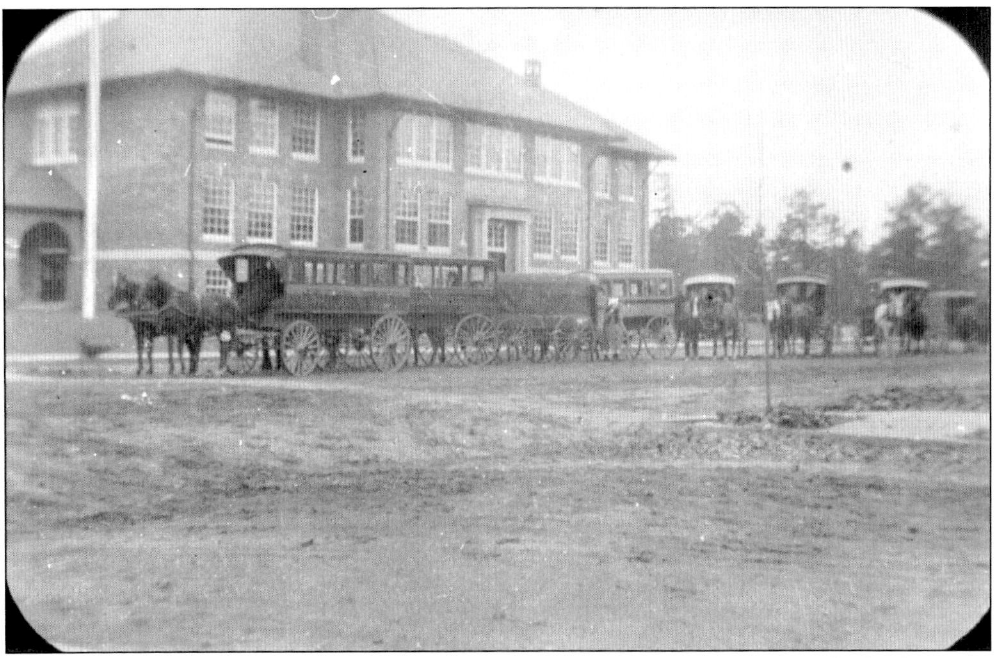

In 1911, the original section of the high school at Princeton Avenue was built; later on, additions were constructed. In this early picture, the student transportation is waiting outside for the children at the end of another school day. Today, the building houses the Lakewood Board of Education and Lakewood Community School. (Photograph by R. Steele, courtesy of the OCHS.)

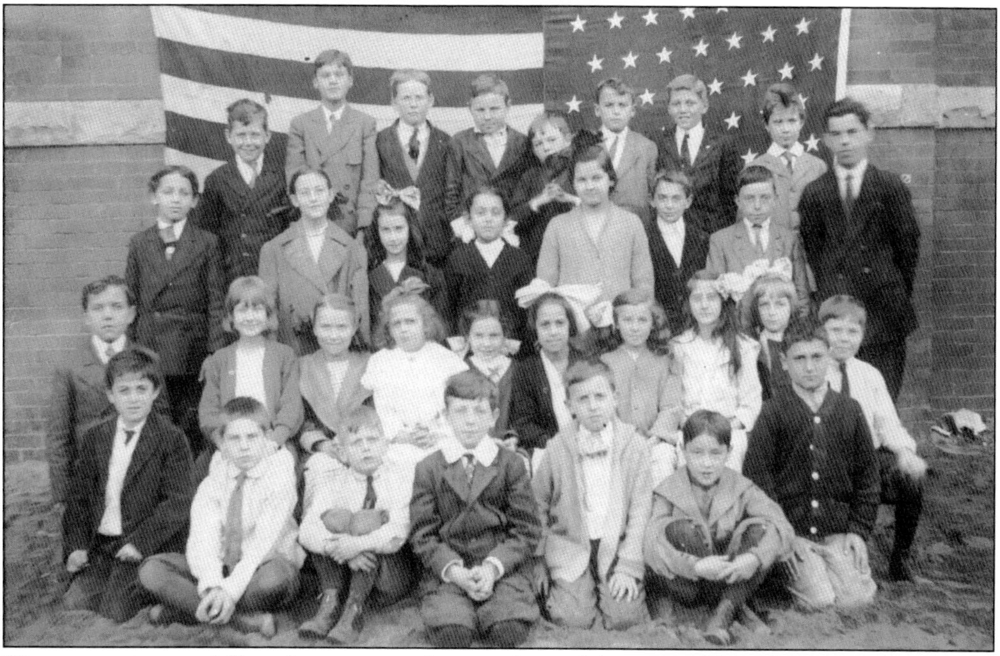

These two pictures follow the progress of young Bessie Johnson and her classmates through the years at the No. 5 School. Above, nine-year-old Bessie Johnson is photographed in the fourth grade in 1912; below, 12-year-old Bessie Johnson is shown as a sixth-grader in Miss Royal's class in 1915. (Photographs courtesy of Betsy Dudas.)

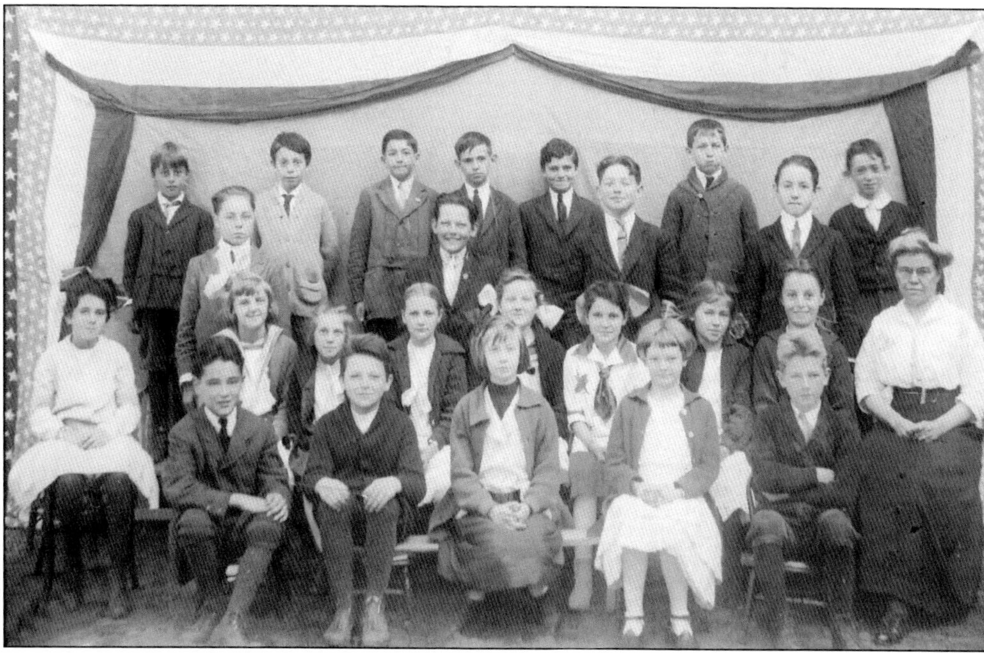

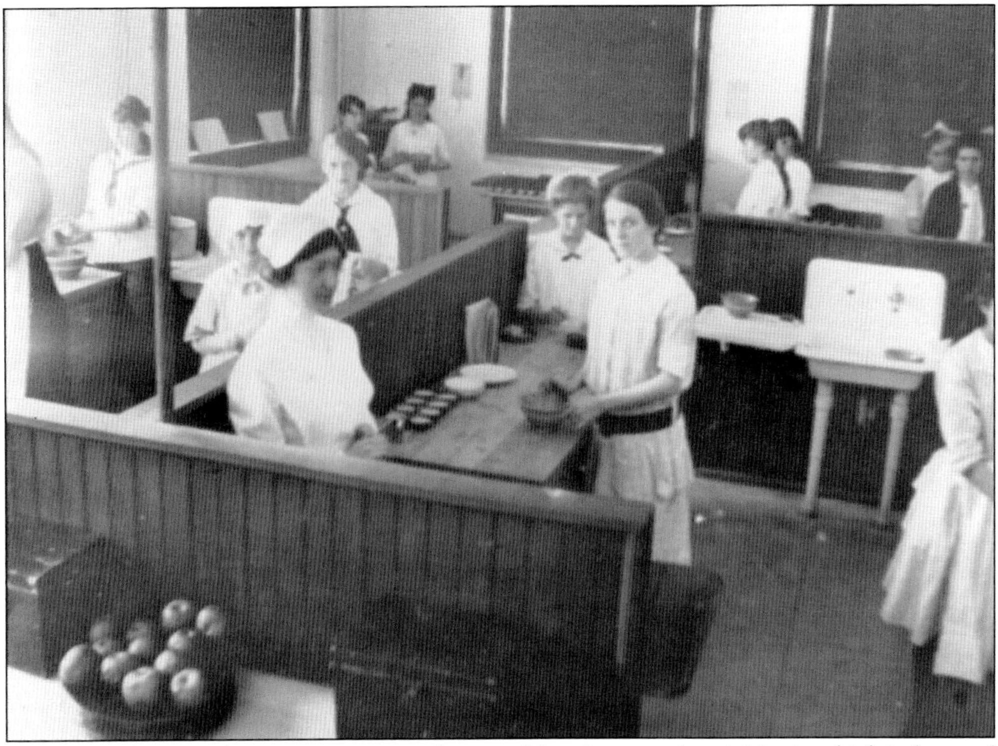

These two photographs give an account of some of the classes and activities in which Lakewood High School students participated in the past. Above, students are hard at work making apple pastries during their Domestic Science class. Below, students are working on projects during the meeting of the sewing club after school. (Top photograph by R. Steele and bottom photograph by C.A. Morris, courtesy of the OCHS.)

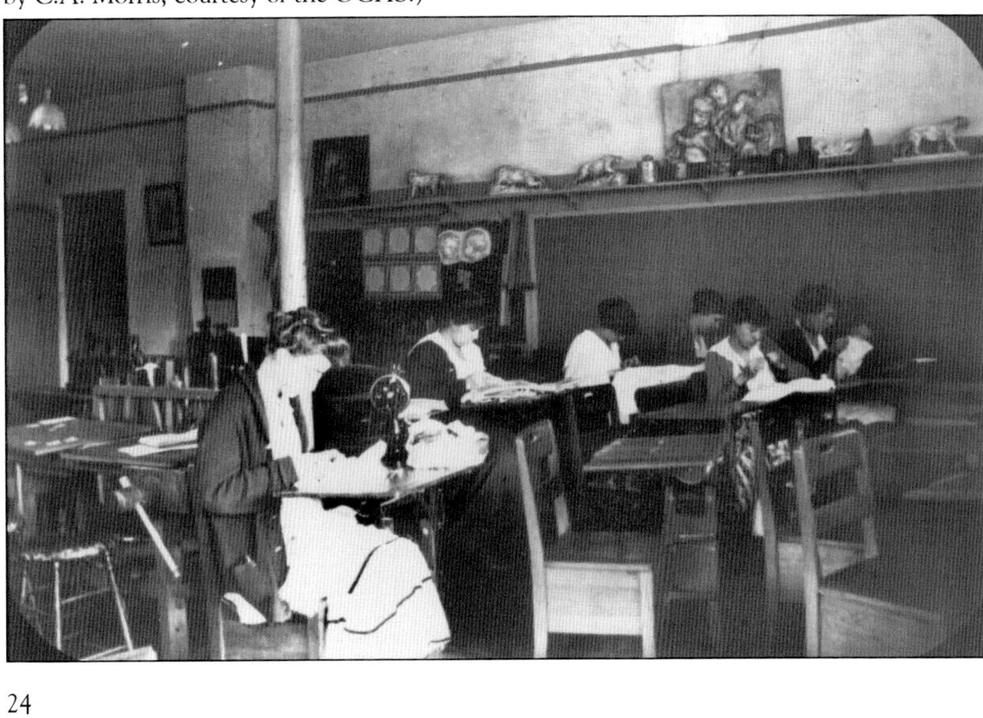

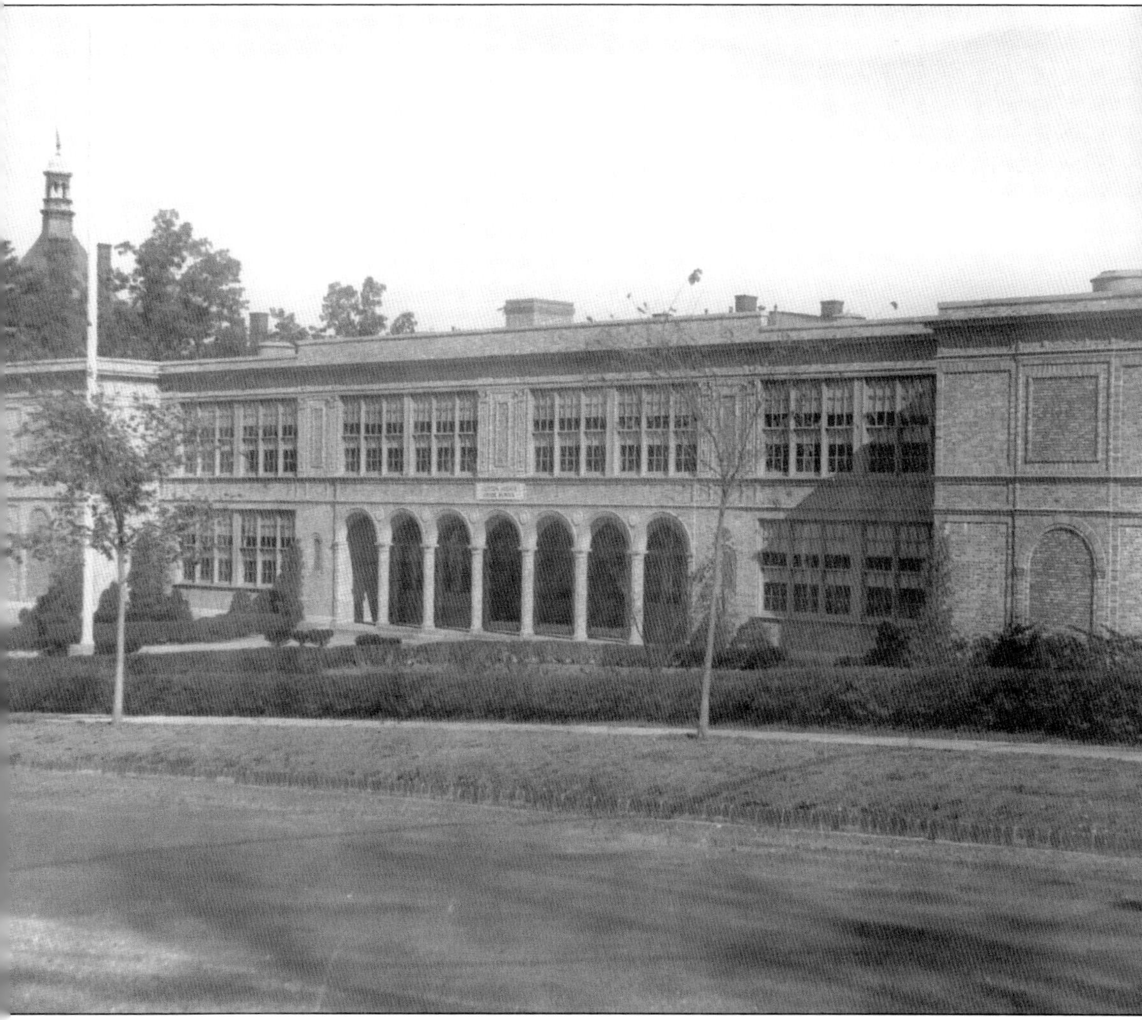

The Clifton Avenue Grade School was constructed in 1923. It is still used today as one of Lakewood's four elementary schools. Its architecture and detailed design make it one of the most aesthetically unique schools in Ocean County. Notice the Lakewood Hotel in the upper left-hand corner of the photograph. (Photograph courtesy of the OCHS.)

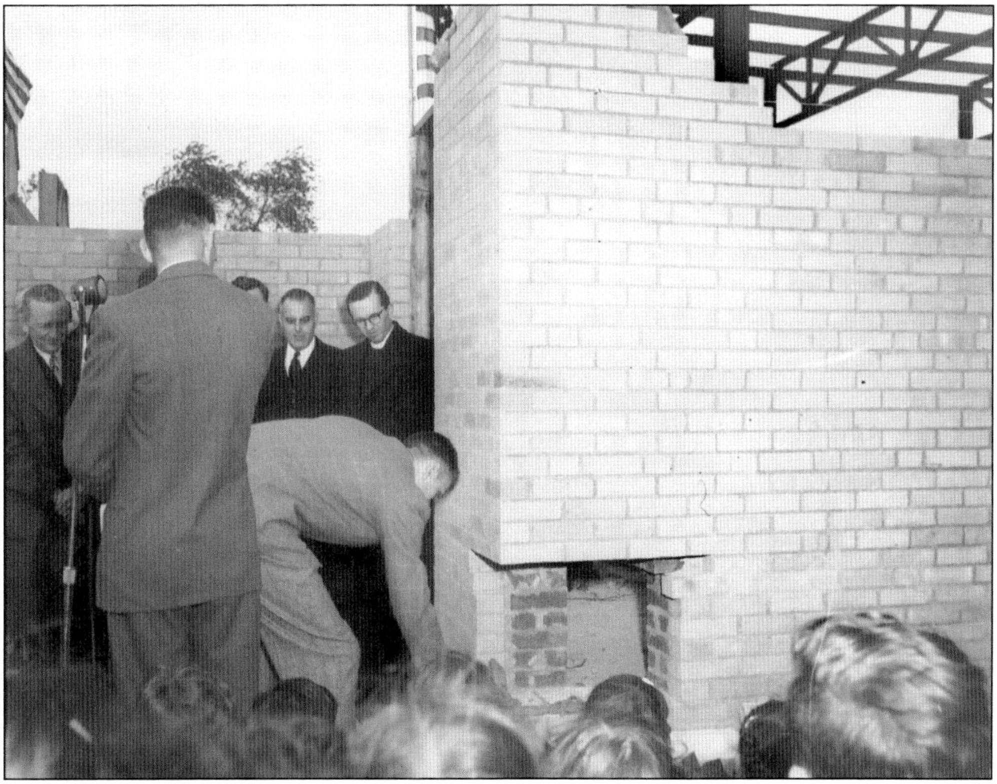

The growing population of Lakewood Township increased the need for the construction of new schools. In 1948, the construction of the Ella G. Clark School was under way. Above, participants engage in activities at the cornerstone ceremony for the new school *c.* 1948. Below, Principal William Apetz, his wife, Mary Apetz, and their son inspect the construction of the school. (Photographs by F.W. Tupper, courtesy of the OCHS.)

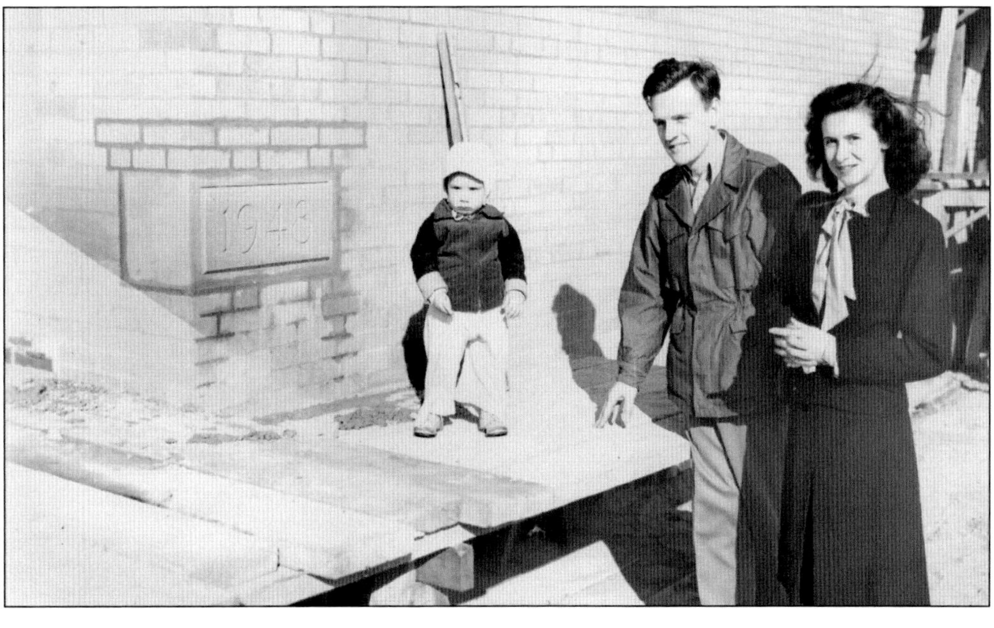

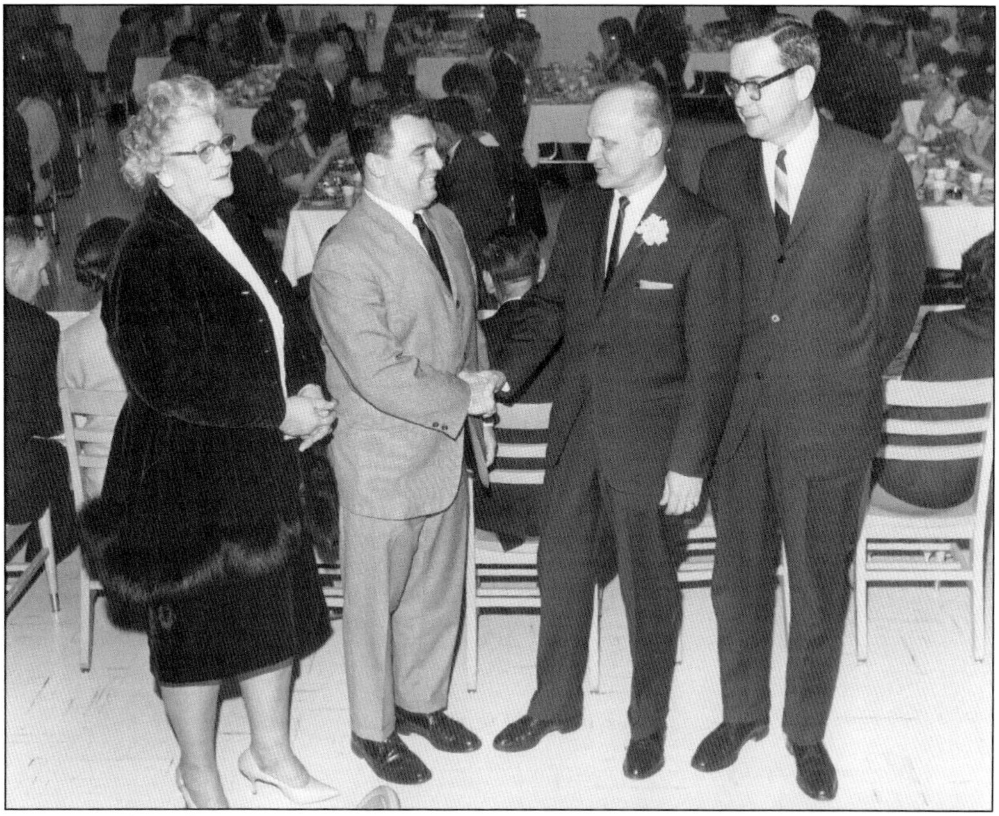

Principal Edmund Casey (far right) of the Spruce Street School exchanges ideas with other county educators at an Ocean County Educational Association meeting. Casey served as the principal of Spruce Street School from 1965 to 1980. (Photograph by Bob Bliss, courtesy of the OCHS.)

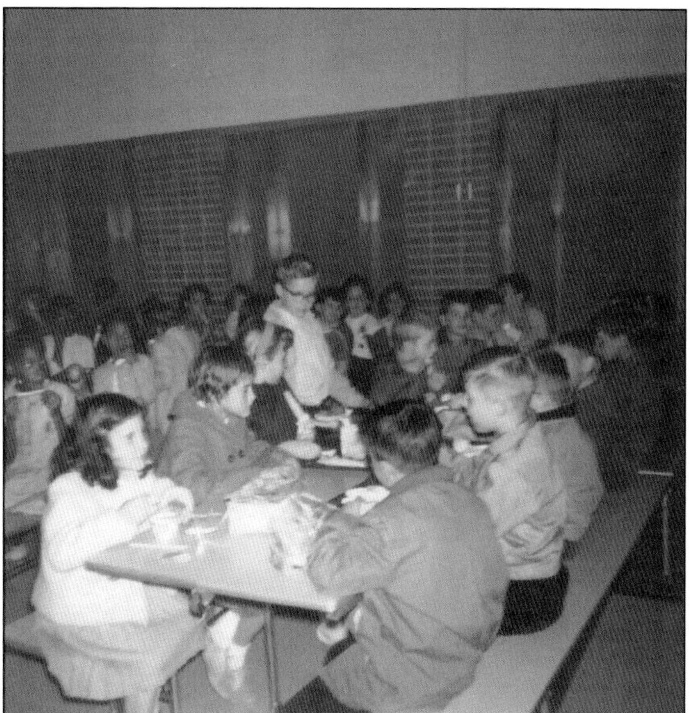

It's lunchtime at the Spruce Street School. A unique aspect of this lunchroom is that after lunch was finished for the day, the tables were folded up and rolled into storage inside the walls. (Photograph courtesy of the OCHS.)

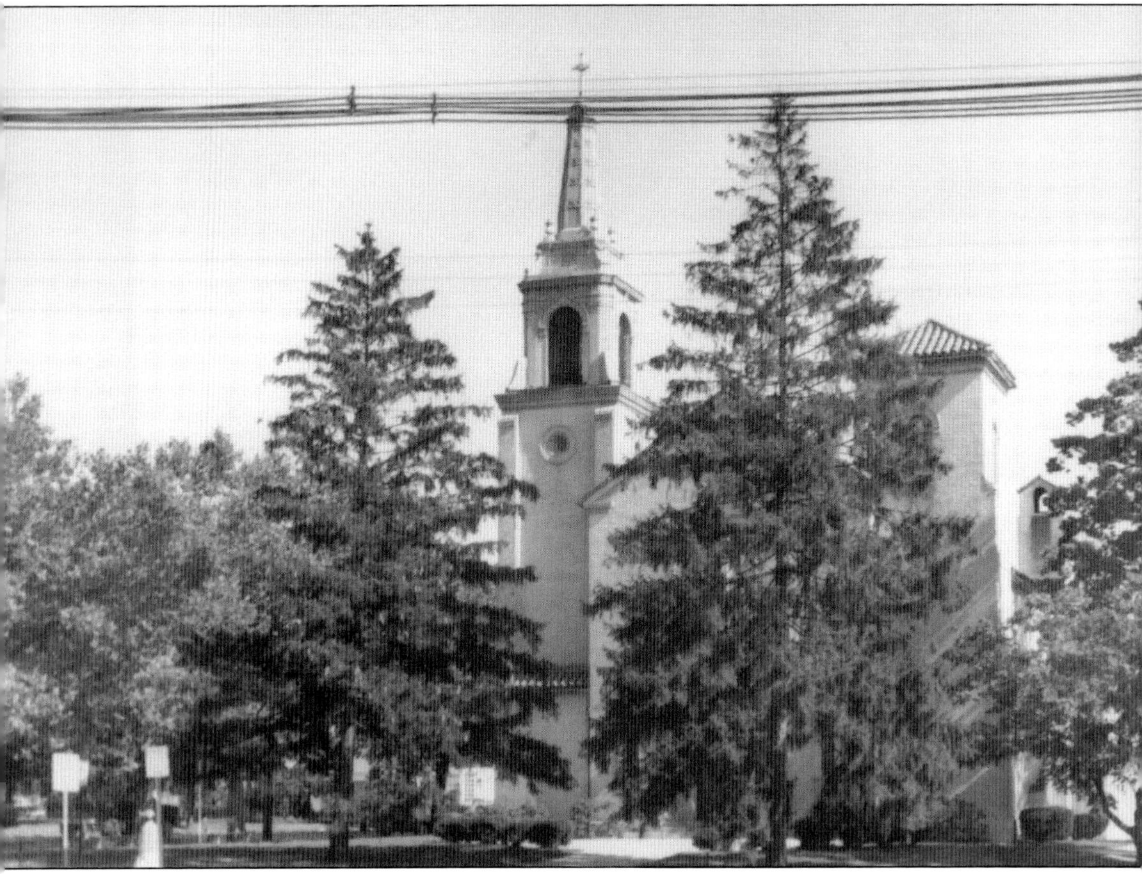

St. Mary's Catholic Church is located diagonally across the street from Lake Carasaljo on Madison Avenue and Main Street. The church was constructed in 1923. One of the most memorable figures of the church was Msgr. George Everitt. Monsignor Everitt spent close to 30 years as pastor of the church, helping children in the community by initiating latchkey, Scouting, and educational programs.

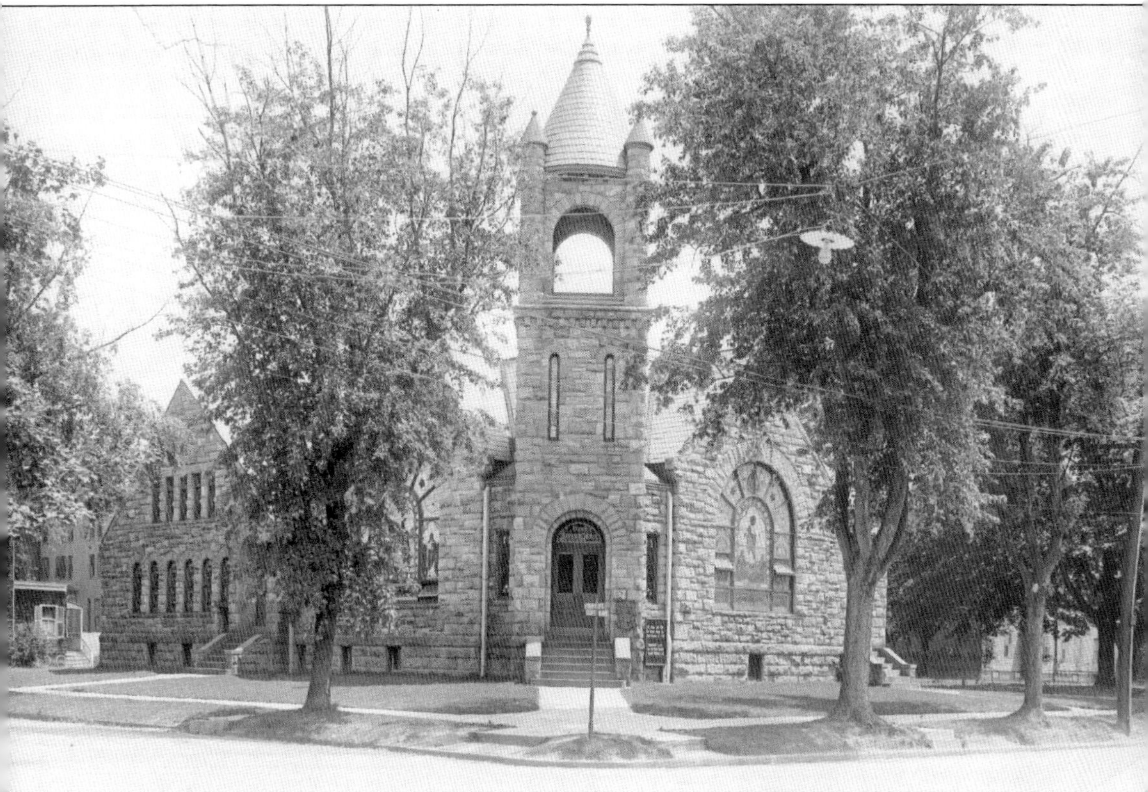

The First Baptist Church is located on First Street and Clifton Avenue. In the early part of 1869, there were close to 20 Baptist churches located in the Lakewood area. The cornerstone of the First Baptist Church was laid on June 7, 1897. One of the church's most famous patrons was John D. Rockefeller. Sometimes Rockefeller had to leave the church by back door to avoid the swarms of photographers who were hoping to capture his image. (Photograph courtesy of the OCHS.)

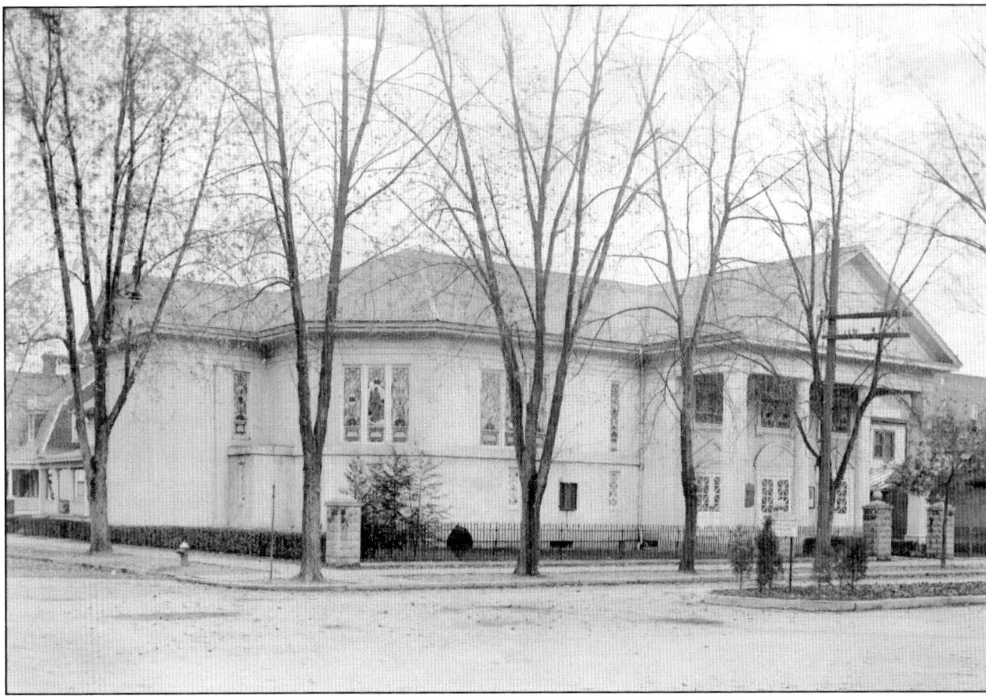

The First Methodist Church was located on Clifton Avenue. The Methodists were the first denomination to establish a religious presence in Lakewood. (Photograph courtesy of the OCHS.)

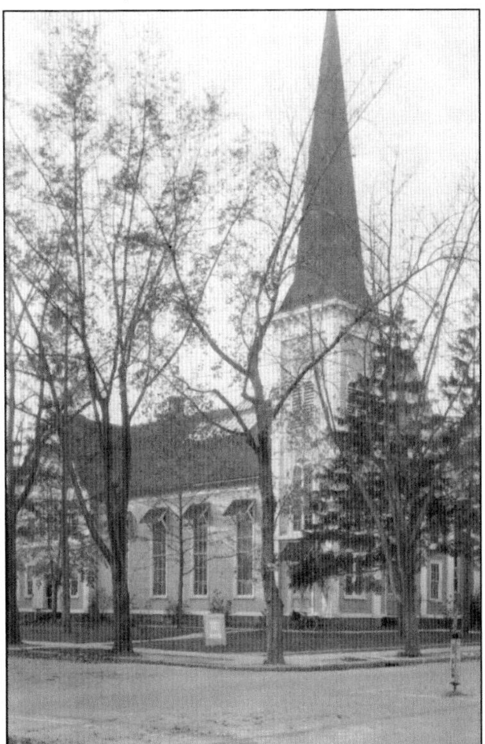

The First Presbyterian Church was constructed in 1884. Riley Brick, the son of Joseph Brick, was responsible for bringing Reverend Alfred Dashiell, the first Presbyterian pastor, to Lakewood in 1867. (Photograph courtesy of the OCHS.)

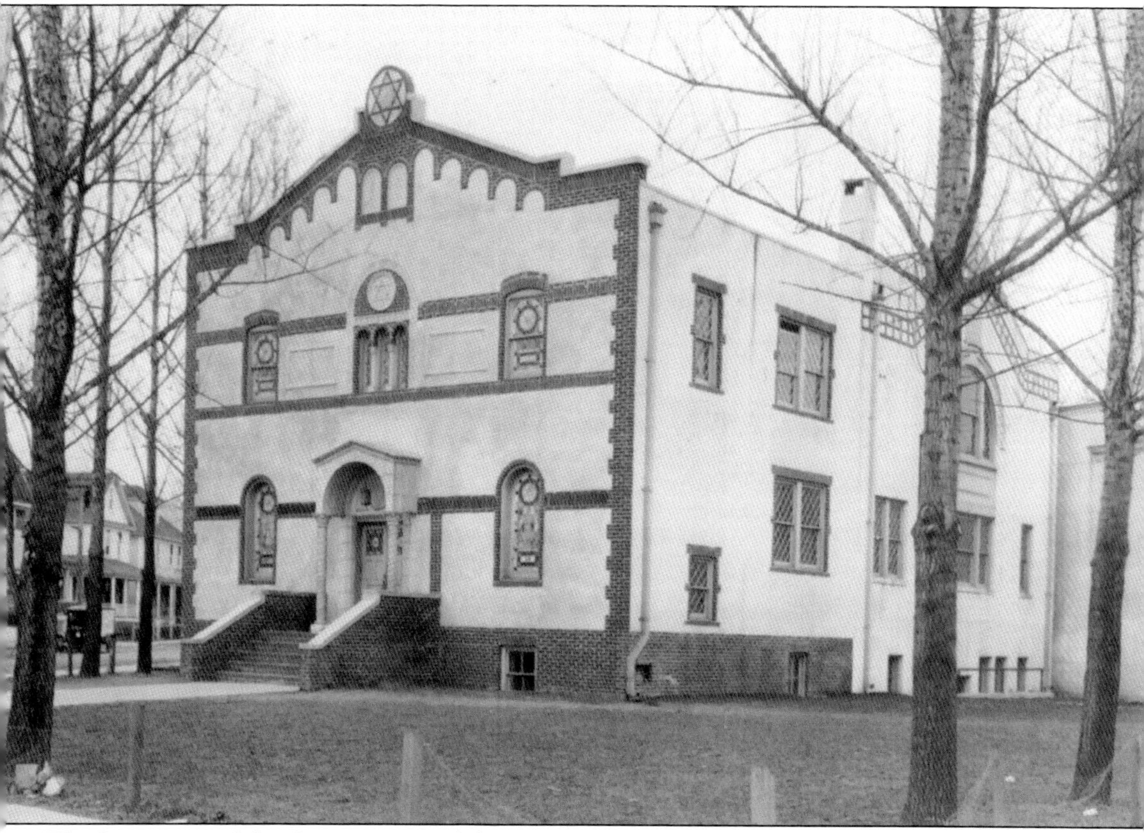

The Synagogue of the Congregation of the Sons of Israel was the first structure of its kind in Lakewood. The building was erected in 1907. Located on Ridge Avenue and East Fourth Street, the church is one of the oldest, if not the oldest Jewish houses of worship in Ocean County.

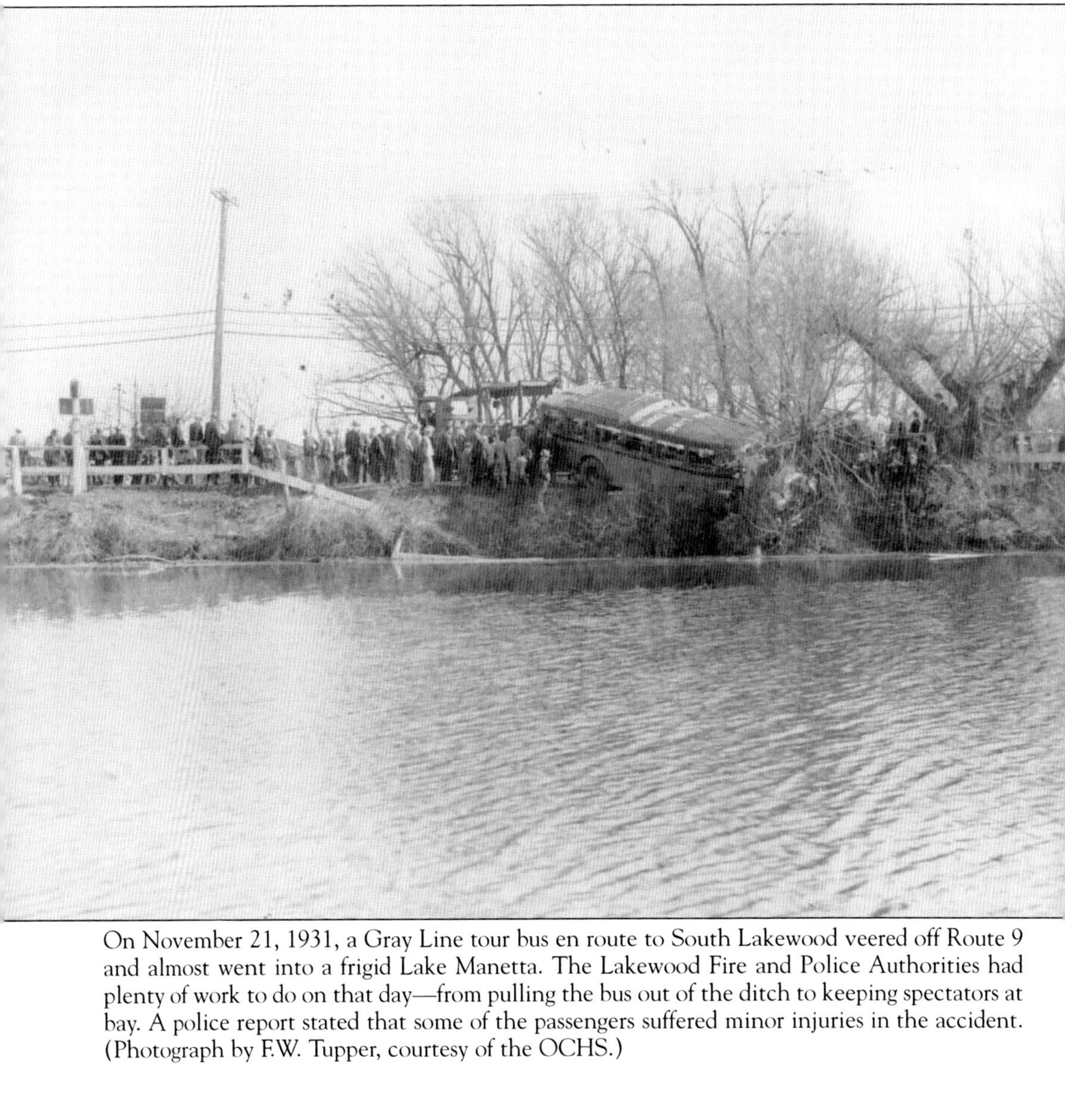

On November 21, 1931, a Gray Line tour bus en route to South Lakewood veered off Route 9 and almost went into a frigid Lake Manetta. The Lakewood Fire and Police Authorities had plenty of work to do on that day—from pulling the bus out of the ditch to keeping spectators at bay. A police report stated that some of the passengers suffered minor injuries in the accident. (Photograph by F.W. Tupper, courtesy of the OCHS.)

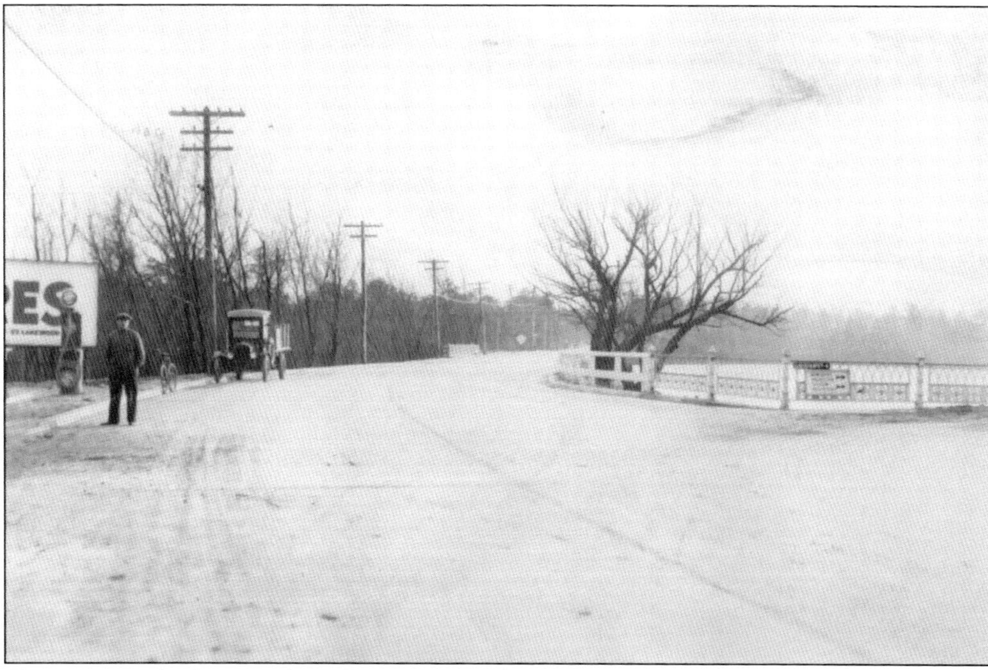

This is a view looking south on River Avenue (Route 9) with the Central Avenue bridge and Lake Manetta to the right. The road sign on the bridge directs travelers west to Lakehurst, New Egypt, Philadelphia, Trenton, and Wrightstown. (Photograph courtesy of the OCHS.)

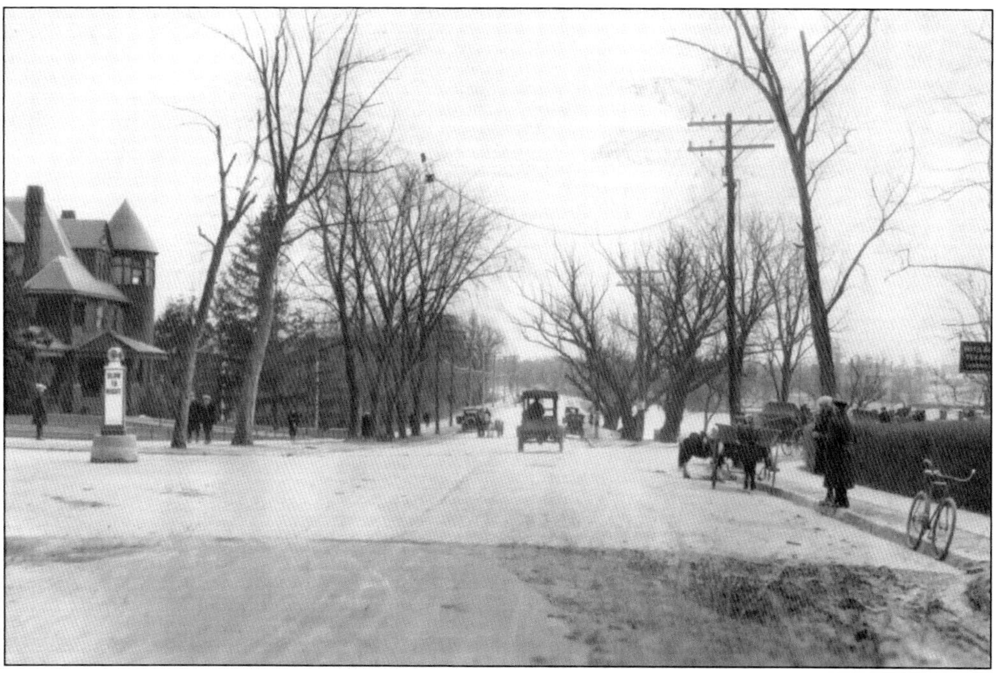

Another view looks south from the intersection of River Avenue (Route 9), Main Street, and North Lake Drive. On the right is the Hotel Armen, with Lake Carasaljo in the background. (Photograph courtesy of the OCHS.)

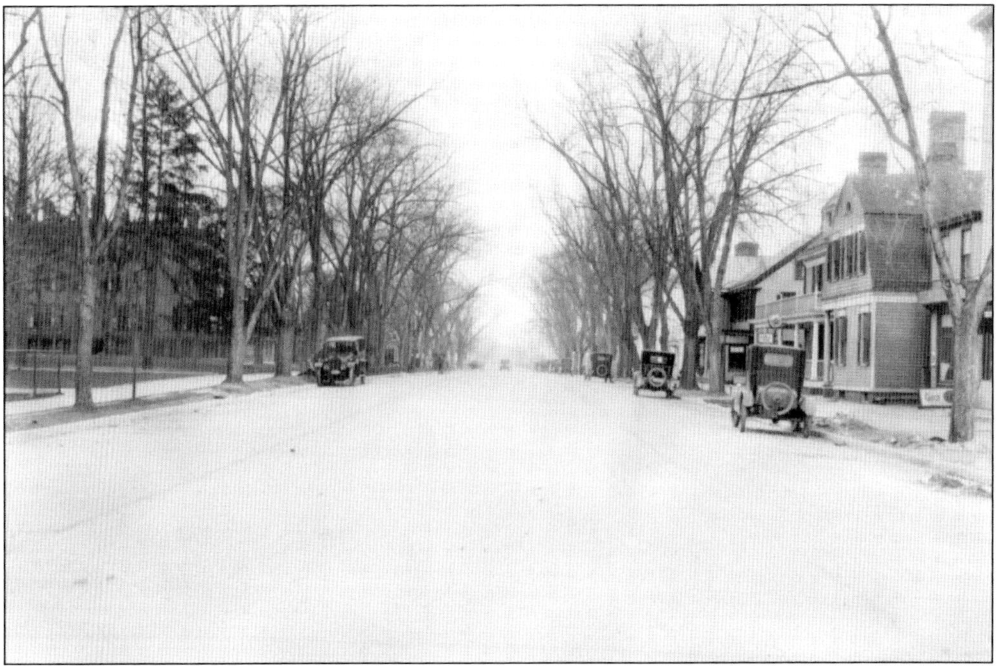

A view from Main Street shows the Laurel House situated on the left. On the right is a Gulf station, which offered free air and water: air for customers with automobiles and water for customers with horses. (Photograph courtesy of the OCHS.)

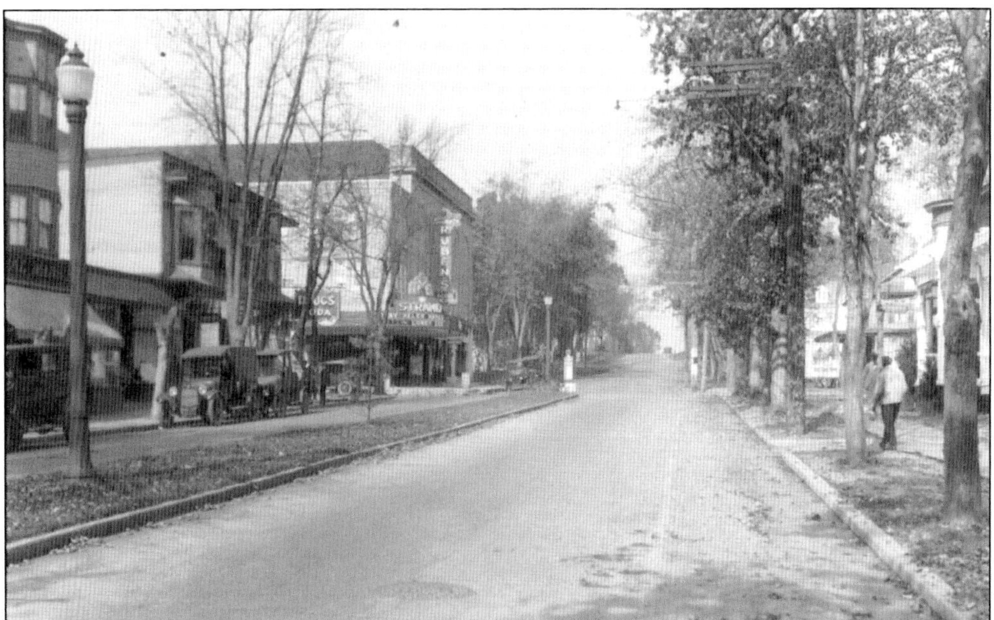

This is a view looking north on Clifton Avenue at the intersection of Fourth Street. The Strand Theater can be seen down the street, on the left. (Photograph courtesy of the OCHS.)

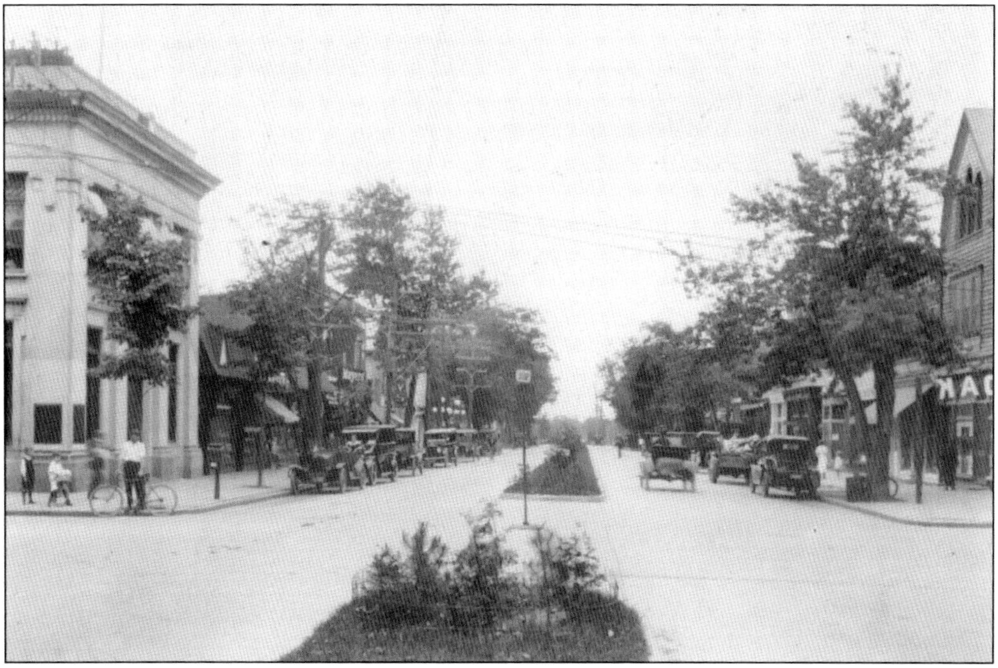

This is a view at the intersection of Clifton Avenue and Second Street. On the left is the Peoples Bank. The northbound and southbound lanes of Clifton Avenue are divided by a grassy median. During the holidays the medians were adorned with festive decorations. (Photograph courtesy of the OCHS.)

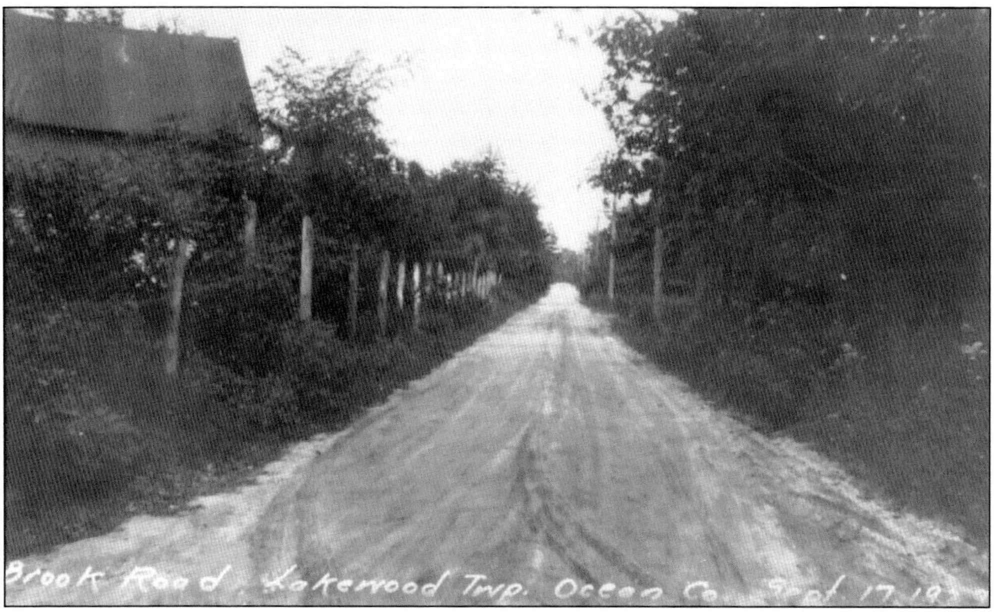

Brook Road used to be a rural, unpaved dirt road, like many of the old avenues of travel in Ocean County. The barn on the left is the only structure that can be seen from the road. This picture was taken on September 17, 1929. (Photograph courtesy of the OCHS.)

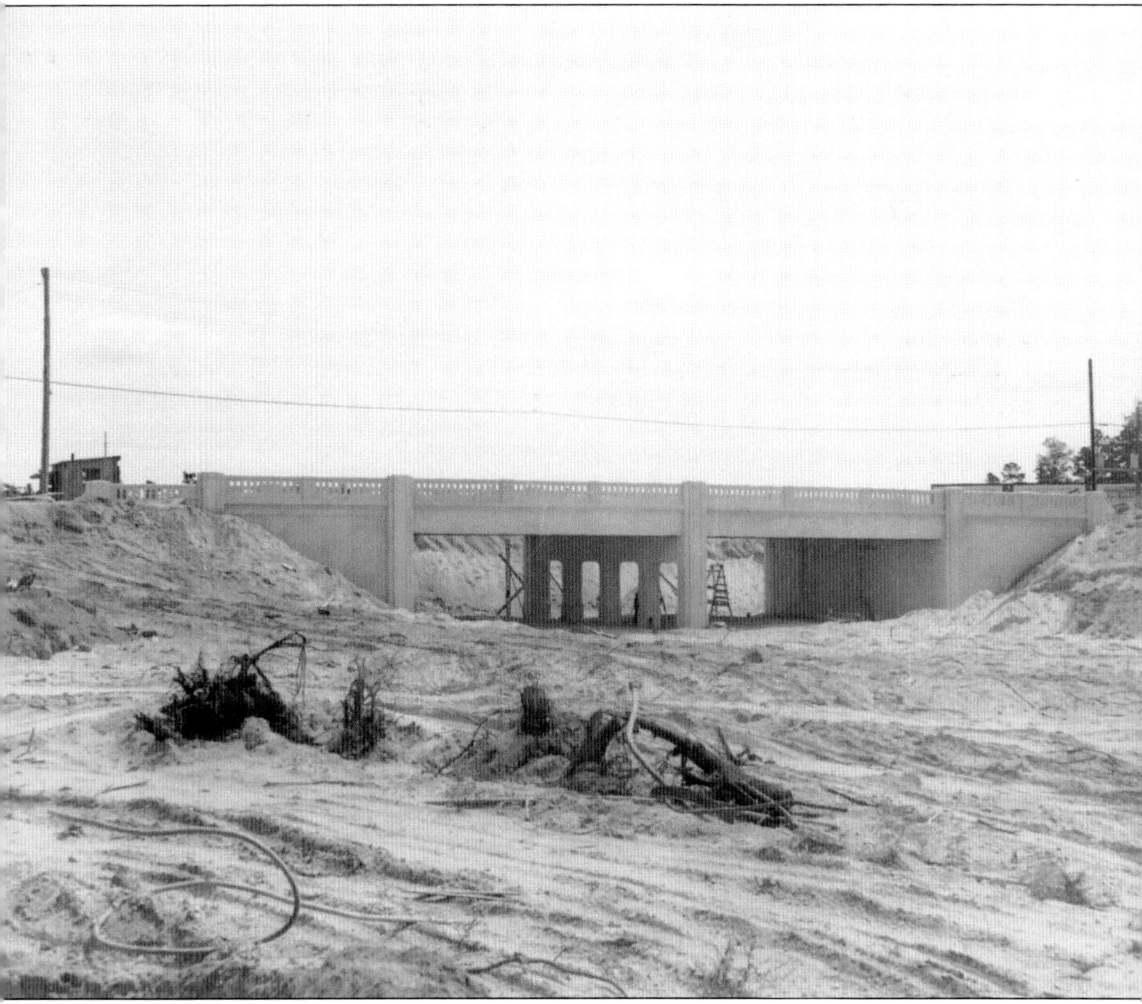

A photograph taken on August 18, 1936, shows the construction of the Route 9 overpass above Route 70. Today, Routes 70 and 9 are major highways that intersect in Lakewood. Route 70 stretches east to west across the state; Route 9 runs north and south. (Photograph by F.W. Tupper, courtesy of the OCHS.)

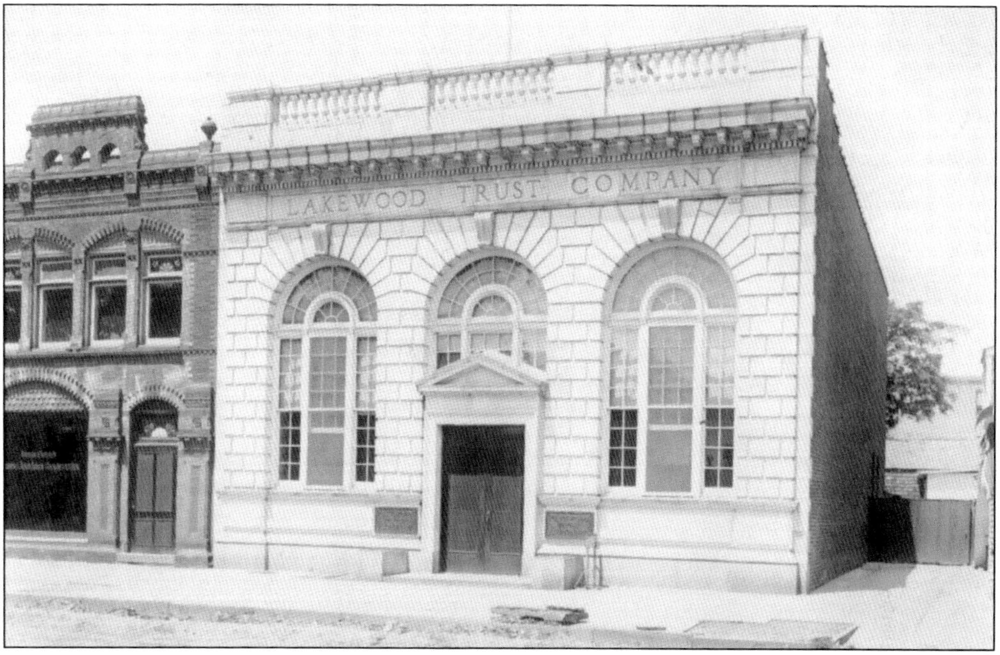

The Lakewood Trust Company was located on Main Street between Madison and Clifton Avenues. The building remains, though it has gone through several name changes. In 1963, the name was changed to the Trust Company of Ocean County. Today, the building houses a branch of the First Union Bank. (Photograph courtesy of the OCHS.)

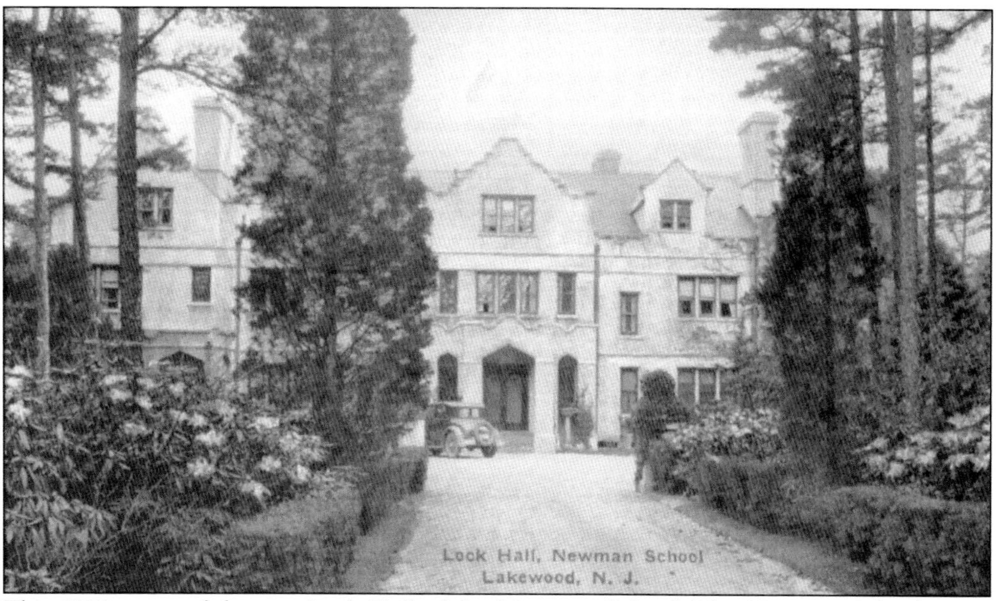

This 1929 postcard features Lock Hall of the Newman School. The Newman School was a prestigious Catholic preparatory school for boys. Some of the names that could be found on the attendance rosters included author F. Scott Fitzgerald and William Vanderbilt. The school's last class graduated during World War II. During the war, the U.S. Navy used the school to train its sailors and meteorologists. Some of these historic buildings are still standing in Pine Park. (Postcard courtesy of the OCHS.)

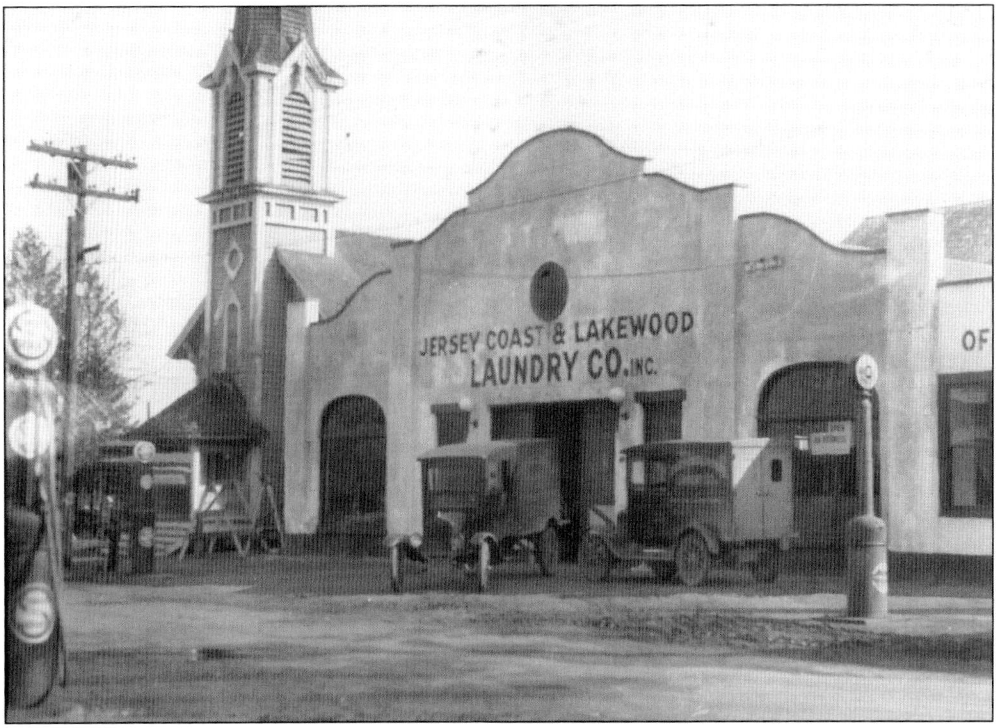

The Jersey Coast & Lakewood Laundry Company, above, was located on 114 First Street and Lexington Avenue. Laundry from different locations around the town and the county were serviced at the plant. Below, a Jersey Coast & Lakewood Laundry Company delivery and pickup truck awaits its next call. (Photographs by F.W. Tupper, courtesy of the OCHS.)

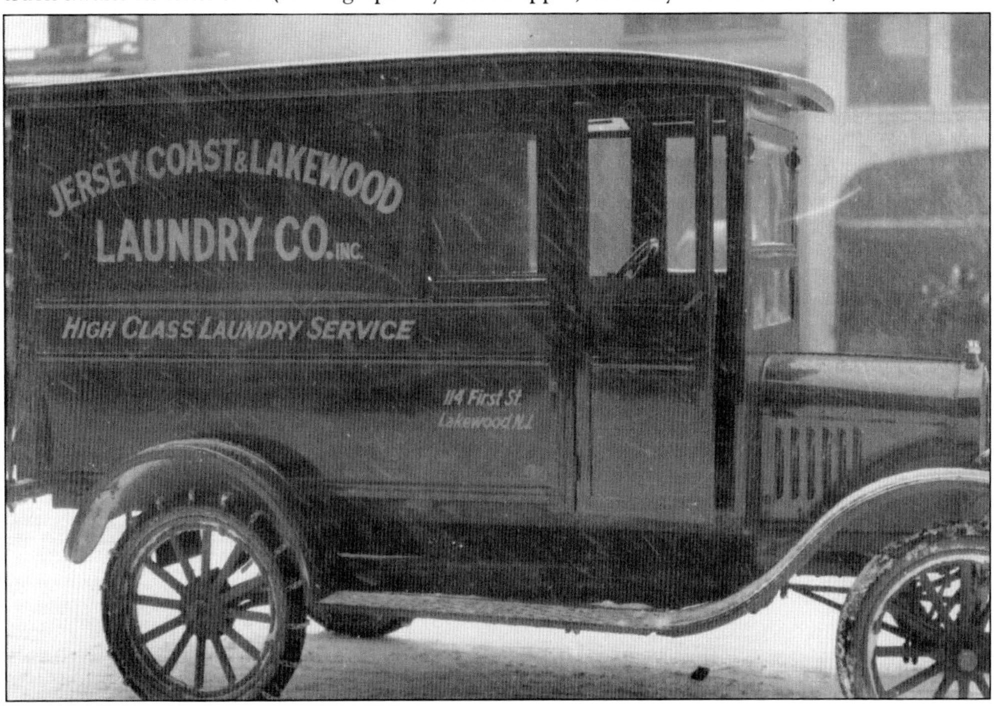

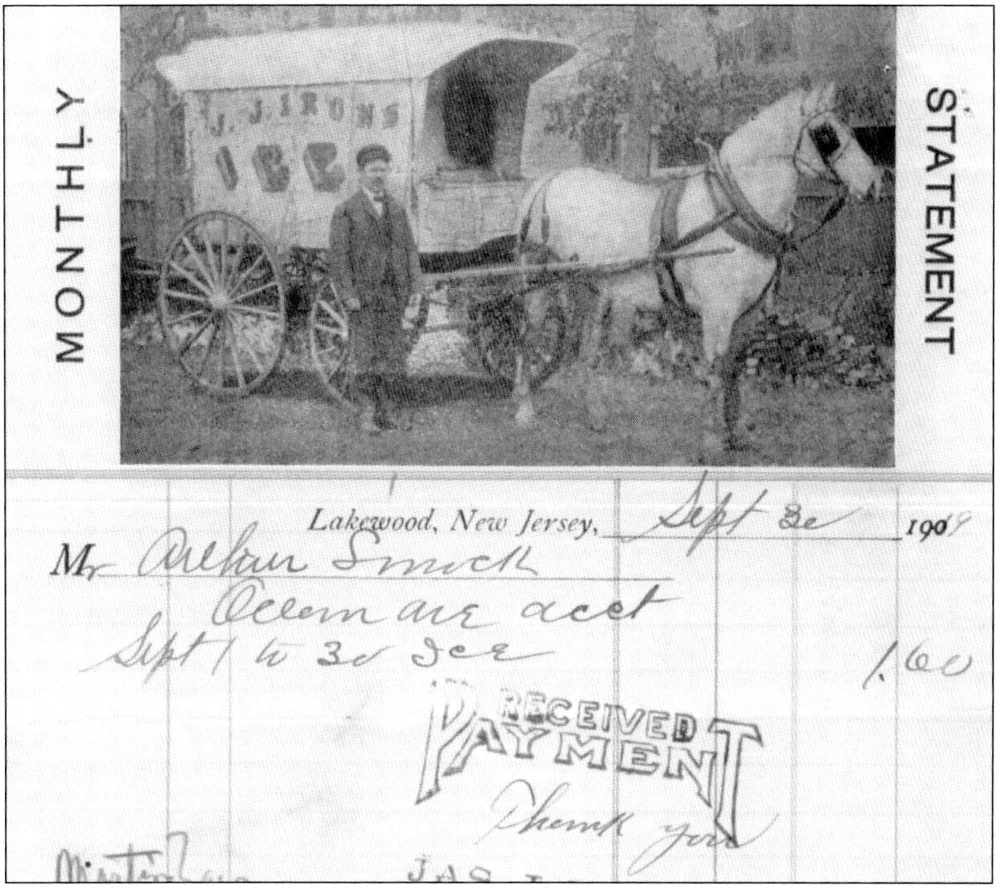

This monthly statement from the J.J. Irons Ice Company was issued to Arthur Smock for an ice delivery. The horse-and-wagon delivery service charged Smock $1.60 for the service rendered in September 1919. (Photograph courtesy of the OCHS.)

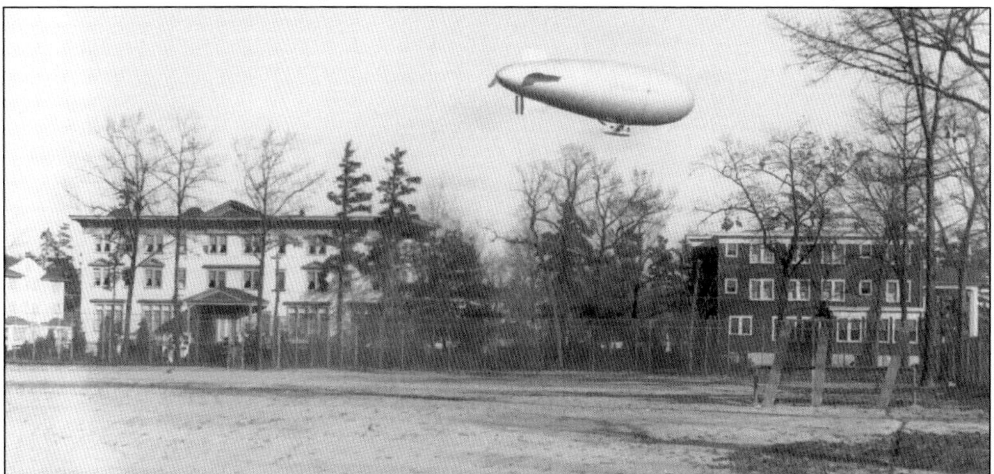

A U.S. Navy blimp is seen over Lakewood on its way to Lakehurst. The view is from the Clifton Avenue School playground. (Photograph by F.W. Tupper, courtesy of the OCHS.)

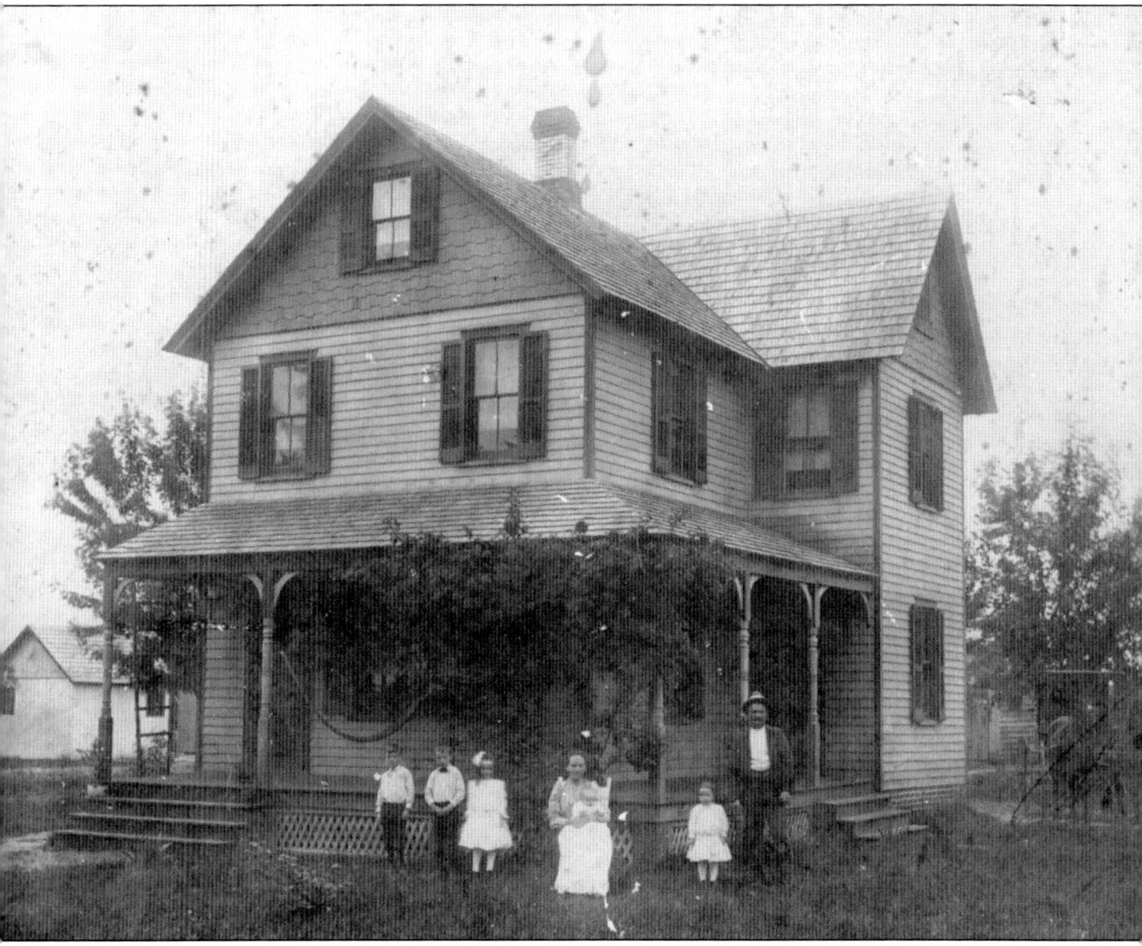

This portrait of the Johnson family at their home dates from c. 1903. The Johnson household was located at 614 County Line Road. Members of the family are, from left to right, George Johnson, O. Johnson, Dorothy Johnson, Lizzie Johnson, Bessie Johnson, Sadie Johnson, and Benjamin Johnson. (Photograph courtesy of Betsy Dudas.)

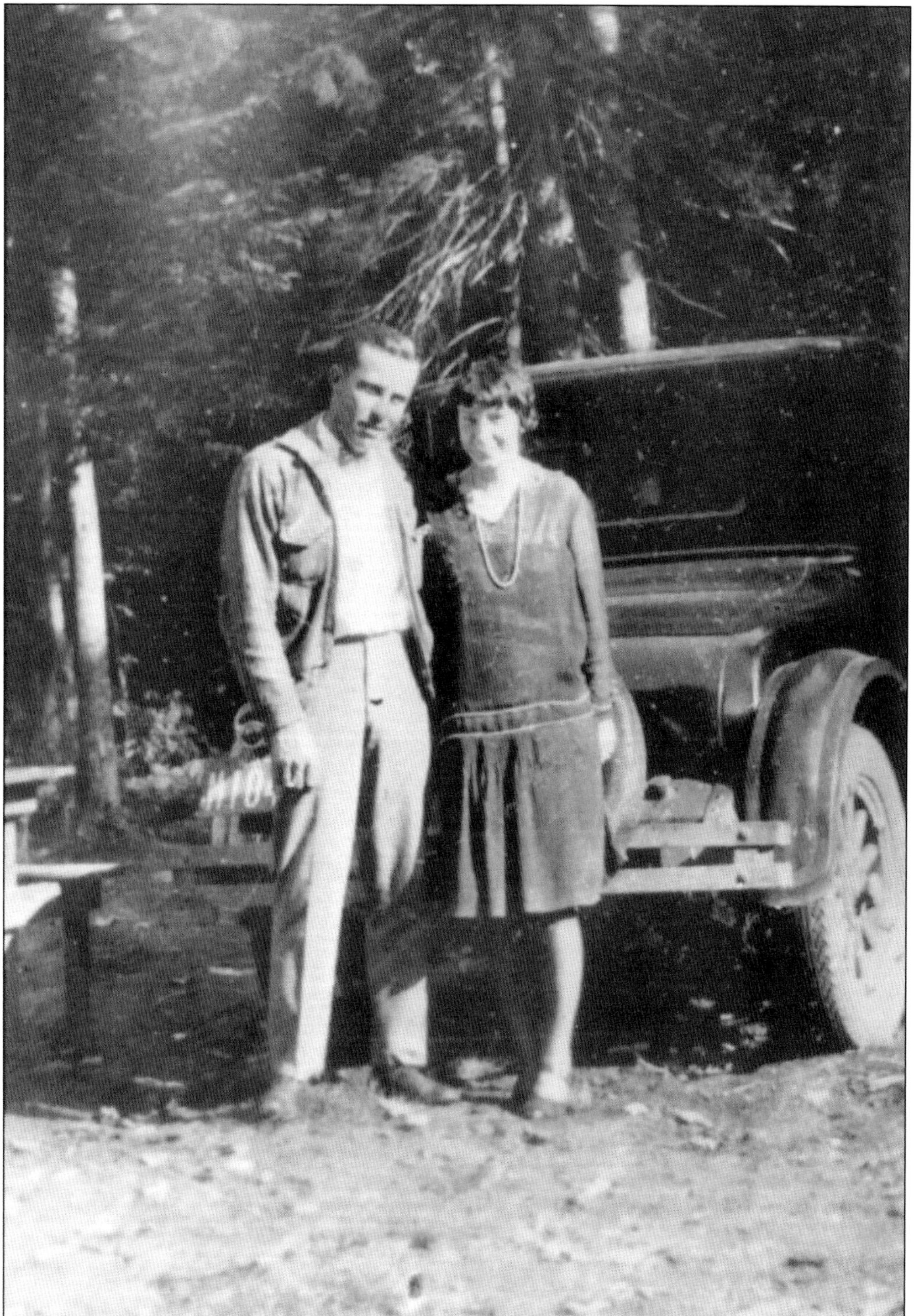

This photograph is of Ralph H. and Florence E. Clayton, *c.* the late 1920s. Ralph H. Clayton was the founder of the Clayton Block Company, which is located on Route 528 in Lakewood. (Photograph courtesy of Leisa Clayton.)

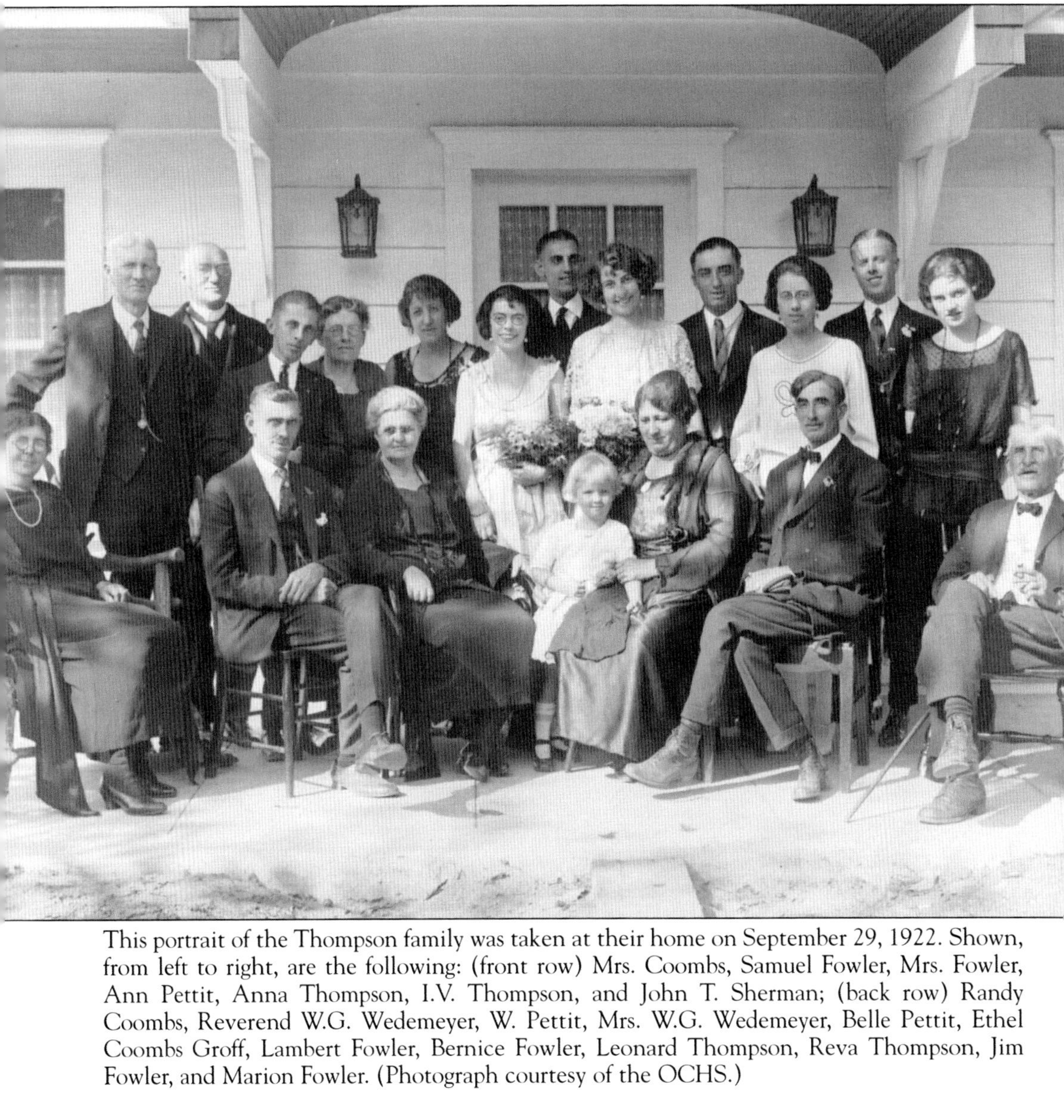

This portrait of the Thompson family was taken at their home on September 29, 1922. Shown, from left to right, are the following: (front row) Mrs. Coombs, Samuel Fowler, Mrs. Fowler, Ann Pettit, Anna Thompson, I.V. Thompson, and John T. Sherman; (back row) Randy Coombs, Reverend W.G. Wedemeyer, W. Pettit, Mrs. W.G. Wedemeyer, Belle Pettit, Ethel Coombs Groff, Lambert Fowler, Bernice Fowler, Leonard Thompson, Reva Thompson, Jim Fowler, and Marion Fowler. (Photograph courtesy of the OCHS.)

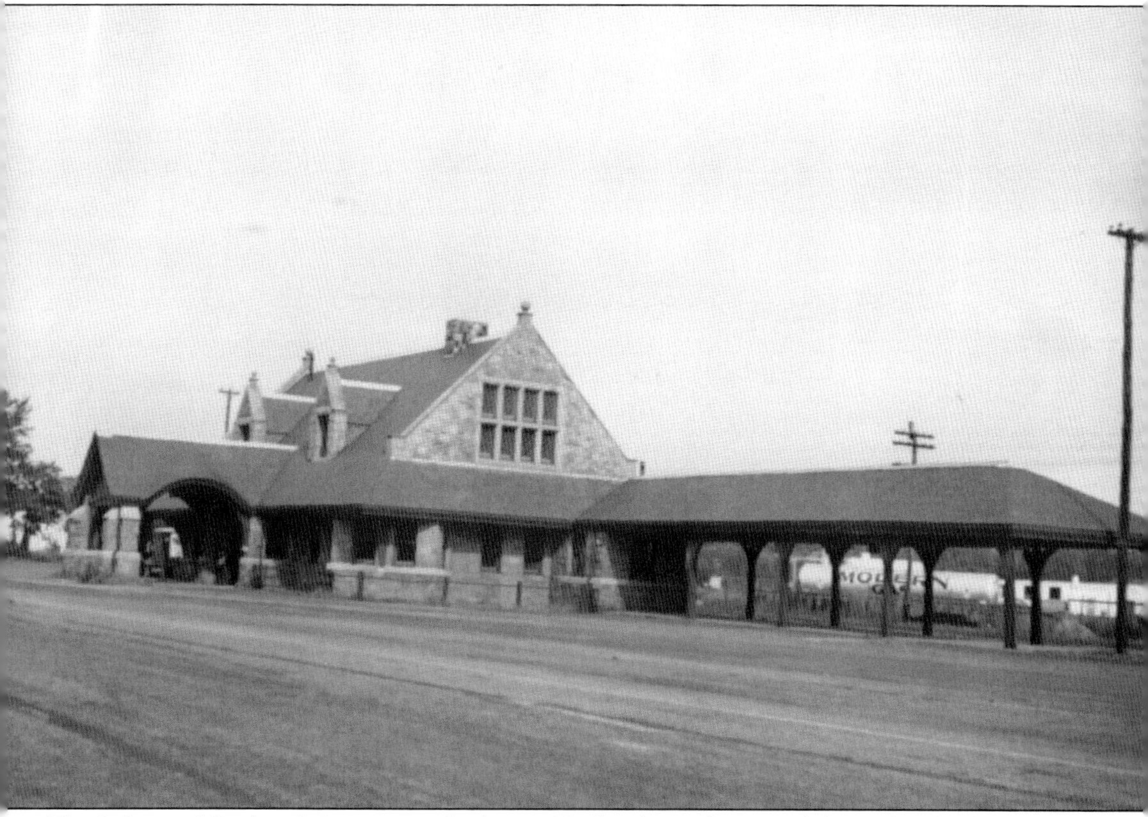

The Lakewood Railroad Station was built in 1891 by the architectural firm of Peabody and York. The station was located on Monmouth Avenue between First and Second Streets. Inside the station were large rest areas for both men and women and fabulous cathedral ceilings. The most eye-catching object in the station was the large fireplace that was used to keep people warm while they were waiting for or arriving from their trains. (Photograph courtesy of the OCHS.)

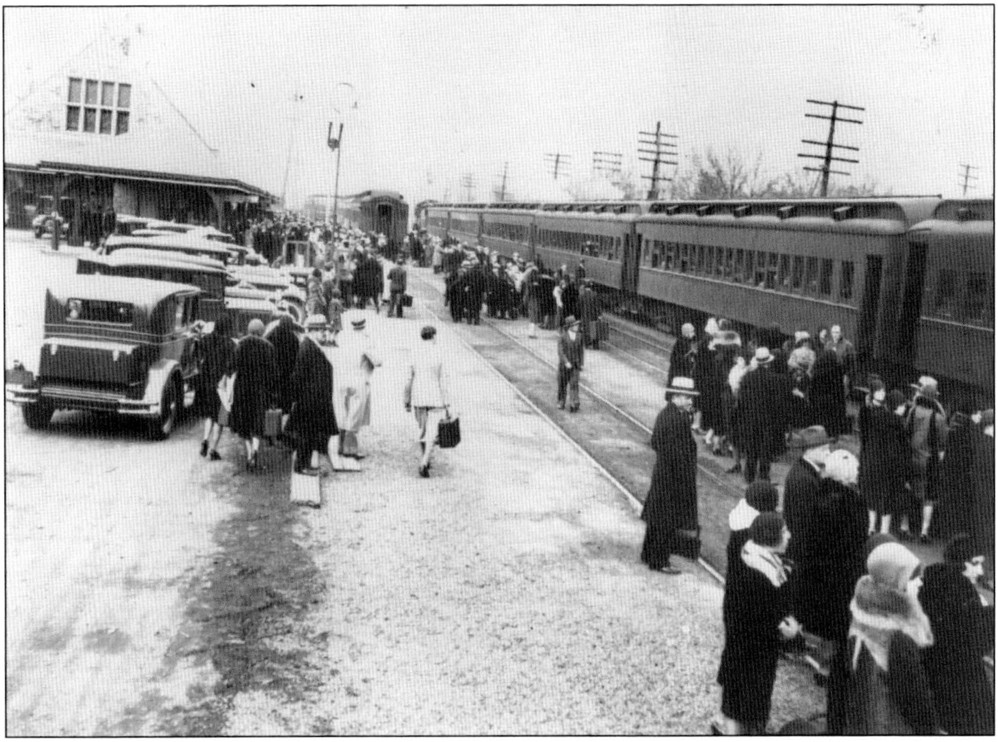

These two pictures show passengers waiting at the Lakewood Railroad Station for the Blue Comet of the New Jersey Central Railroad's Southern Division. The Blue Comet stopped at stations in Elizabethport, Red Bank, Lakewood, Lakehurst, and Hammonton. (Photographs by F.W. Tupper, courtesy of the OCHS.)

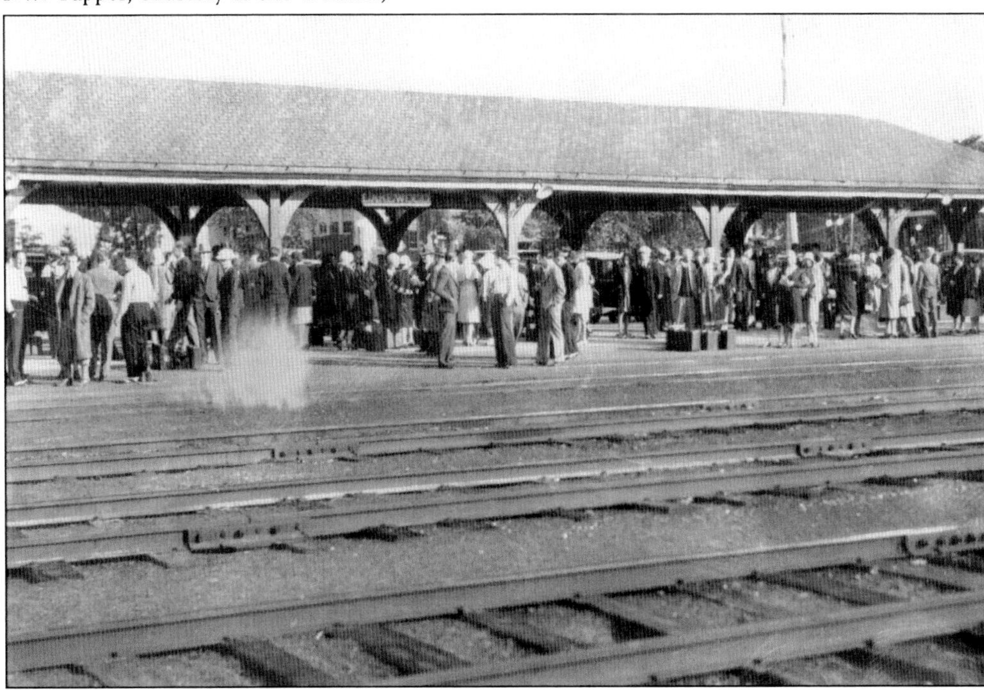

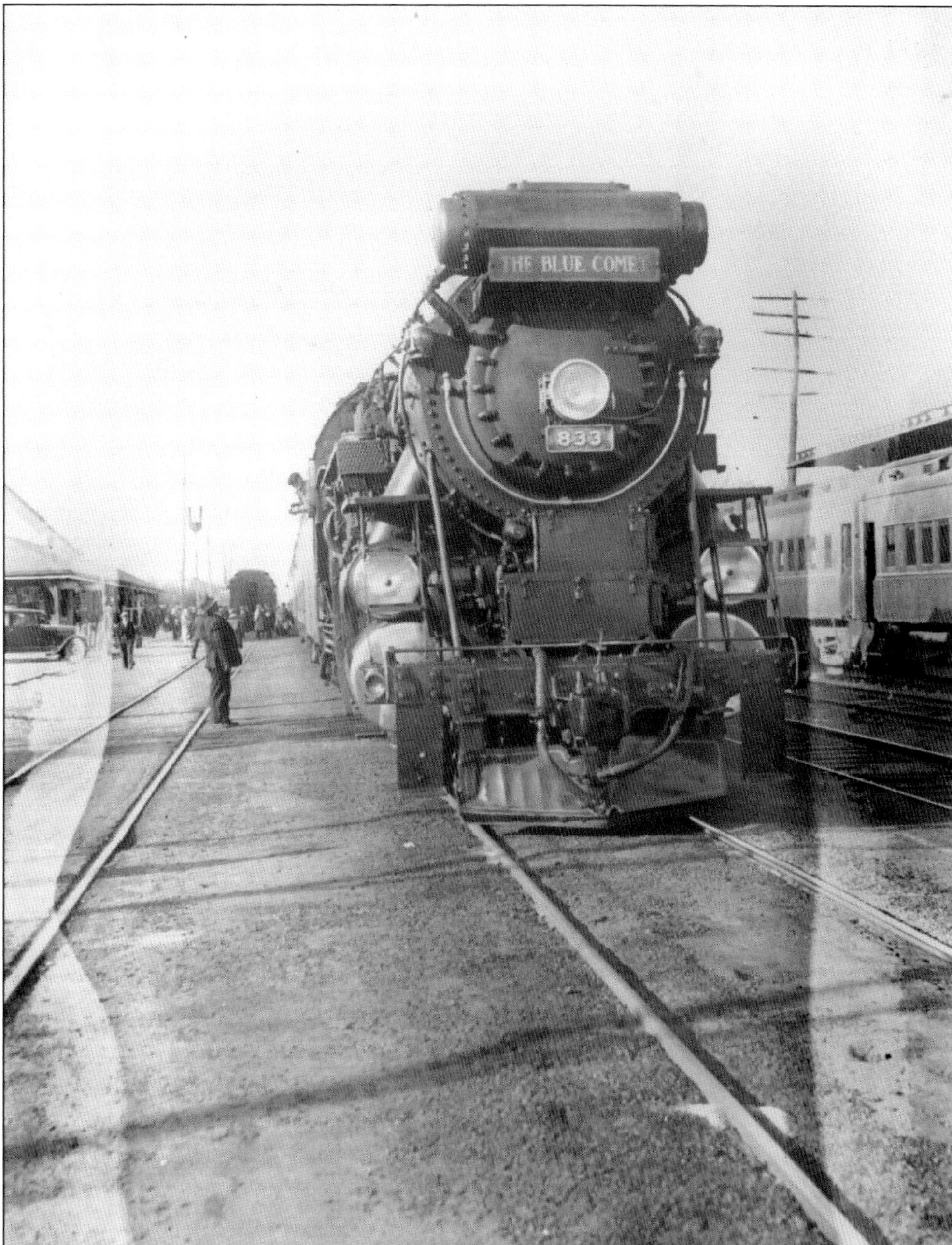

The Blue Comet is shown at the Lakewood Railroad Station. It was the finest long-distance train that the New Jersey Central Railroad's Southern Division produced. The train was painted blue with gold lettering, and the outer part of the windows was cream colored. The Blue Comet replaced the old Atlantic City express routes. (Photograph courtesy of the OCHS.)

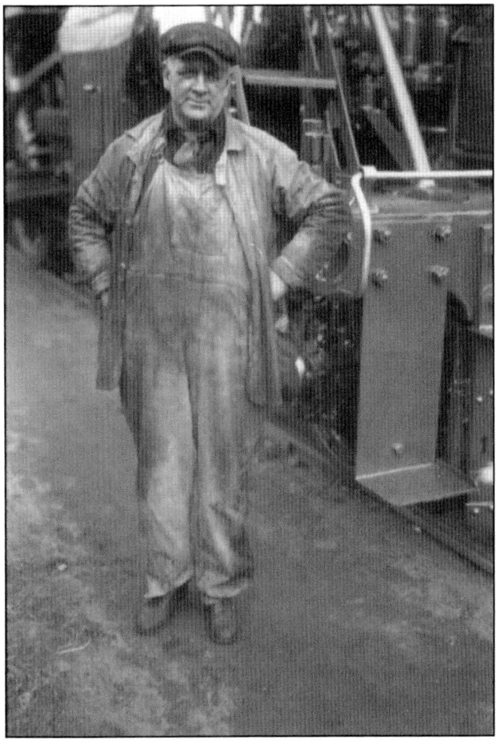

An unidentified train yard worker, covered in soot and coal dust, poses next to the Blue Comet, which had just arrived in town at the station.

On February 22, 1930, these trains of the New Jersey Central Railroad were building up enough power to roll out of the Lakewood Railroad Station and on to their destinations. The trains traveled as far north as New York City and as far south as Atlantic City. (Photograph courtesy of the OCHS.)

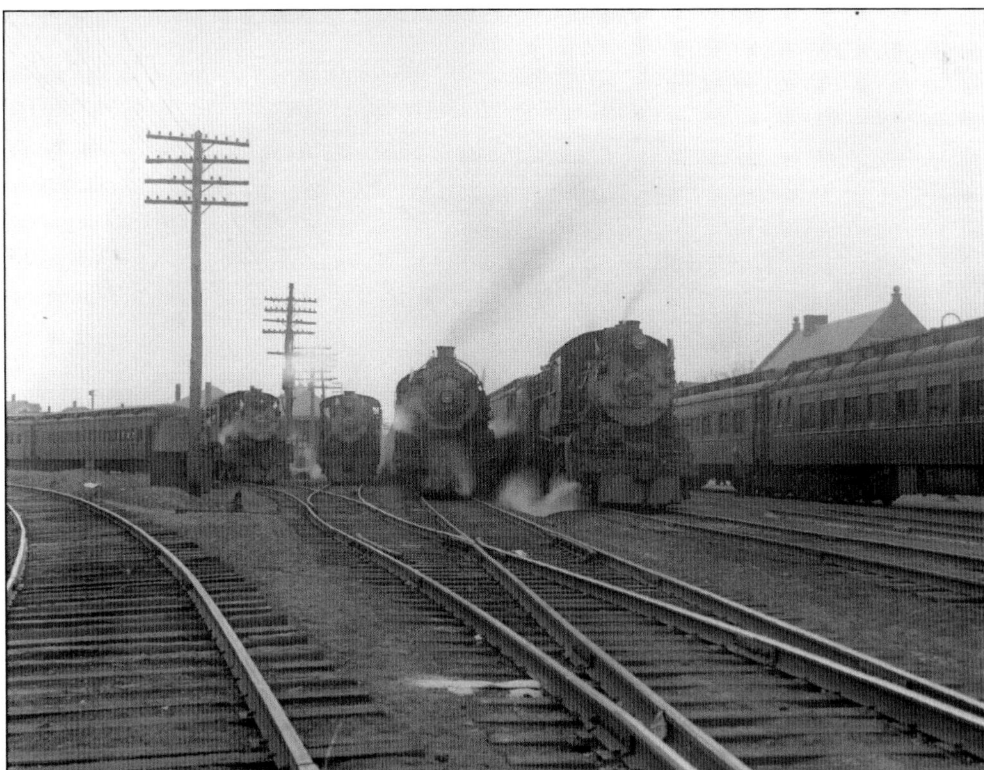

Two

SPORTS AND LEISURE

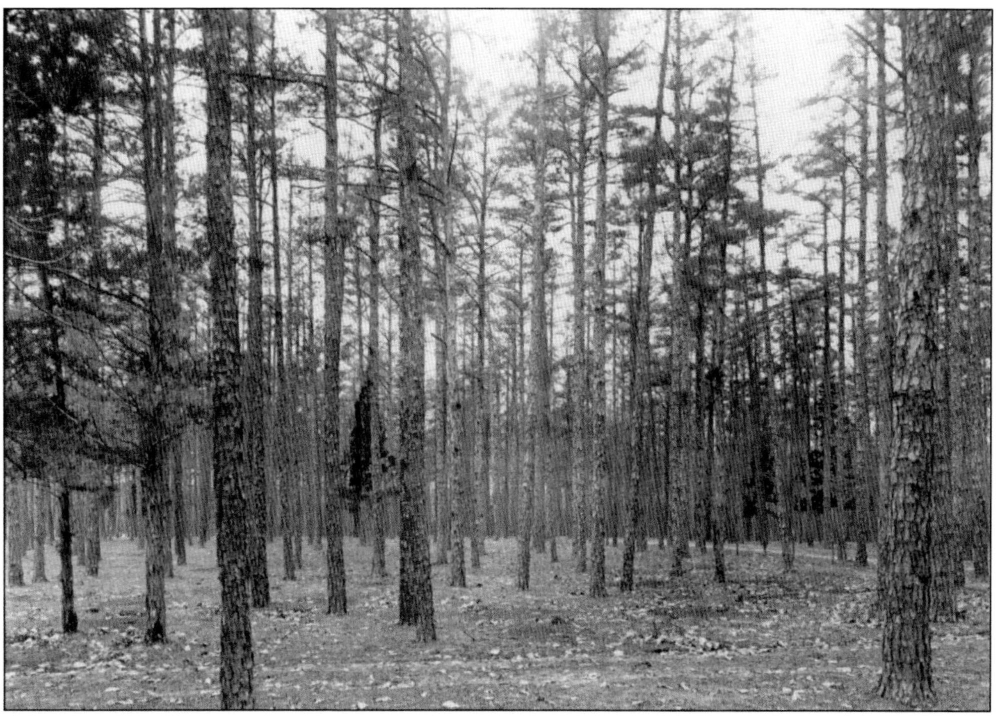

Most of the leisure activities in Lakewood took place either in or around the pine forest of the town. This picture, taken on March 13, 1913, shows a variety of species of trees: pitch pines, shortleaf pines, and red cedars.

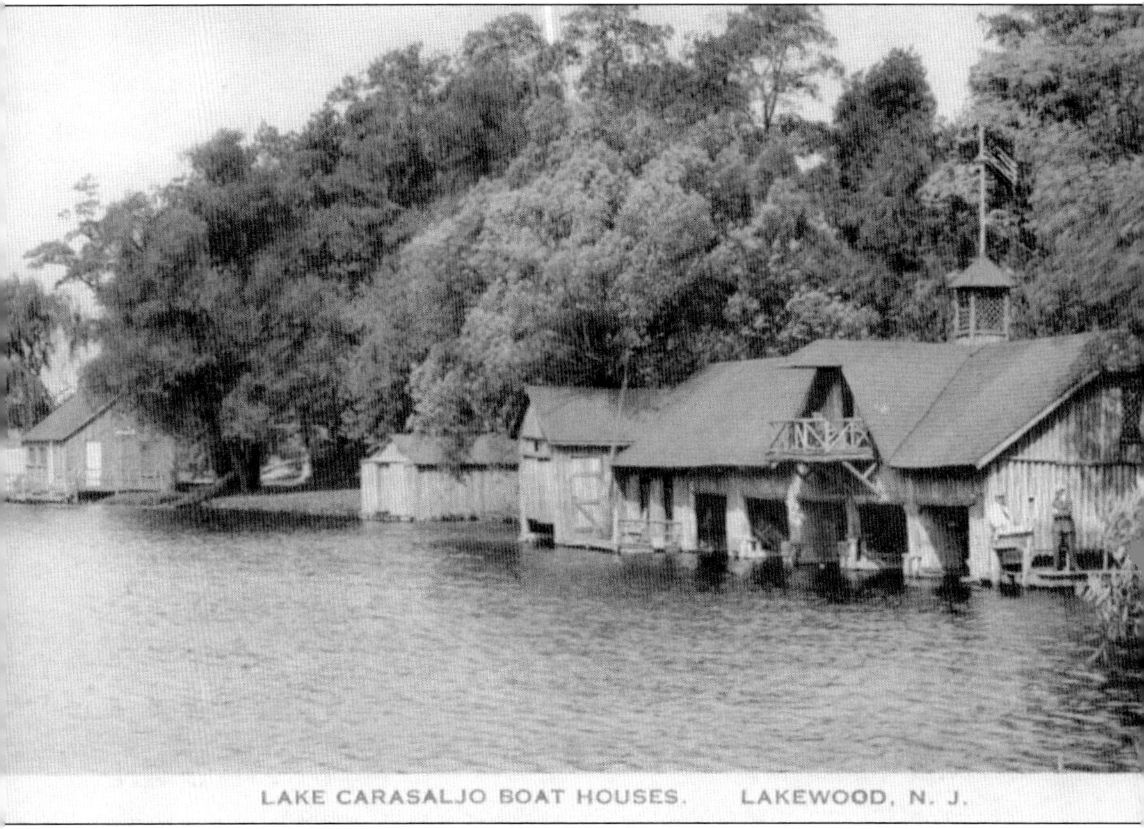

This postcard features the boathouse on Lake Carasaljo. Recreational fisherman who wanted to try their luck in catching the wide variety of fish the lake had to offer launched their crafts from this boathouse. Leisurely boat trips around the lake to take in the natural beauty of the area were very common. (Postcard courtesy of the OCHS.)

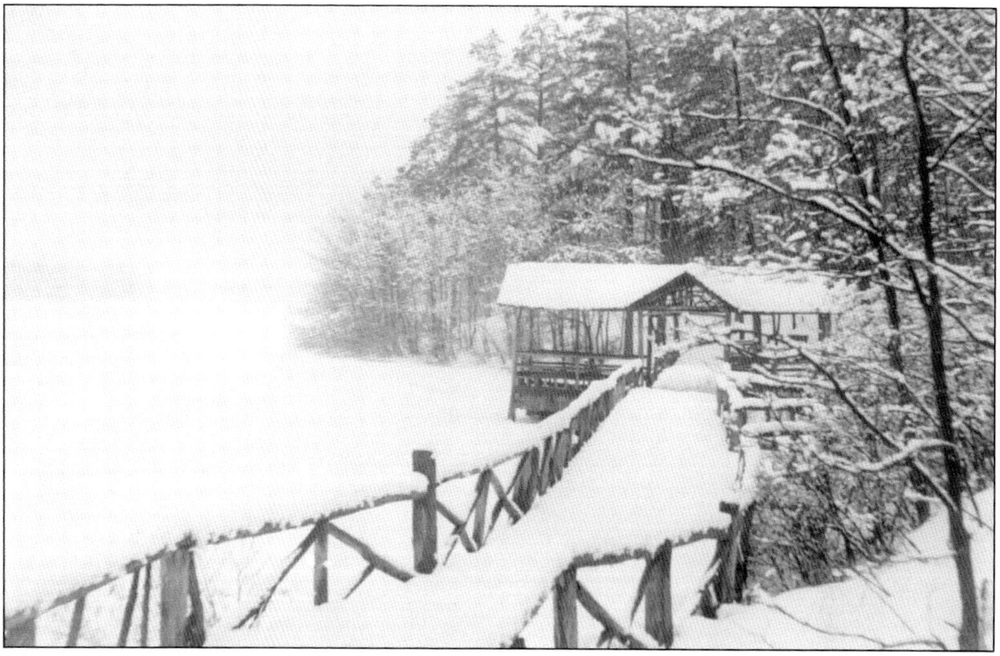

The Kissing Bridge is a well-known landmark to residents and visitors of Lakewood. Anyone who has ever taken a walk through the woods that adorn Lake Carasaljo can easily identify the bridge. The name itself defines the characteristics and nostalgia of the structure. The Kissing Bridge often was covered with snow from a late-winter storm, as shown above; however, a bicyclist could take in the beauty of Lake Carasaljo while resting for a moment on the bridge during the early summer, below. (Photographs courtesy of the OCHS.)

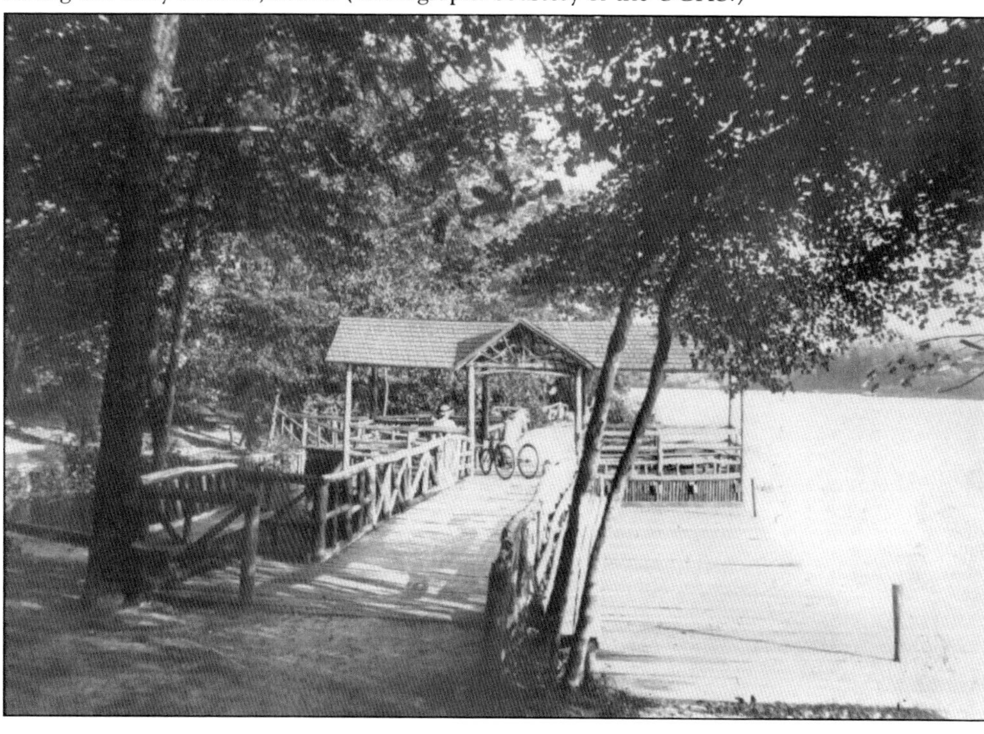

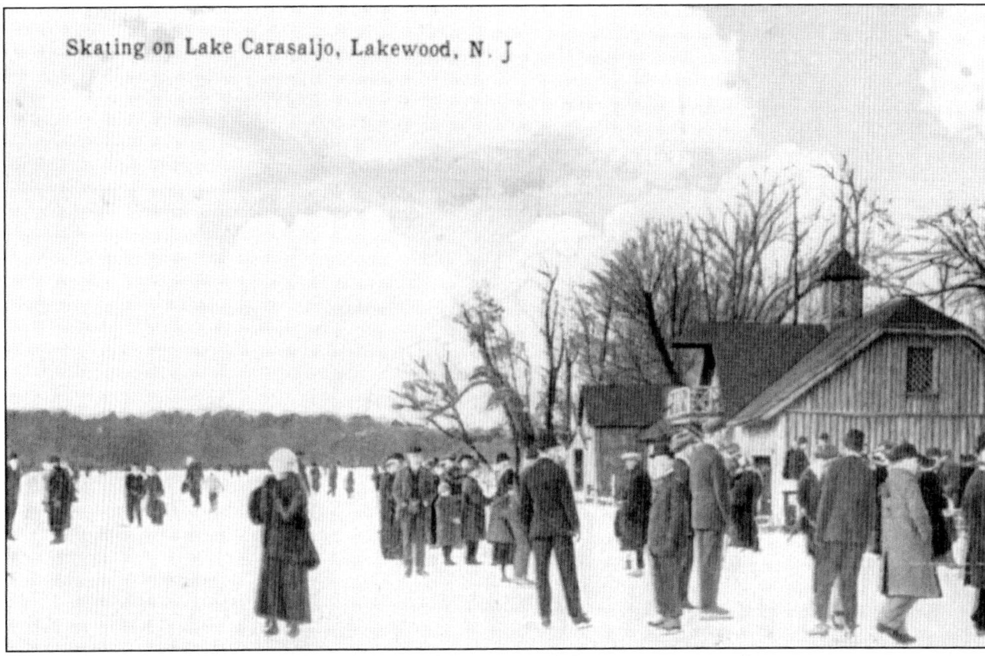

Lakewood's resort season was from early October to late May. During the wintertime, guests at many of the hotels would engage in a selection outdoor winter activities such as ice-skating, iceboat rides, and sleigh riding. The postcard above shows a crowd ice-skating on Lake Carasaljo in the area of the boathouse. Below, an iceboat awaits its next passenger. (Postcards courtesy of the OCHS.)

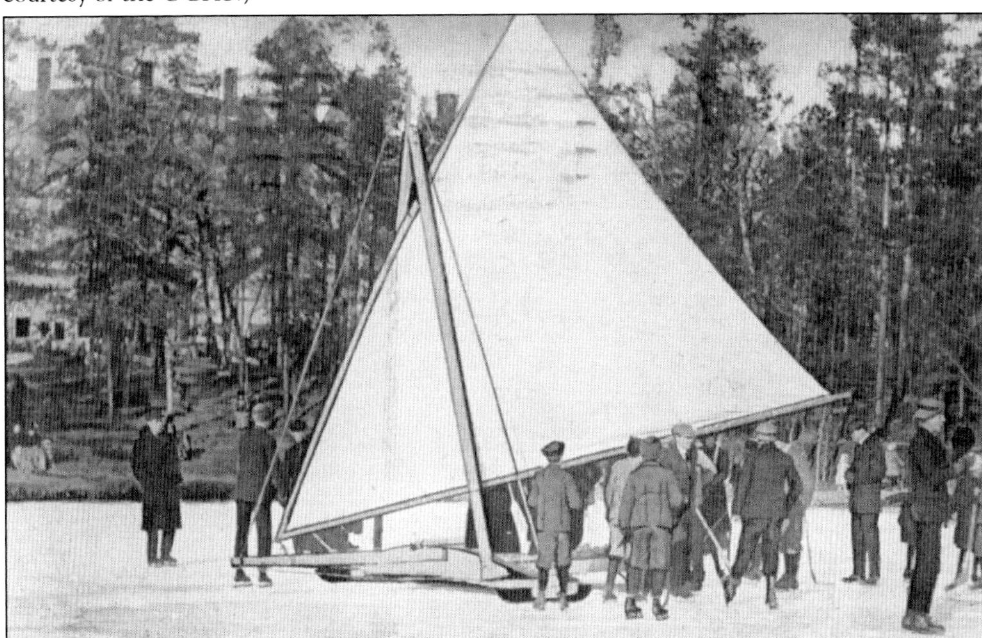

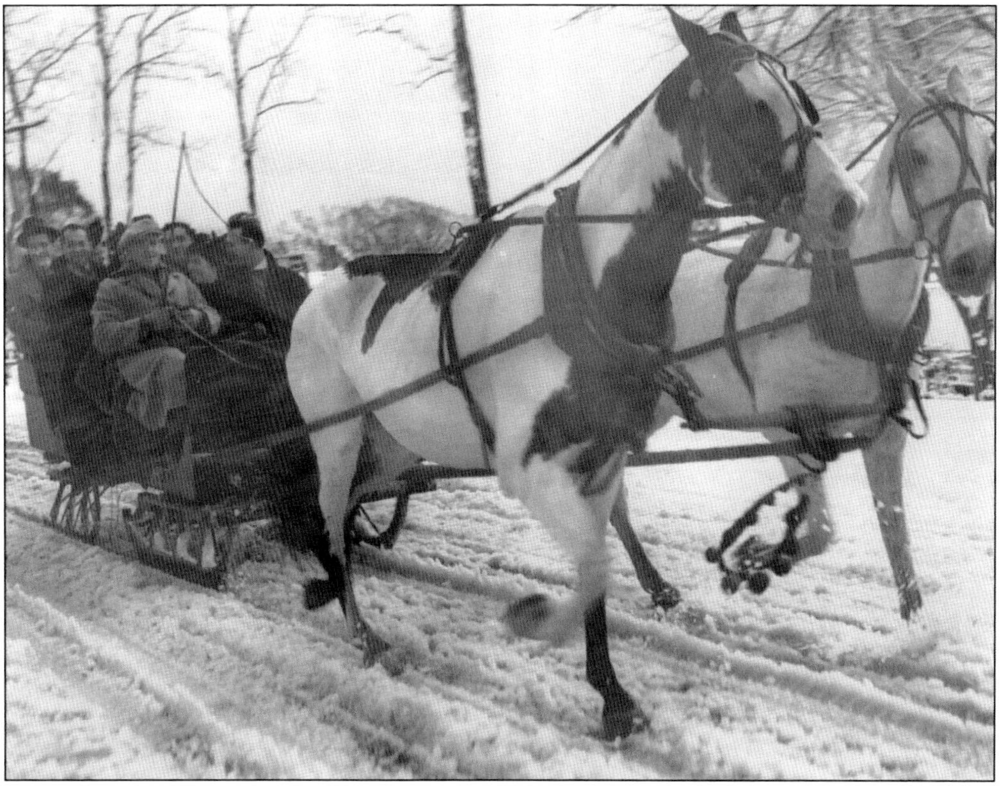

During the winter months, hotel guests were treated to sleigh rides around town. Most of the sleighs would explore the wooded areas around Lake Carasaljo. At certain times during the year, a stretch of Forest Avenue to North Lake Drive was closed to automobile traffic to allow the horse-drawn sleighs to utilize the icy road. Passengers of a crowded sleigh enjoy the exhilaration of a brisk winter's day, above. Below, sleigh drivers prepare for another day of sightseeing as they rush through town to pick up eagerly waiting passengers. (Lower photograph by F.W. Tupper, courtesy of the OCHS.)

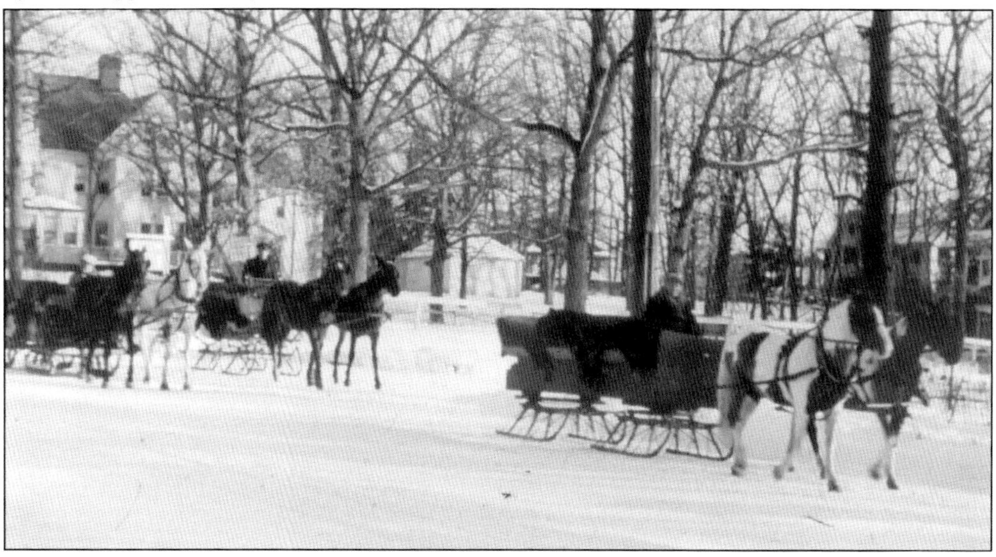

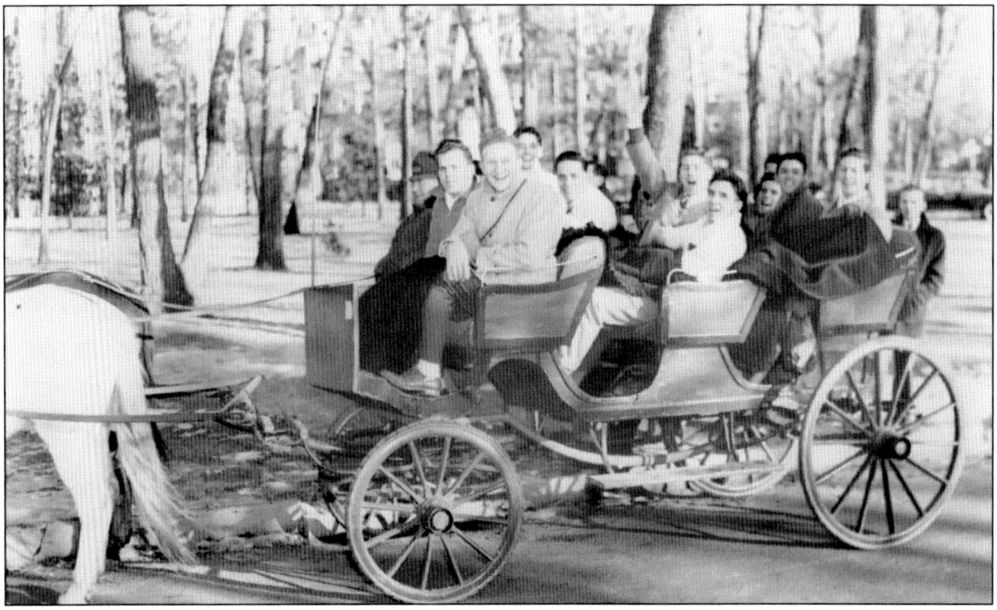

In the early fall and late spring, when there was not a trace of ice or snow on the ground, horse-drawn carriages were used to give tours of the town. Above, a group of college students, probably on a break, excitedly ride by on a crowded horse-drawn carriage. The photograph below was taken during the fall of 1936. Carriages often took passengers on a tour around Lake Carasaljo to see the changing colors of the foliage on the trees. (Photographs by F.W. Tupper, courtesy of the OCHS.)

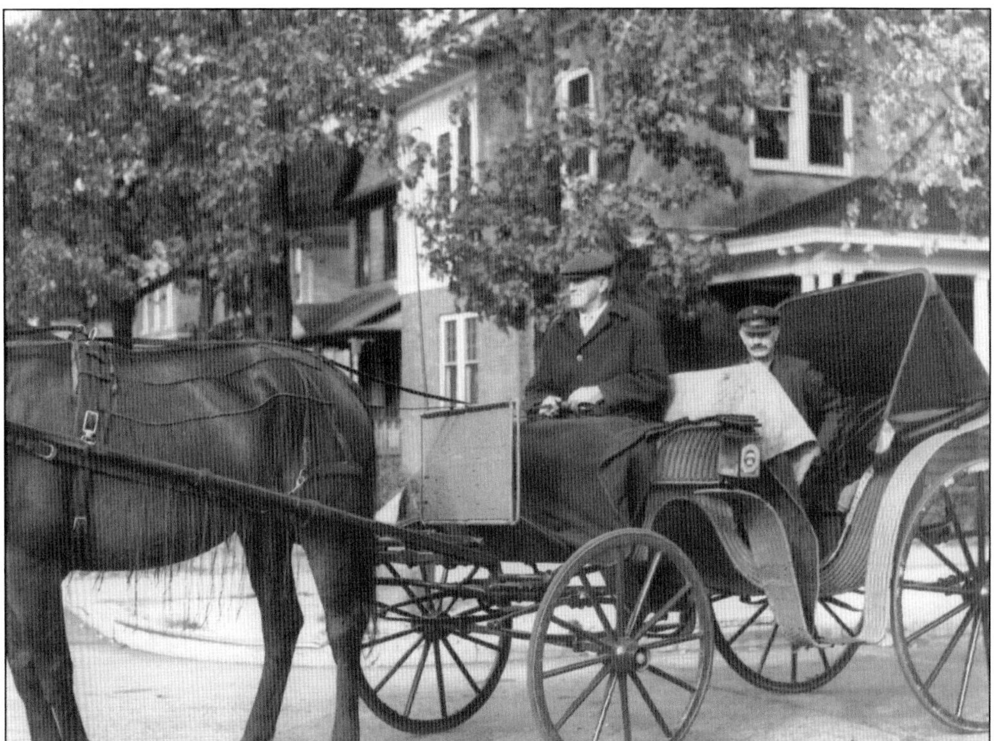

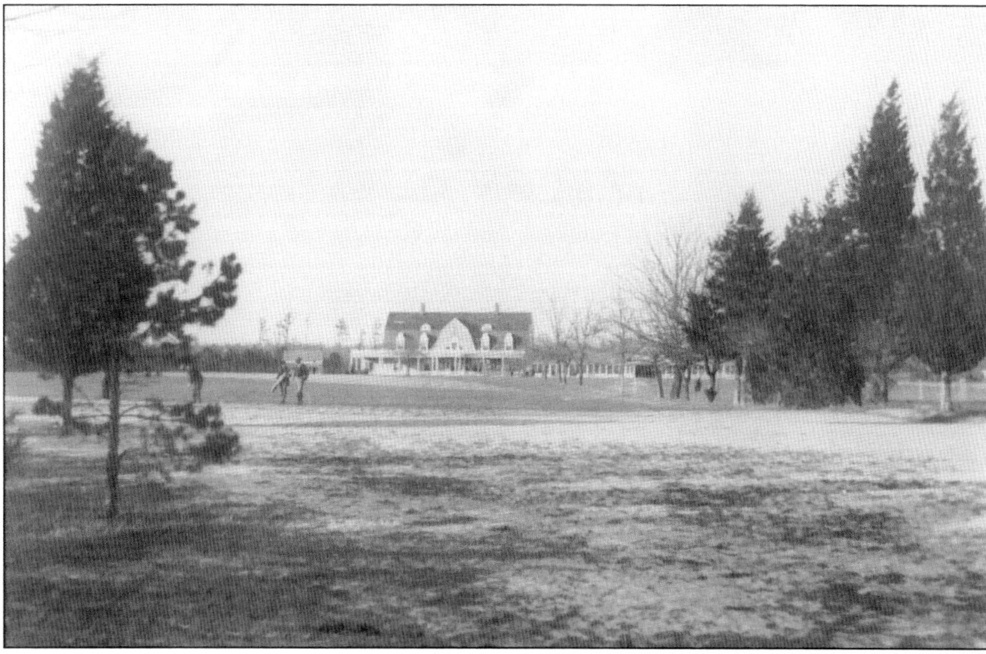

The Country Club of Lakewood was incorporated on June 26, 1902. The five original shareholders of the club were George Jay Gould, Henry A. James, Albert M. Bradshaw, Jasper Lynch, and William A. Hamilton. They all agreed that the insignia of the club should be a pine cone, and the colors of the club should be black and yellow. According to the constitution of the Country Club of Lakewood, the main objective of the club was to purchase, acquire, lease, and provide land, buildings, or structures, golf clubs, golf balls, and other implements, devices, and facilities for golf grounds and games. (Photograph by R. Steele, courtesy of the OCHS.)

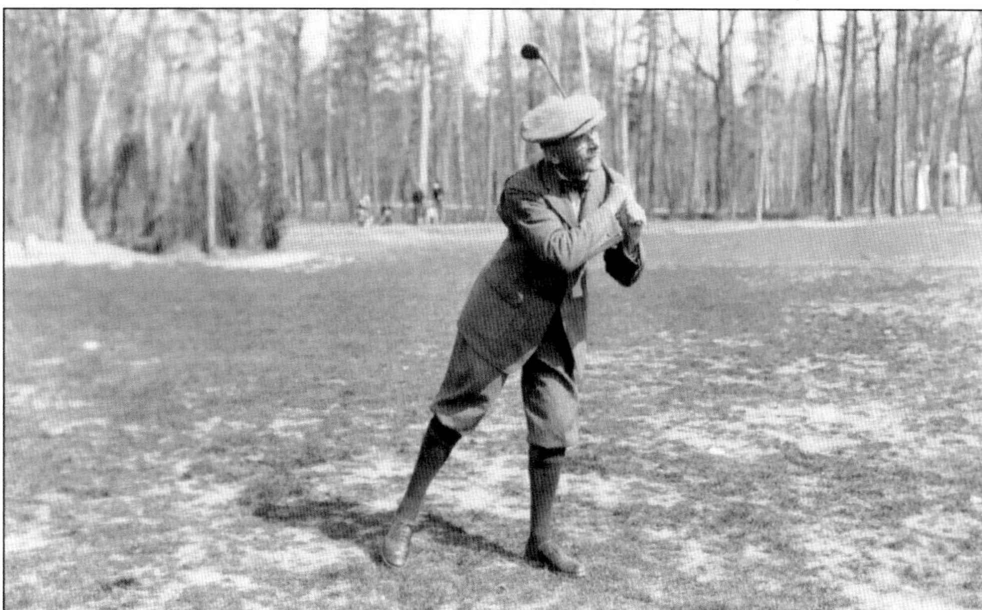

Professional golfer Charles Gardiner follows through on his swing while wondering if the ball will land in his favor. (Photograph courtesy of the OCHS.)

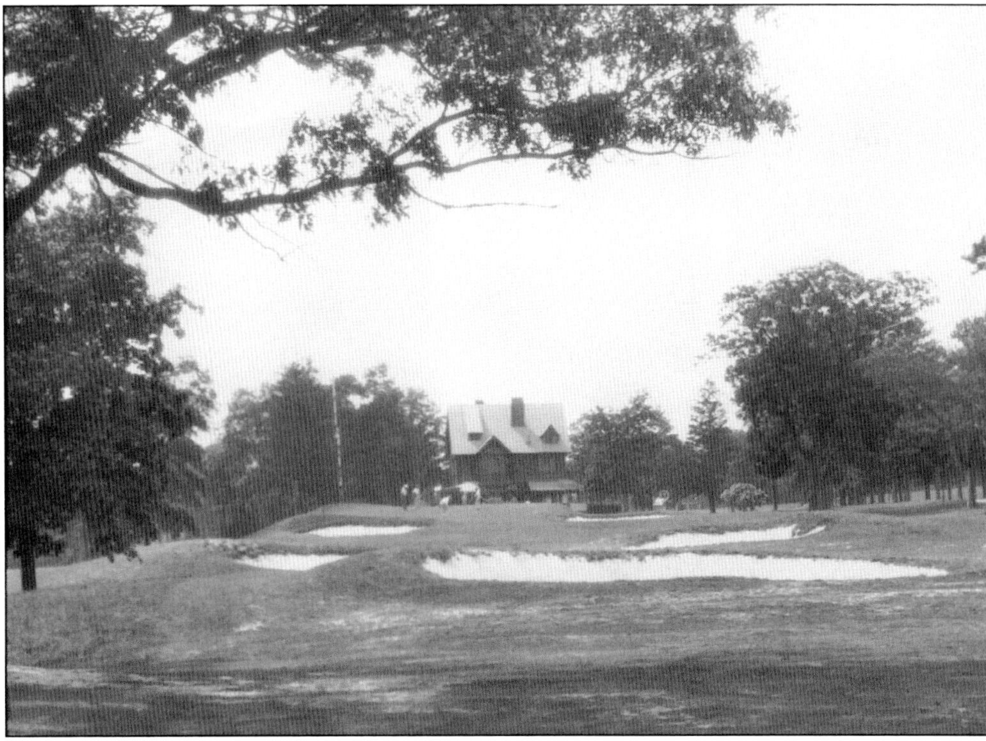

On January 1, 1898, the first professional golf tournament ever played in America took place in Lakewood at the Ocean County Hunt and Country Club's nine-hole golf course. The tournament included ten professional golfers who played three rounds, and competed for the prize purse of $150. The winner of the tournament was a gentleman by the name of Val Fitzjohn. (Photograph courtesy of the OCHS.)

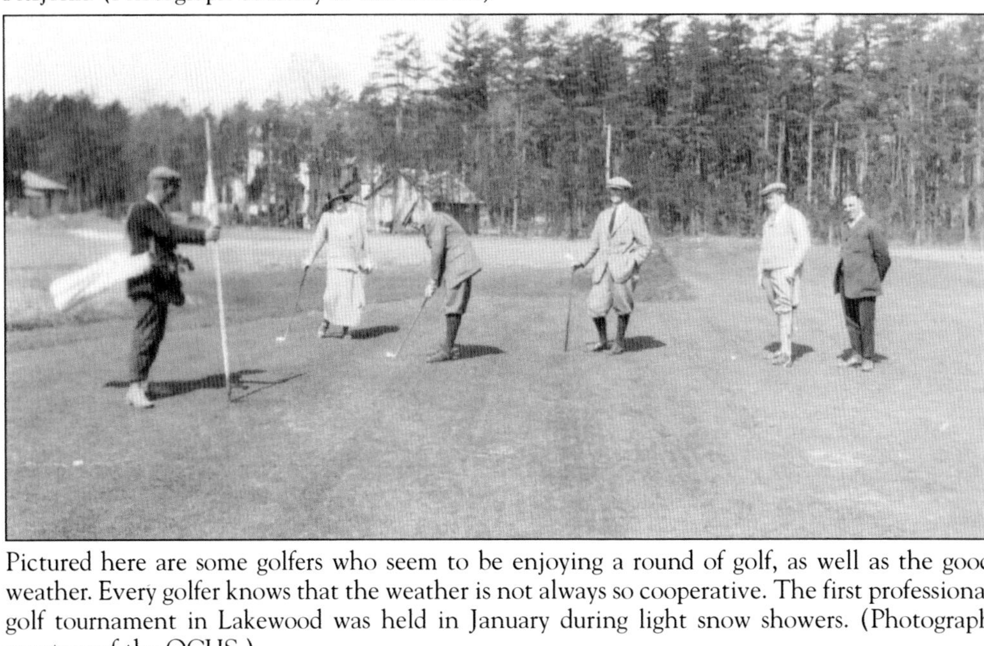

Pictured here are some golfers who seem to be enjoying a round of golf, as well as the good weather. Every golfer knows that the weather is not always so cooperative. The first professional golf tournament in Lakewood was held in January during light snow showers. (Photograph courtesy of the OCHS.)

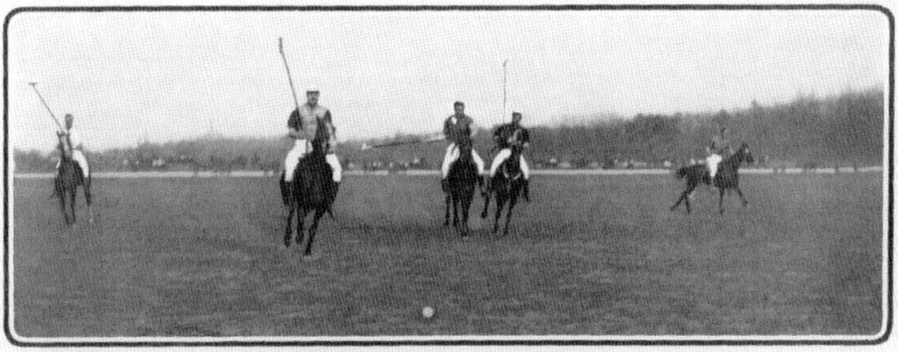

Camden vs. the Second Lakewood Team

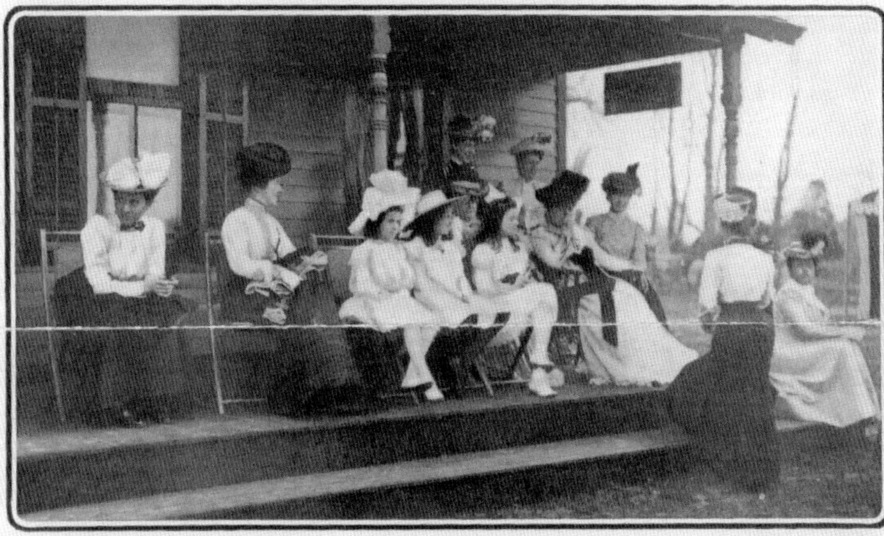

Mrs. Gould and her Guests on the Club-house Veranda

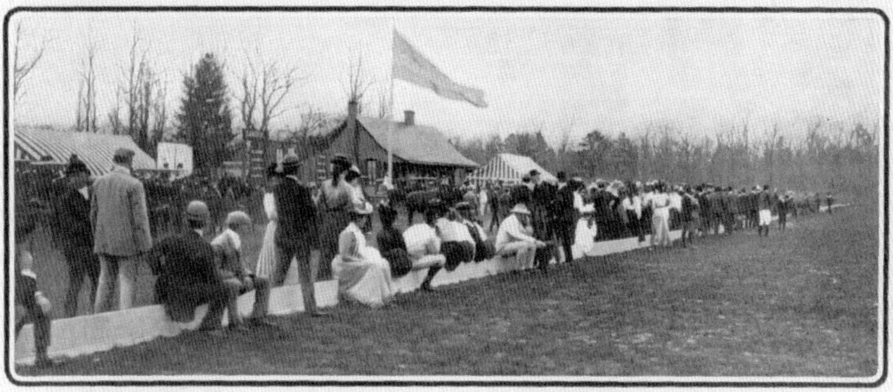

The Gallery

Besides golf and fox hunting, the next most popular sport at the country club was polo. George J. Gould and his polo team participated in matches against teams from all over the United States, Canada, and England. Pictured here are scenes from a match between teams from Lakewood and Camden. Droves of spectators came to see these events.

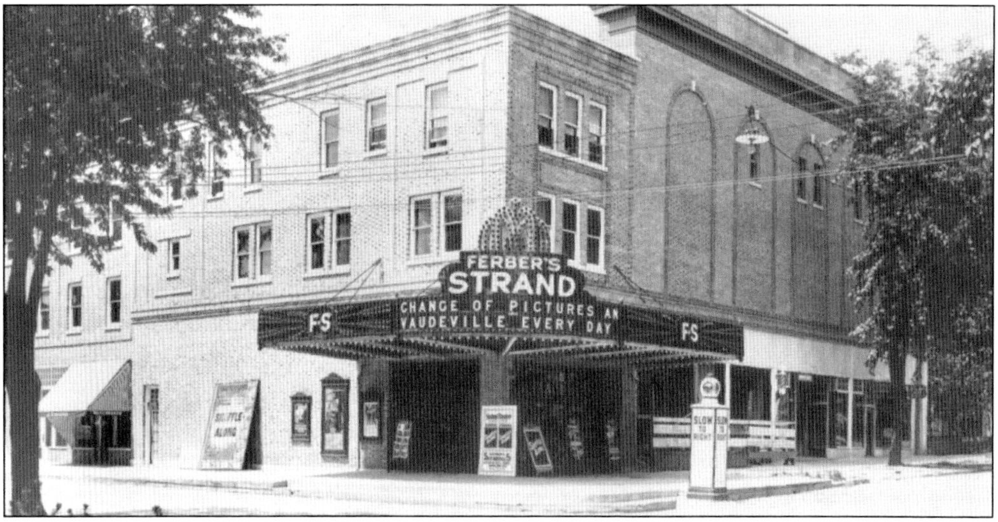

The Strand Theater is located at 401 Clifton Avenue in the heart of downtown Lakewood. The theater was designed by architect Thomas Lamb and constructed by the Ferber Amusement Company in 1922. The theater has a capacity to hold 1,000 patrons. In the spring of 1981, the theater was added to the New Jersey Register of Historic Places, and one year later the National Park Service placed the theater on the National Register of Historic Places. (Photograph courtesy of the OCHS.)

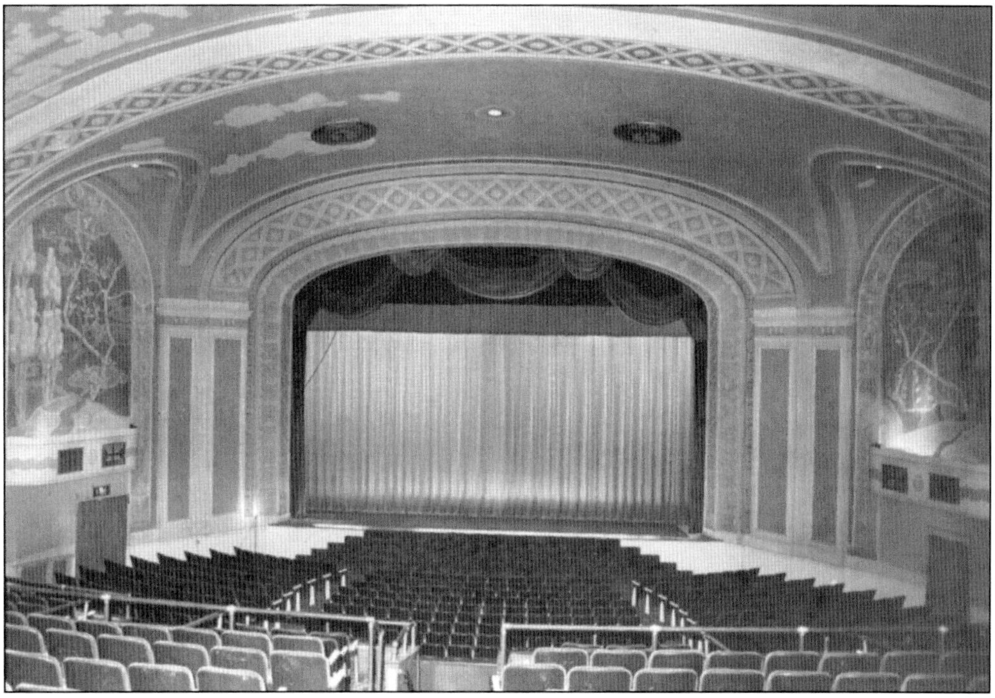

The acoustics inside of the Strand Theater are so excellent that shows can be performed without microphones. The theater was home to a plethora of Broadway and vaudeville shows, silent films, and finally movies with sound. It was not uncommon for five vaudeville acts to be performed in one day. Tickets for the shows ranged from 25¢ to 40¢. The theater is still used today. (Photograph courtesy of the OCHS.)

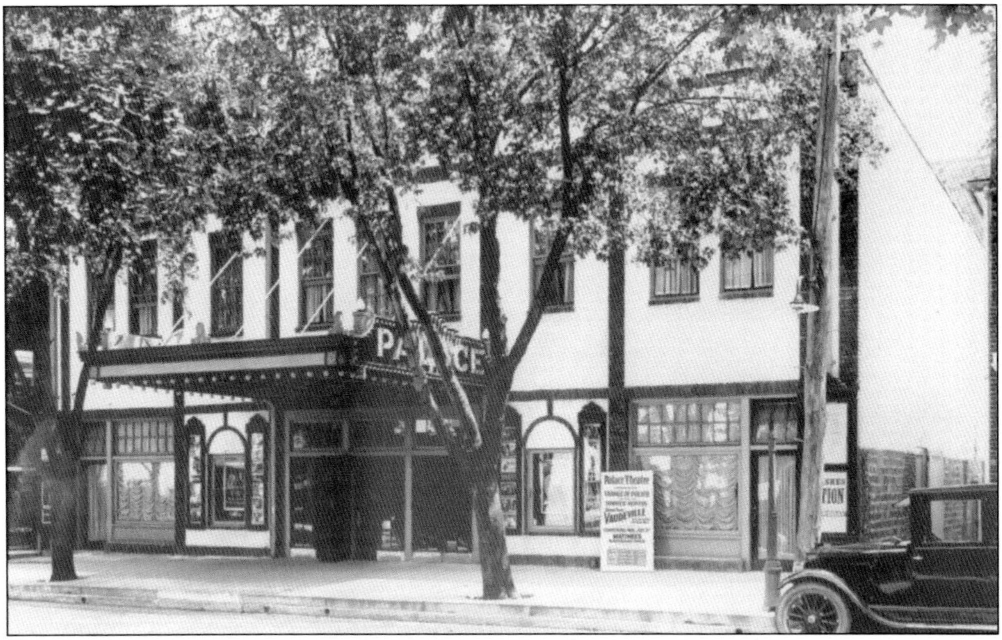

The Palace Theater was located on Second Street close to Monmouth Avenue. The theater used to entertain its guests with vaudeville acts. During the summer, patrons enjoyed the Saturday matinees, when the price for an orchestra box was 35¢ and a loge or mezzanine box was 55¢. At night, an orchestra seat cost 40¢. (Photograph courtesy of the OCHS.)

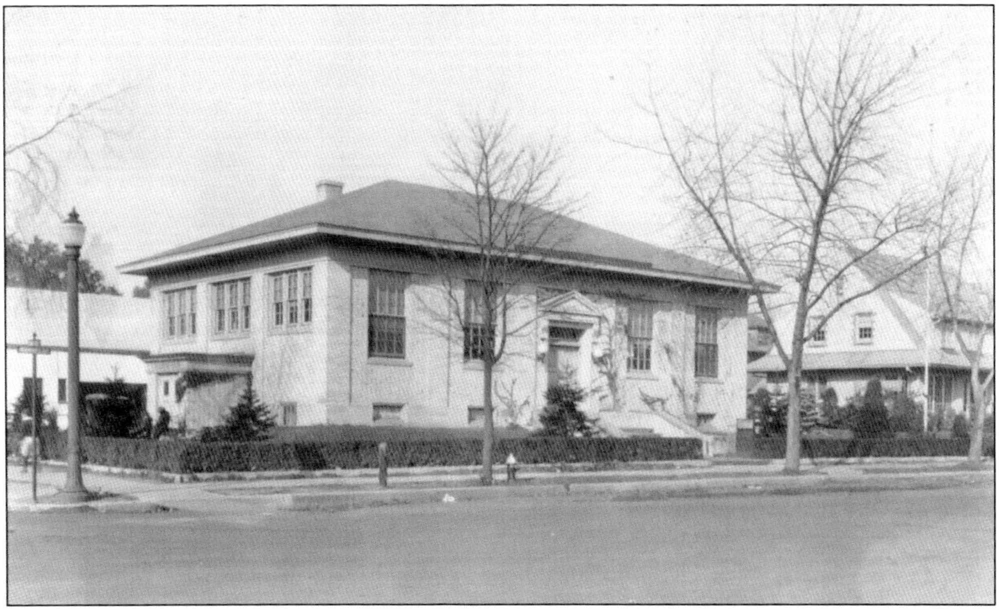

This is the former Lakewood Public Library on Second Street and Monmouth Avenue. The library was constructed using public funds and grants from the Carnegie Foundation. In 1918, the library first opened its doors. This library had ties to the Bricksburg Library Association, which was established in 1869. Recently, a new Lakewood Library was built on Lexington Avenue and was absorbed into the Ocean County Library System. (Photograph courtesy of the OCHS.)

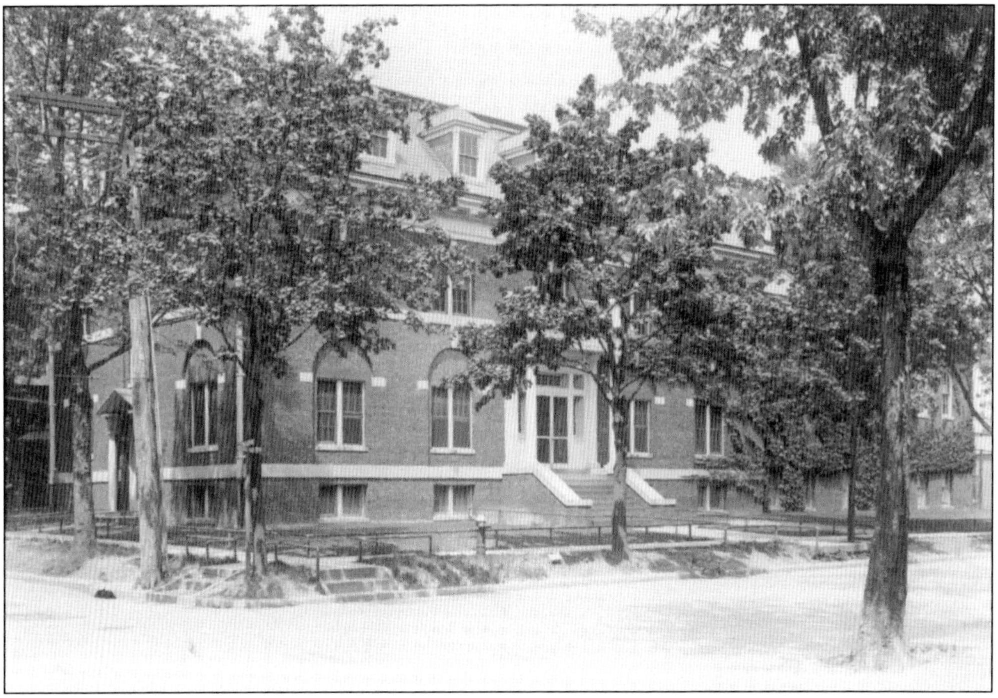

The YMCA in Lakewood, located on Monmouth Avenue, was incorporated in 1905. The building that housed the organization opened its doors in 1908. The YMCA included a swimming pool, gymnasium, bowling alley, and rooms that were used for reading, meetings, and other indoor activities. (Photograph courtesy of the OCHS.)

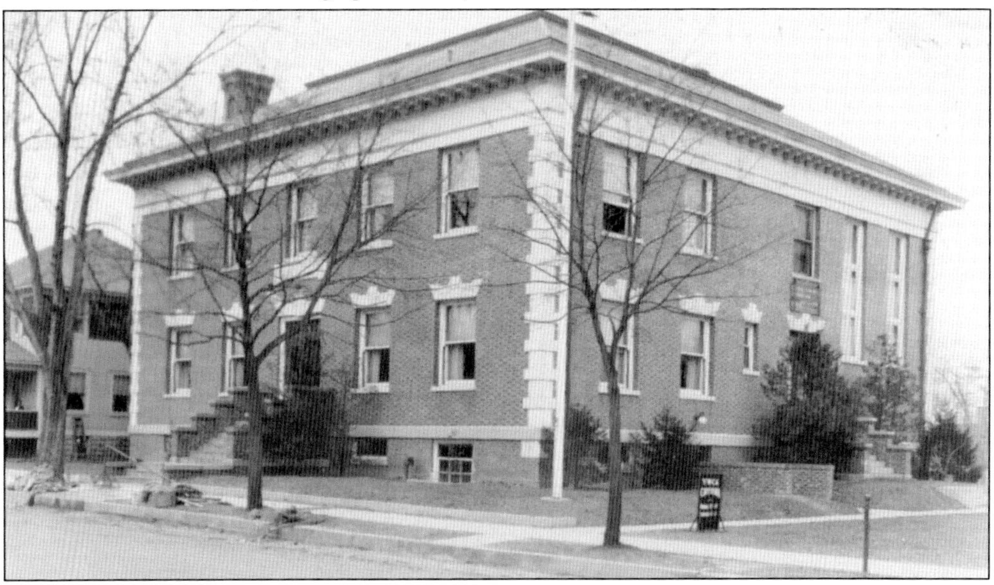

The YWCA was located at 299 Monmouth Avenue. The organization opened during the spring of 1912. The YWCA offered informational and educational classes to its patrons. During World War I, the YWCA aided the war effort by supplying prepared bandages and linens to France. The YWCA also held dances for World War I serviceman when they were in the area. (Photograph courtesy of the OCHS.)

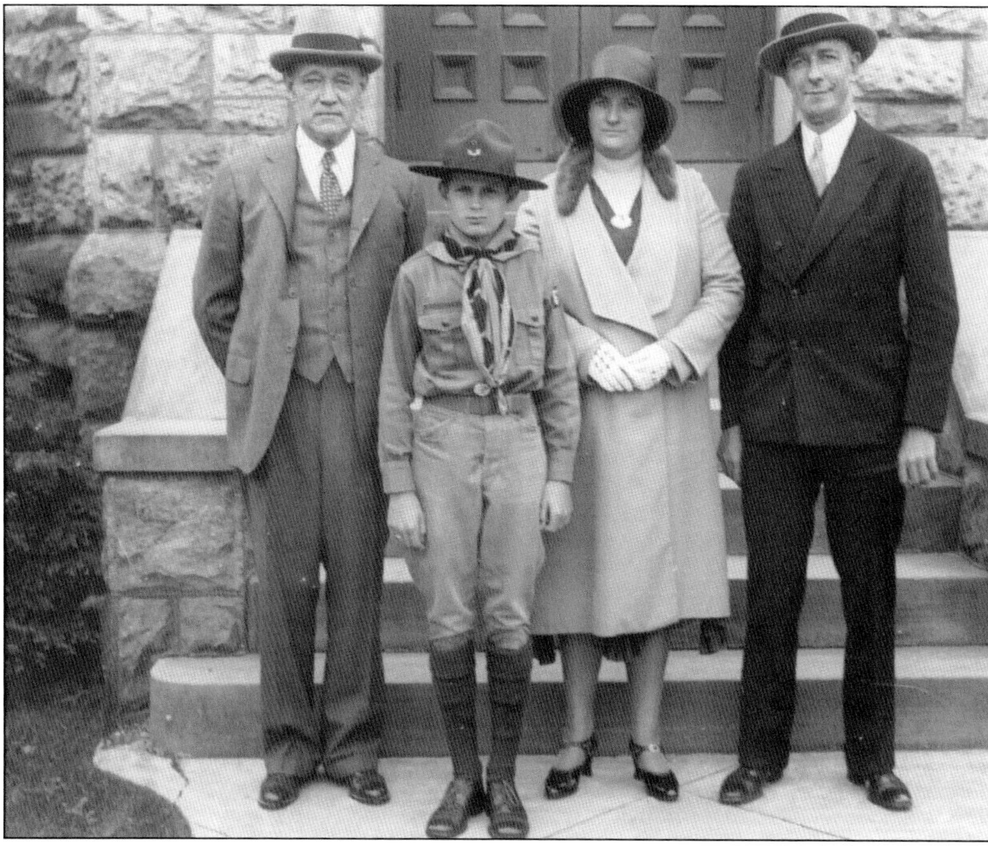

The Boy Scouts of America positively influenced the lives of the many young Lakewood men who decided to join. This picture was taken on May 25, 1930. Standing in front of the First Baptist Church are, from left to right, Mr. Holbrook, Boy Scout William, Mrs. Margaret, and Mr. Foster. Holbrook used to hold Boy Scout meetings and activities on his farm, which was located in Lakewood. (Photograph courtesy of the OCHS.)

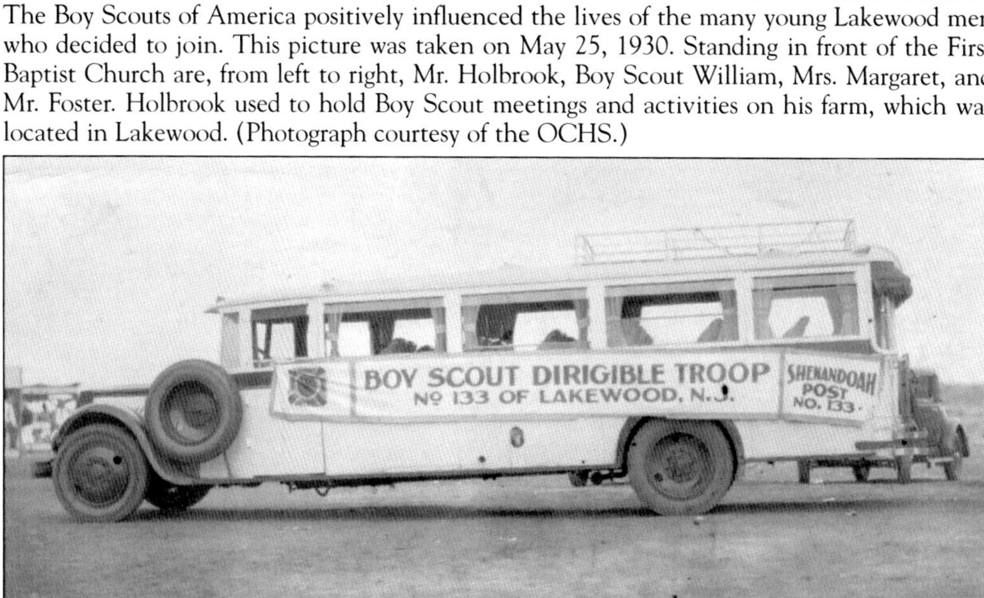

This bus transported Boy Scout Dirigible Troop No. 133 of Lakewood to landing fields throughout the county to help the military and ship crews in the landing of dirigibles. Most of the airships were docked at Lakehurst Naval Air Station. (Photograph courtesy of the OCHS.)

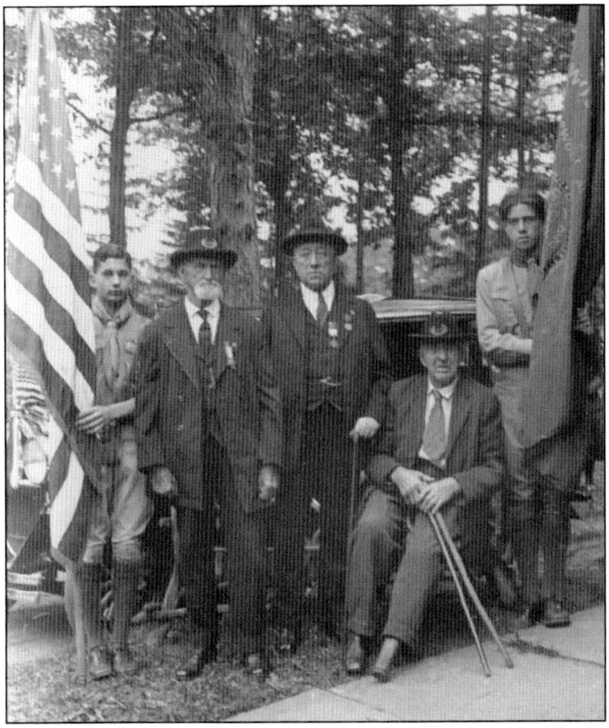

Some Boy Scouts from Lakewood pose with several veterans of the Civil War. It is believed that during that war, the seated gentleman suffered a bad wound to his leg, which later had to be amputated. (Photograph courtesy of the OCHS.)

This photograph is of an American Legion Memorial Day ceremony in Lakewood on May 30, 1930. Several Civil War veterans, American Legion members, local Boy Scouts, and other visitors attended the ceremony to honor America's fallen war heroes. (Photograph courtesy of the OCHS.)

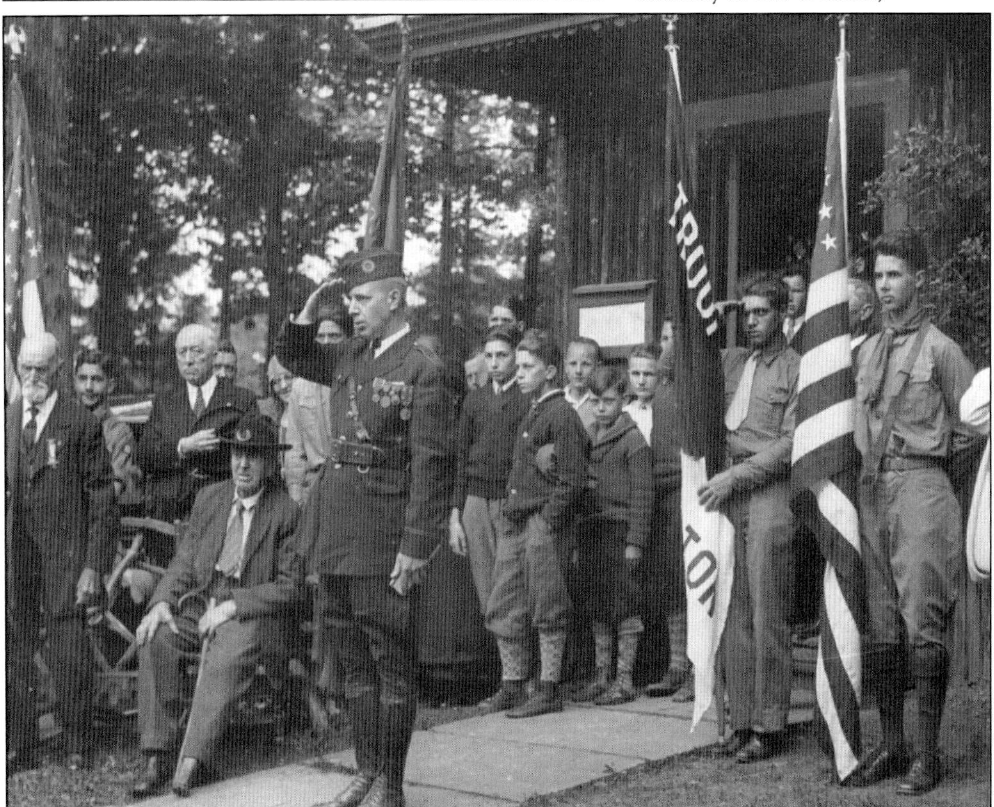

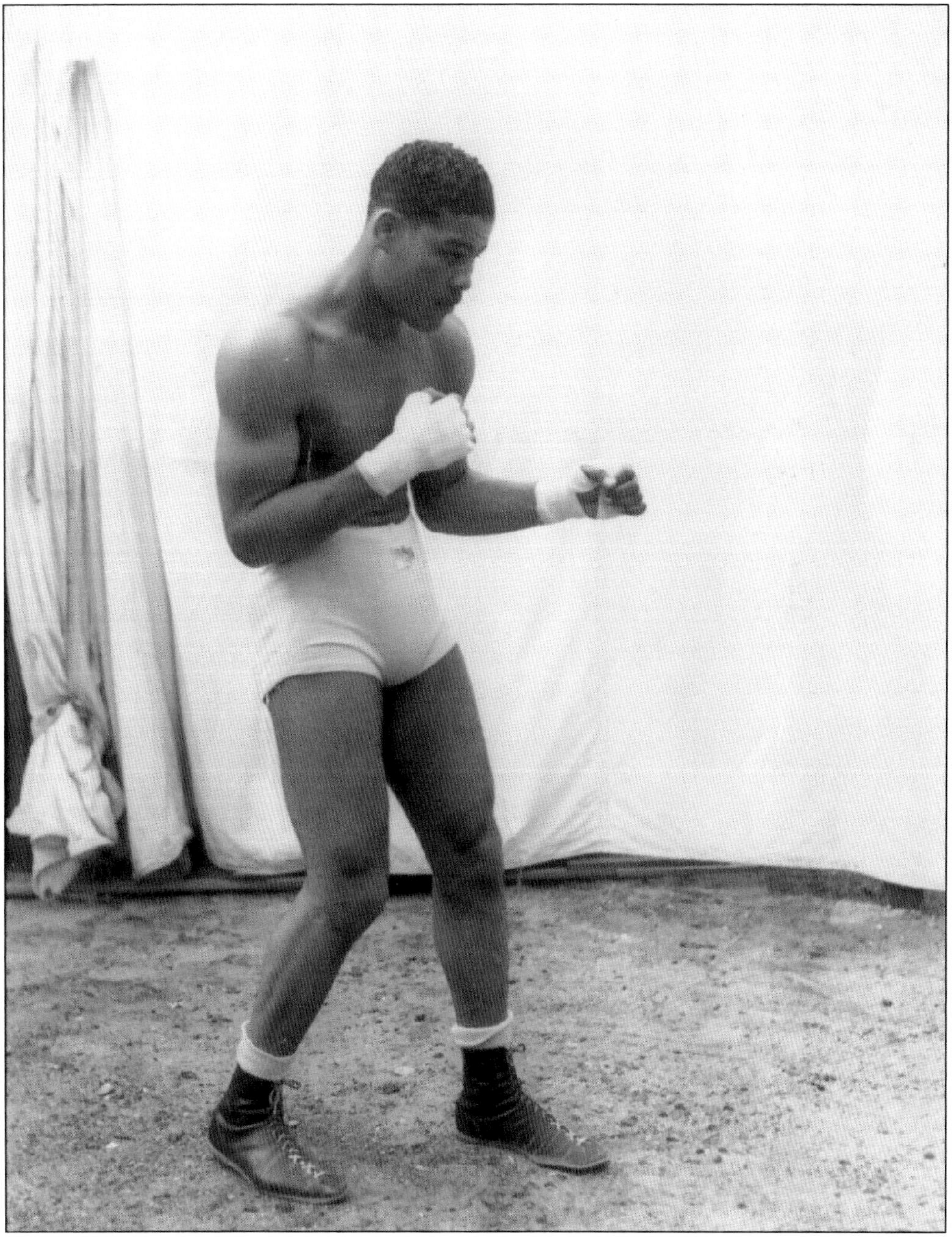

Joe Louis (1914–1981), nicknamed the "Brown Bomber," poses for a picture at the Hotel Stanley training ground on Madison Avenue. Louis was Heavyweight Champion from June 1937 to March 1949. His professional boxing record consisted of 63 wins and 3 losses, with 49 knockouts. (Photograph by F.W. Tupper, courtesy of the OCHS.)

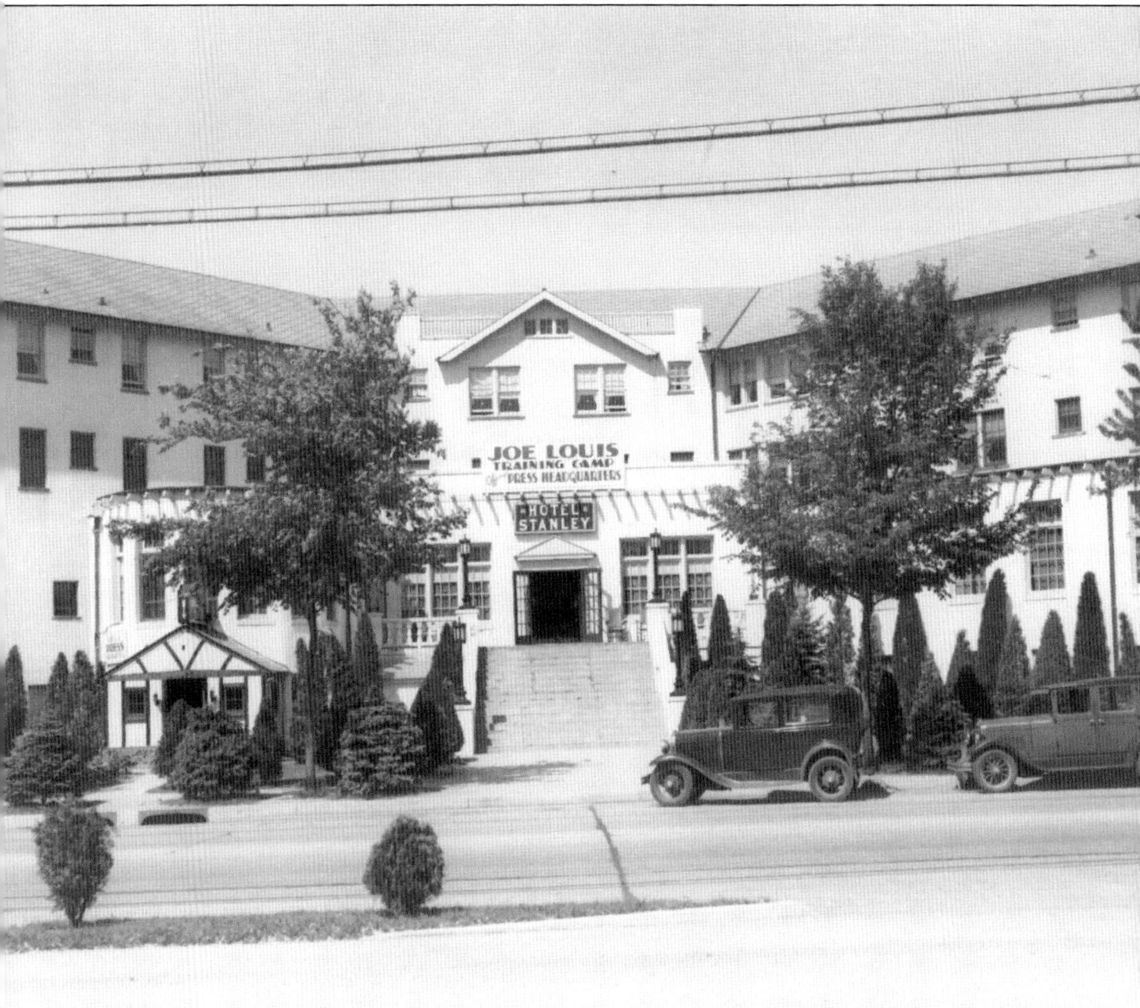

The Hotel Stanley, located on Madison Avenue and Tenth Street, was used as the training facility for Joe Louis. Louis used the grounds to prepare for his 1936 fight against German boxer Max Schmeling. Large tents were constructed and set up to cover the boxing ring that Louis sparred in. Admission to the tents was 50¢. (Photograph by F.W. Tupper, courtesy of the OCHS.)

Joe Louis was at the Hotel Stanley in May 1936. During his stay in Lakewood, Louis jogged around Lake Carasaljo as part of his daily training routine. It is said that he played a round of golf every few days and was scolded by his trainers who cautioned him that his golf swing could damage his punch. On June 19, 1936, he suffered his first defeat at the hands of German boxer Max Schmeling. Louis avenged the loss in 1938 by knocking Schmeling out in the first round. (Photograph by F.W. Tupper, courtesy of the OCHS.)

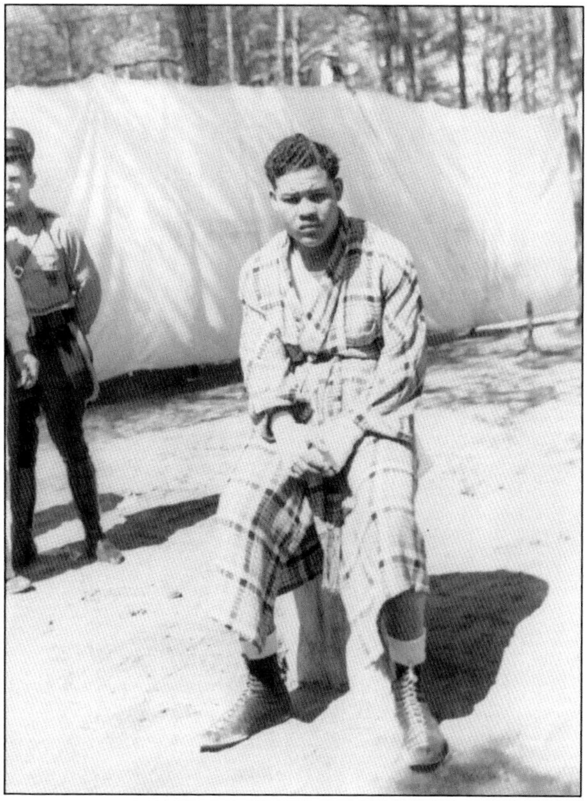

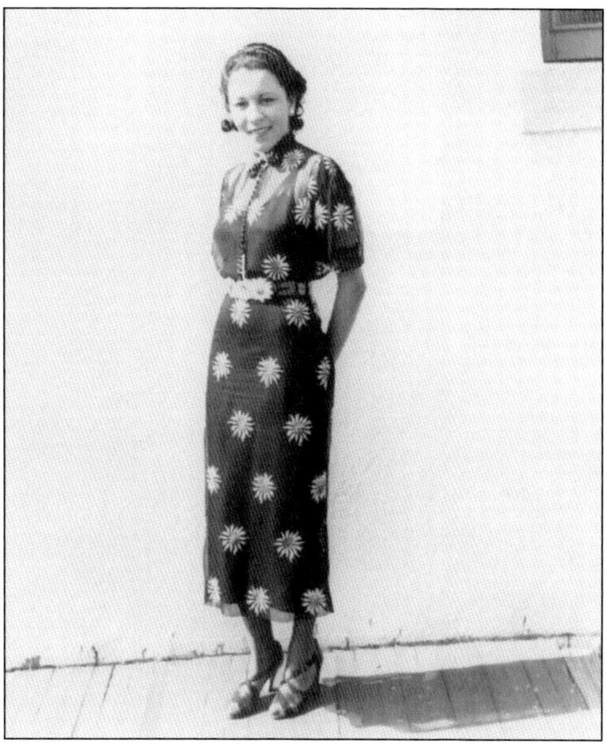

This photograph shows Marva Trotter Louis taking in the Lakewood scenery outside of the Hotel Stanley. Joe Louis married Marva Trotter several hours before one of his fights in September 1935. While in Lakewood, the couple lived in a house on Madison Avenue. (Photograph courtesy of the OCHS.)

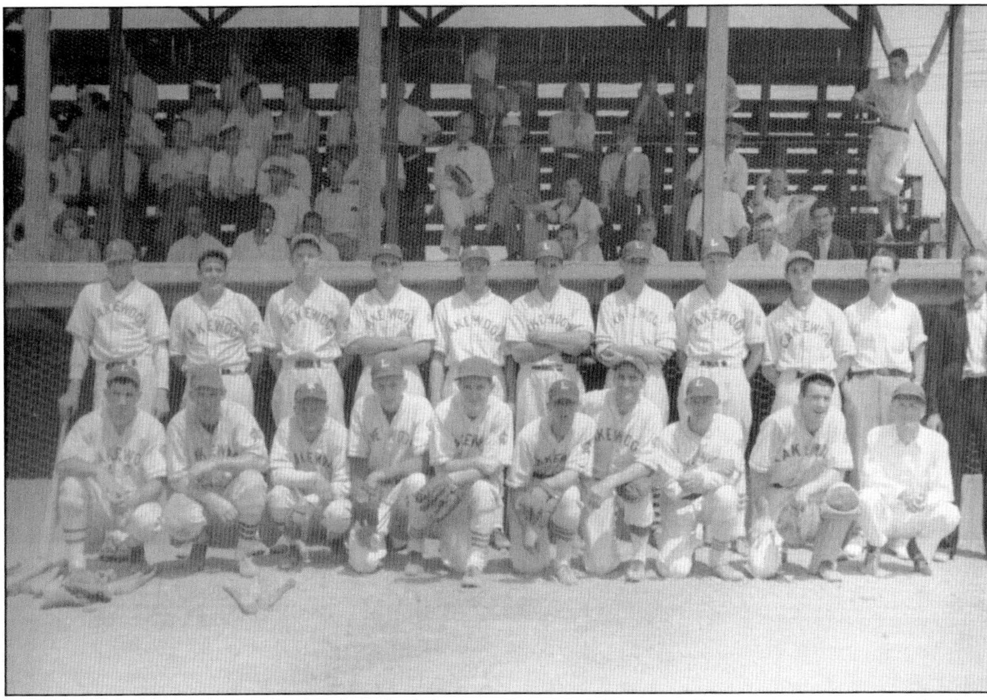

Lakewood's reputation is rich in baseball history. One of the most famous ball games took place on June 9, 1934. Lakewood High School coach Mr. Haley invited the Philadelphia Athletics, with stars such as Jimmy Foxx and Mickey Cochrane, to town for a fund-raising scrimmage against his Lakewood Athletic Club, shown above. The game took place at the old high school athletic field on Princeton Avenue. The A's, shown below, were victorious over the much smaller Lakewood Club. (Photograph courtesy of the OCHS.)

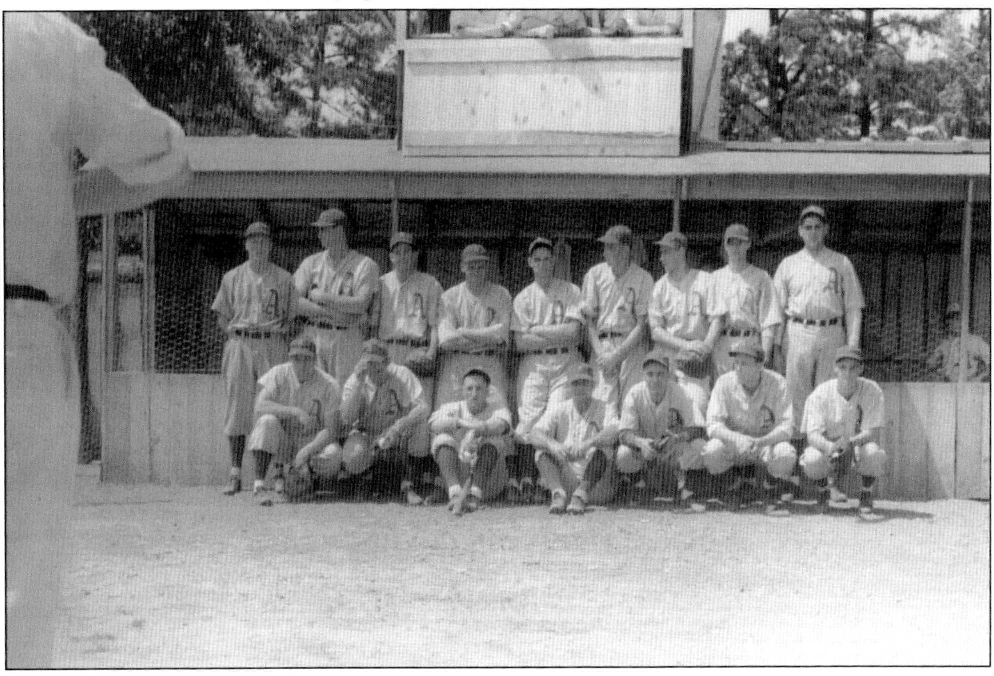

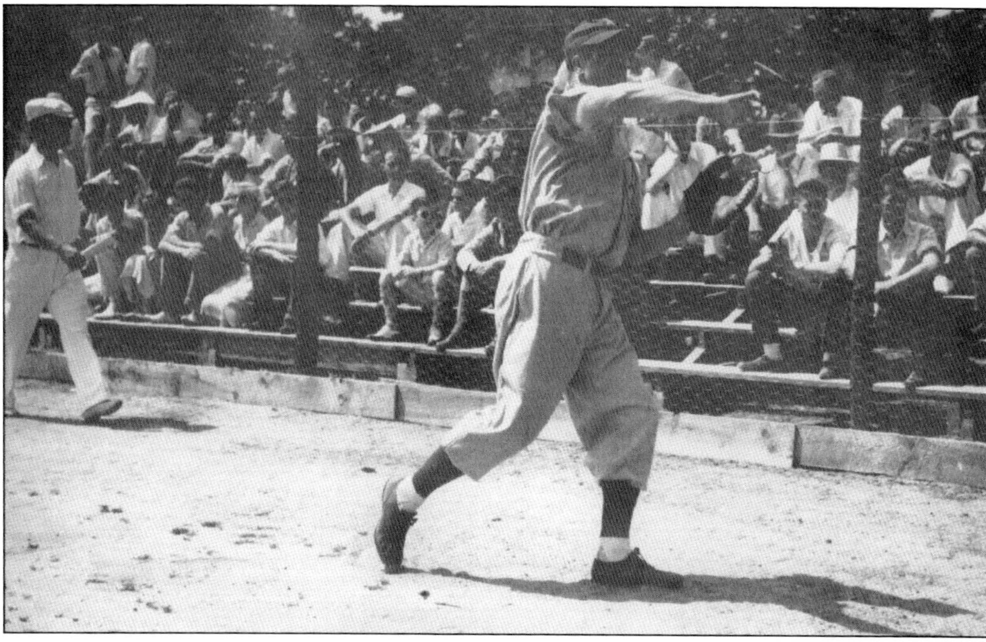

Jimmy Foxx, nicknamed "the Beast," starts to warm up in front of the Lakewood fans. Foxx was voted in as a member of major league baseball's prestigious All Century Team; he became No. 14. He played with the Philadelphia A's from 1926 to 1935. He played or was present at seven All Star Games and captured the Most Valuable Player Award in 1932. His lifetime statistics include 534 home runs and a .325 batting average. (Photograph courtesy of the OCHS.)

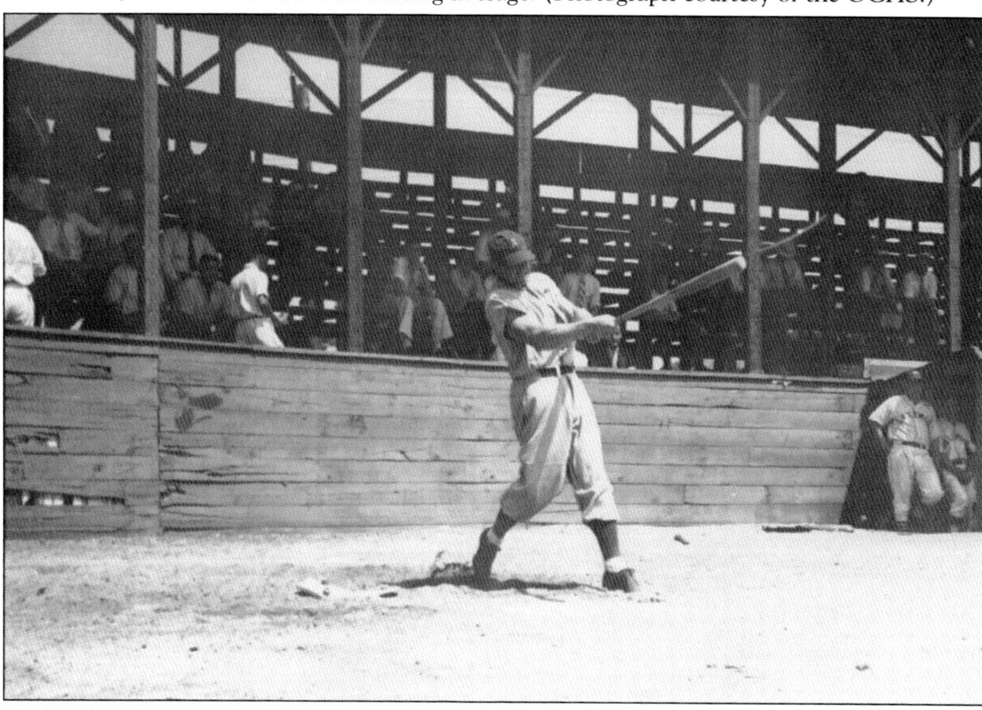

A Philadelphia player takes batting practice before the start of the game while several Lakewood players take notice. (Photograph courtesy of the OCHS.)

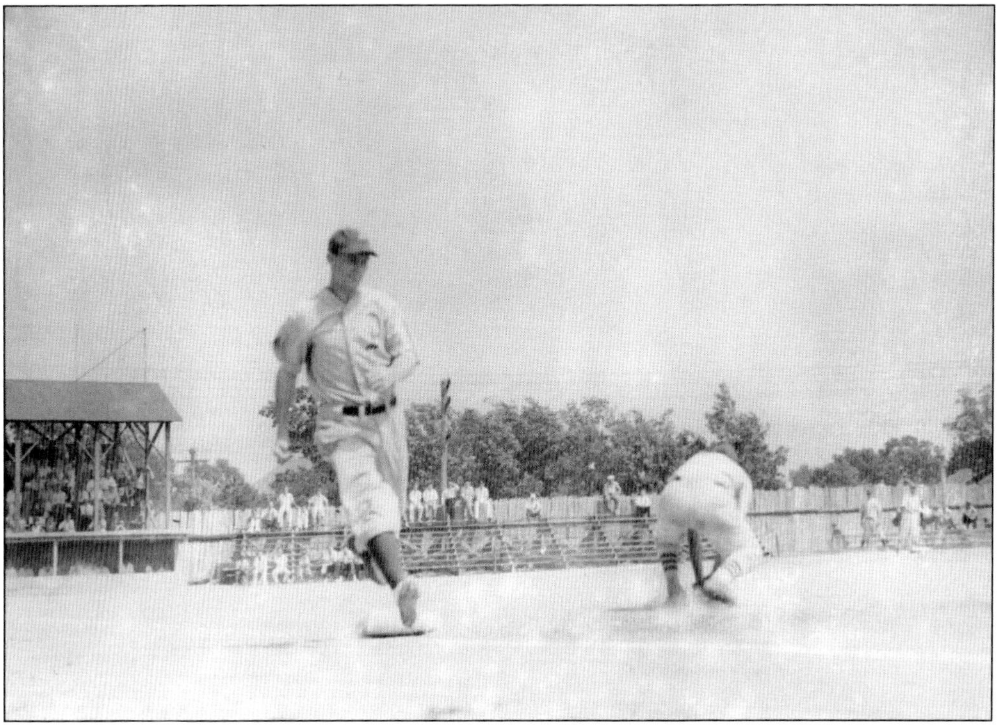

It is a busy day for the Lakewood first baseman, above, scooping the ball out of the dirt, while the runner easily reaches first base. Below, another Philadelphia runner is safe at first base as the throw to the bag is late. (Photograph courtesy of the OCHS.)

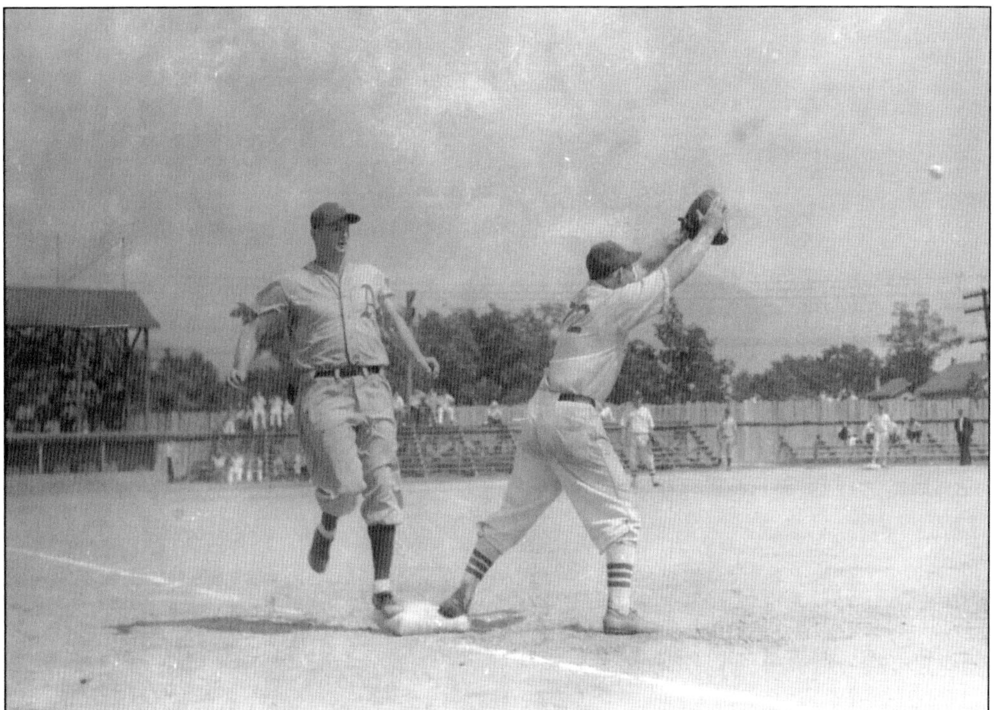

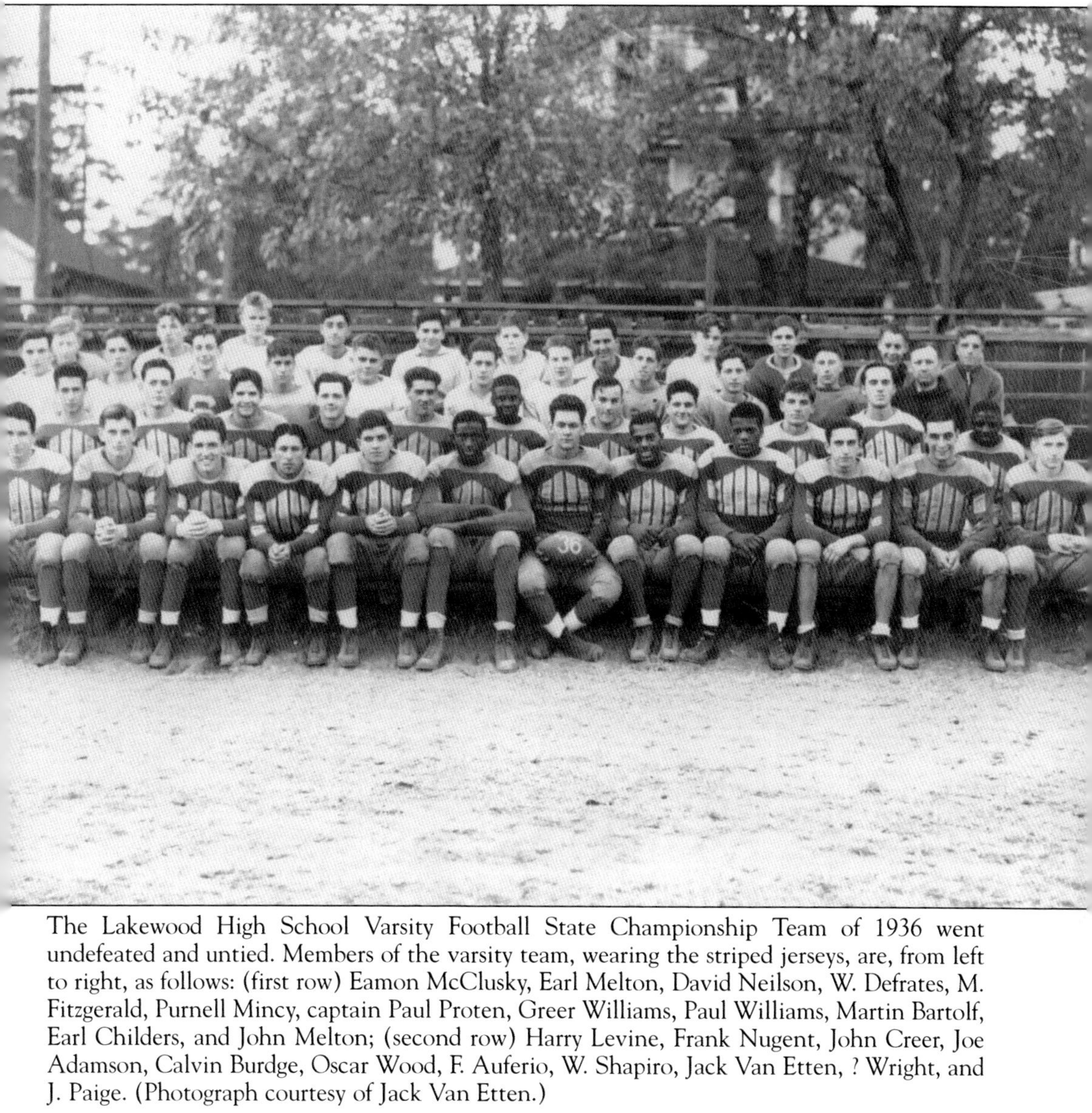

The Lakewood High School Varsity Football State Championship Team of 1936 went undefeated and untied. Members of the varsity team, wearing the striped jerseys, are, from left to right, as follows: (first row) Eamon McClusky, Earl Melton, David Neilson, W. Defrates, M. Fitzgerald, Purnell Mincy, captain Paul Proten, Greer Williams, Paul Williams, Martin Bartolf, Earl Childers, and John Melton; (second row) Harry Levine, Frank Nugent, John Creer, Joe Adamson, Calvin Burdge, Oscar Wood, F. Auferio, W. Shapiro, Jack Van Etten, ? Wright, and J. Paige. (Photograph courtesy of Jack Van Etten.)

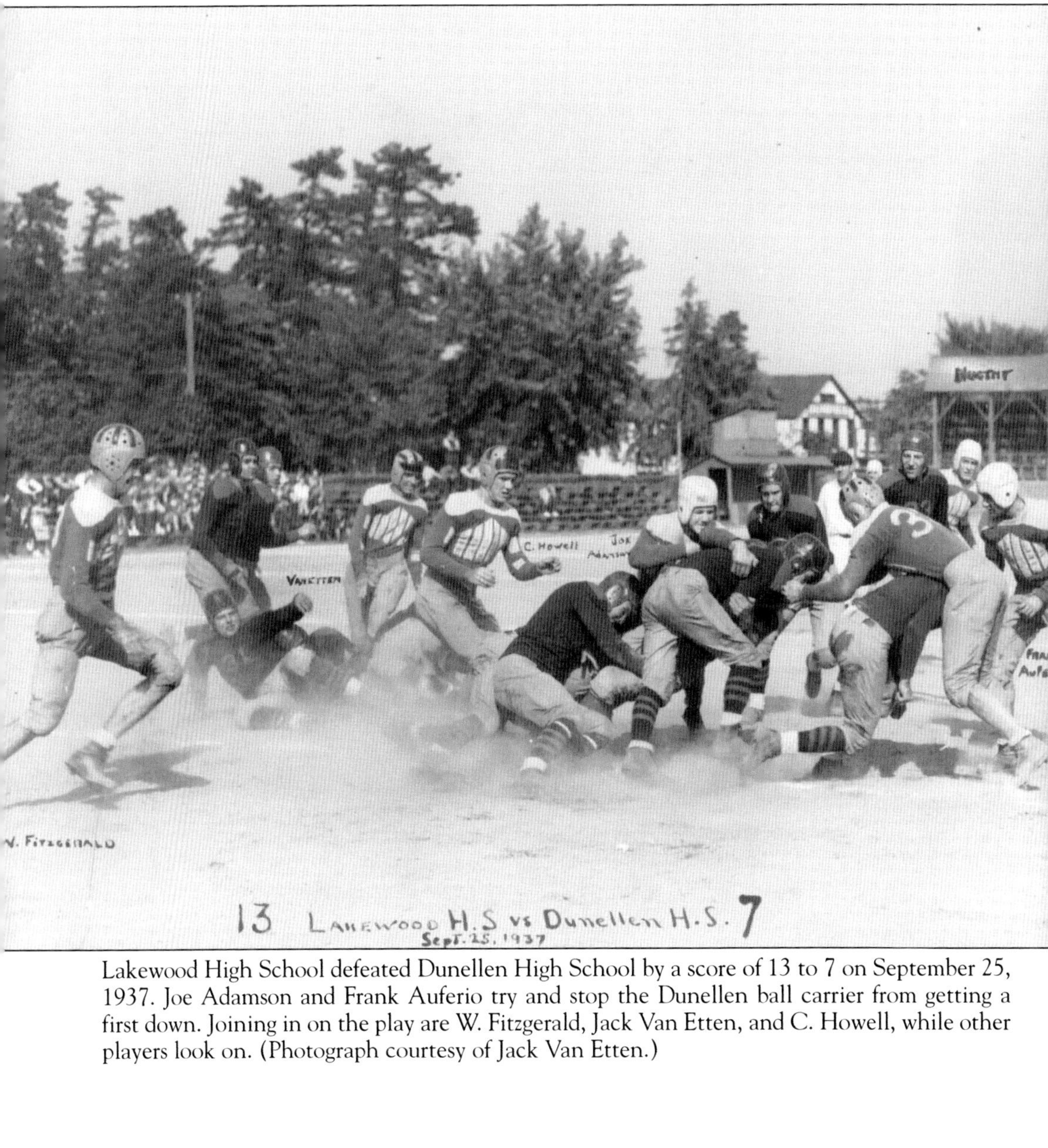

Lakewood High School defeated Dunellen High School by a score of 13 to 7 on September 25, 1937. Joe Adamson and Frank Auferio try and stop the Dunellen ball carrier from getting a first down. Joining in on the play are W. Fitzgerald, Jack Van Etten, and C. Howell, while other players look on. (Photograph courtesy of Jack Van Etten.)

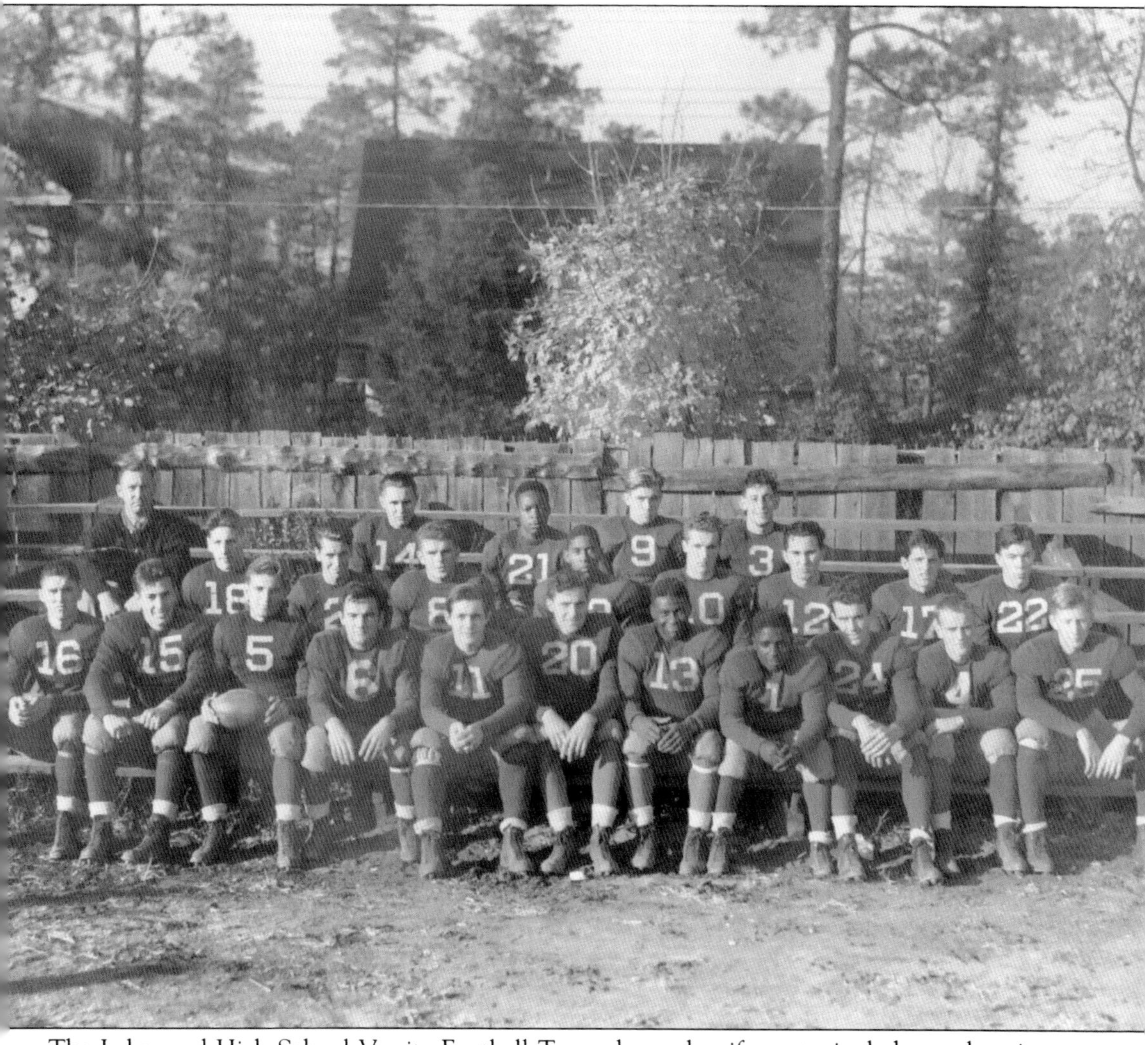

The Lakewood High School Varsity Football Team changed uniforms to include numbers in 1938. Coach Wright is in the back row at the left. The players by number are, from left to right, as follows: (front row) No. 16, Frank Huber; No. 15, Jack Wexler; No. 5, captain Jack Van Etten; No. 6, Frank Auferio; No. 11, Stanford Pfursik; No. 20, Wilbur Bailey; No. 13, Oscar Wood; No. 1, Joe Paige; No. 24, Bill Fitzgerald; No. 4, Robert Lee; and No. 25, Ed Melton; (middle row) No. 18, Francis McNutt; No. 2, Calvin Woolley; No. 8, E. Beers; No. ?, ? Watson; No. 10, Bill Halleck; No. 12, Simon Weber; No. 17, Robert Van Etten; and No. 22, unknown; (back row) No. 14, unknown; No. 21, ? Douglas; No. 9, Tommy ?; and No. 3, Chet Kurinsky. (Photograph courtesy of Jack Van Etten.)

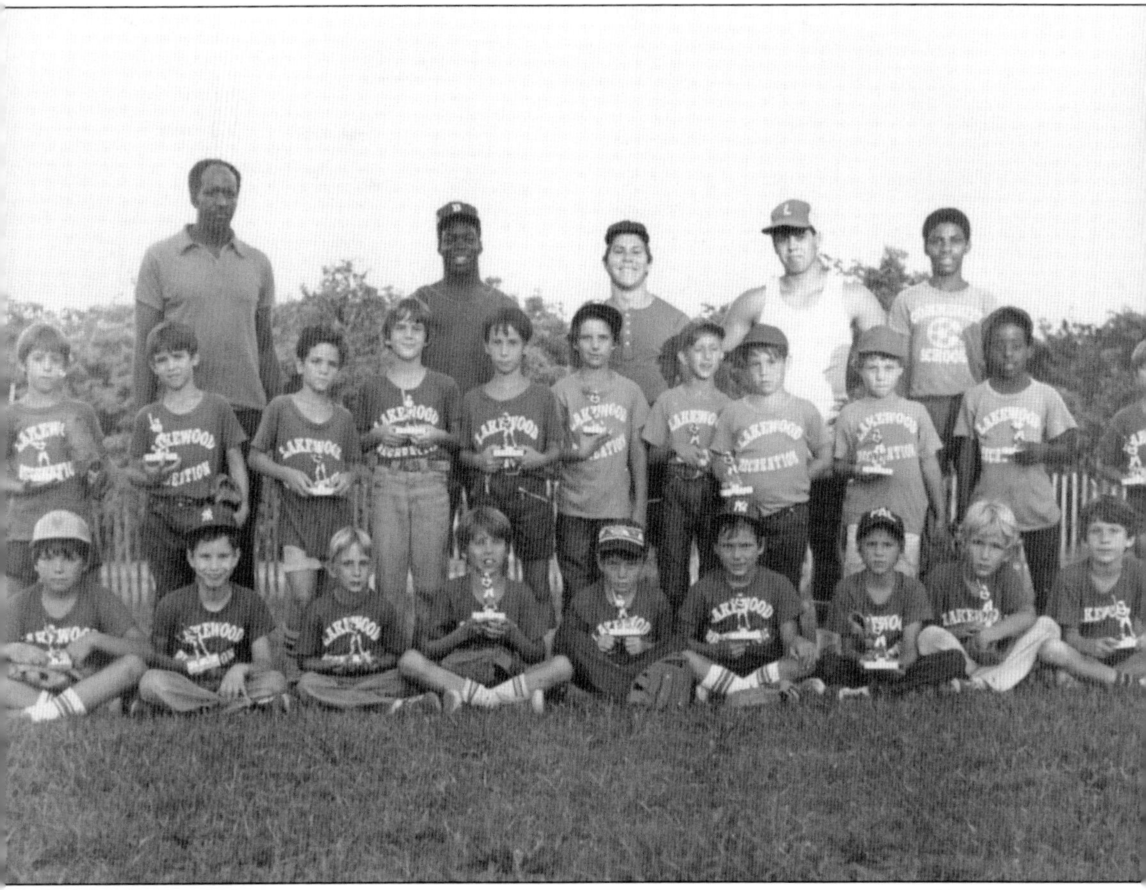

The Lakewood Community Schools 1978 T-Ball All Stars team was supervised by Art Turner, back row at the left. Standing in back with Turner are the team's four coaches, from left to right, Dion Lowe, Scott Schulman, John Reizer, and Wayne Richardson. They were all part of the 1975 Lakewood Little League National Championship Team. (Photograph courtesy of Dan Kozelnik.)

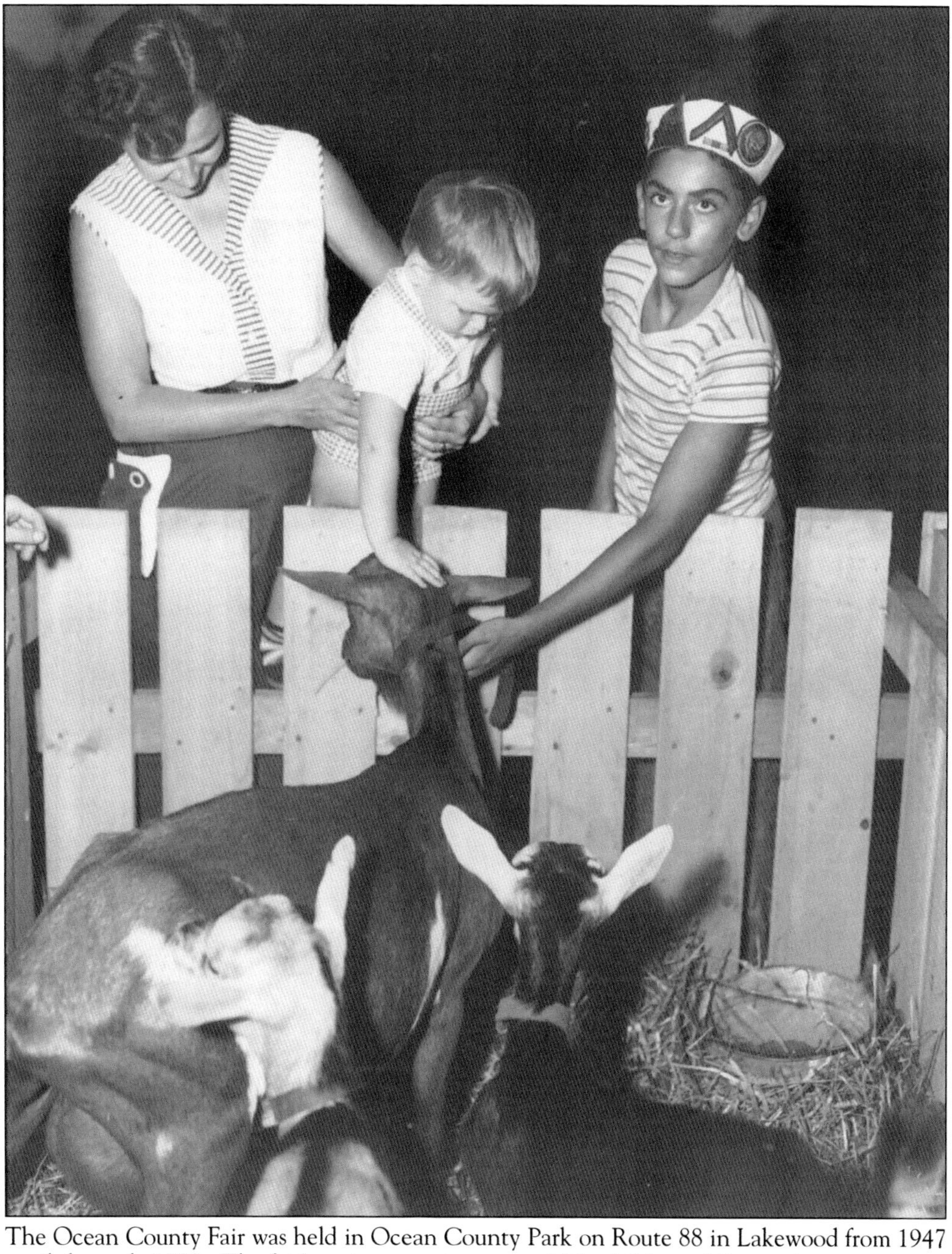

The Ocean County Fair was held in Ocean County Park on Route 88 in Lakewood from 1947 until the early 1980s. The fair's main attractions were 4-H exhibits and livestock competitions. Mrs. Joseph Brugan, her son Stephan, and another young man admire the prizewinning goat owned by Henry Allan of Jackson Township. (Photograph courtesy of the OCHS.)

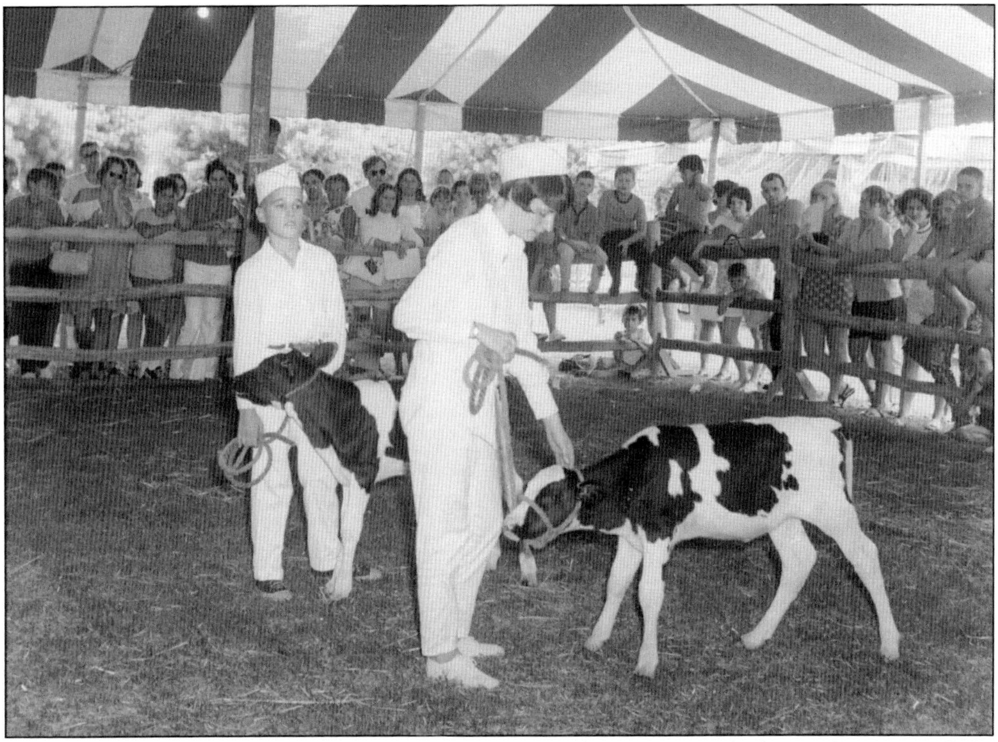

Hoping to take home first prize, contestants No. 17 and No. 16 parade their calves around the 4-H livestock tent in front of an enthusiastic crowd. (Photograph courtesy of the OCHS.)

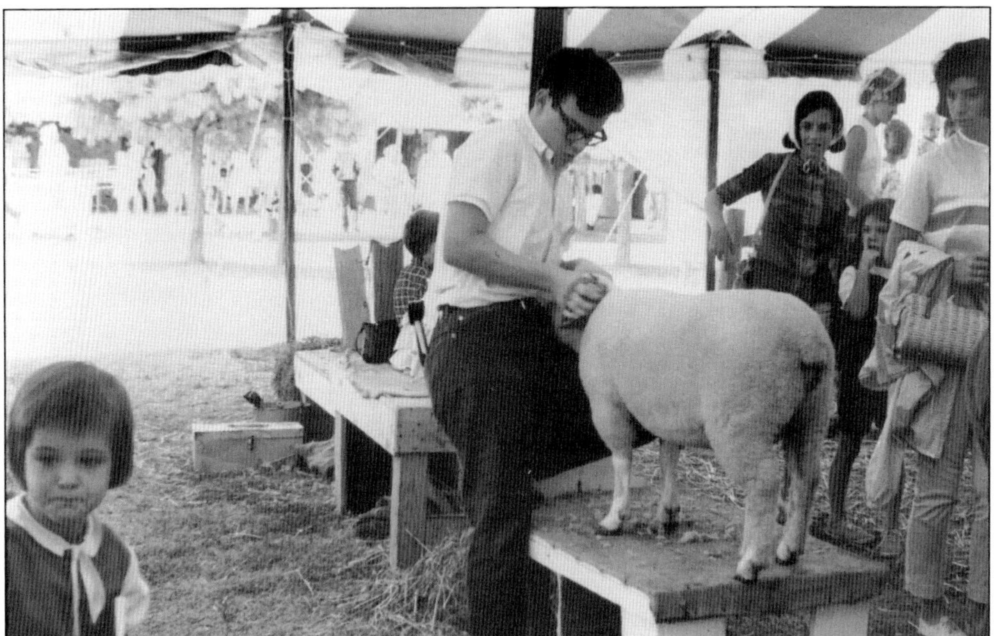

Behind the scenes at the Ocean County Fair on August 3, 1966, a contestant grooms and prepares his entry for the sheep contest to be held later in the day. Onlookers are amused at this spectacle, as they are with the real contest. (Photograph by A.H. Graf, courtesy of the OCHS.)

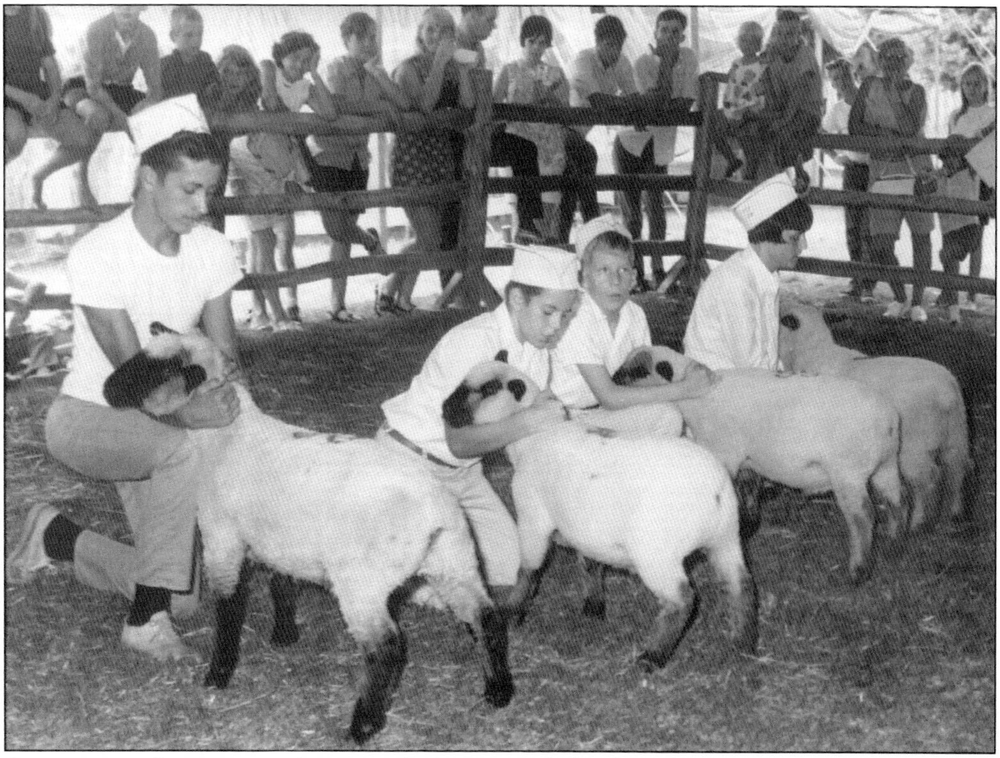

Contestants, above, anxiously wait with their animals for the judges to make a decision. Several of the young contestants make sure that the number on the back of their animal is clearly visible to the judges. Below, contestants No. 89 and No. 90 hope to win a prize. (Photographs courtesy of the OCHS.)

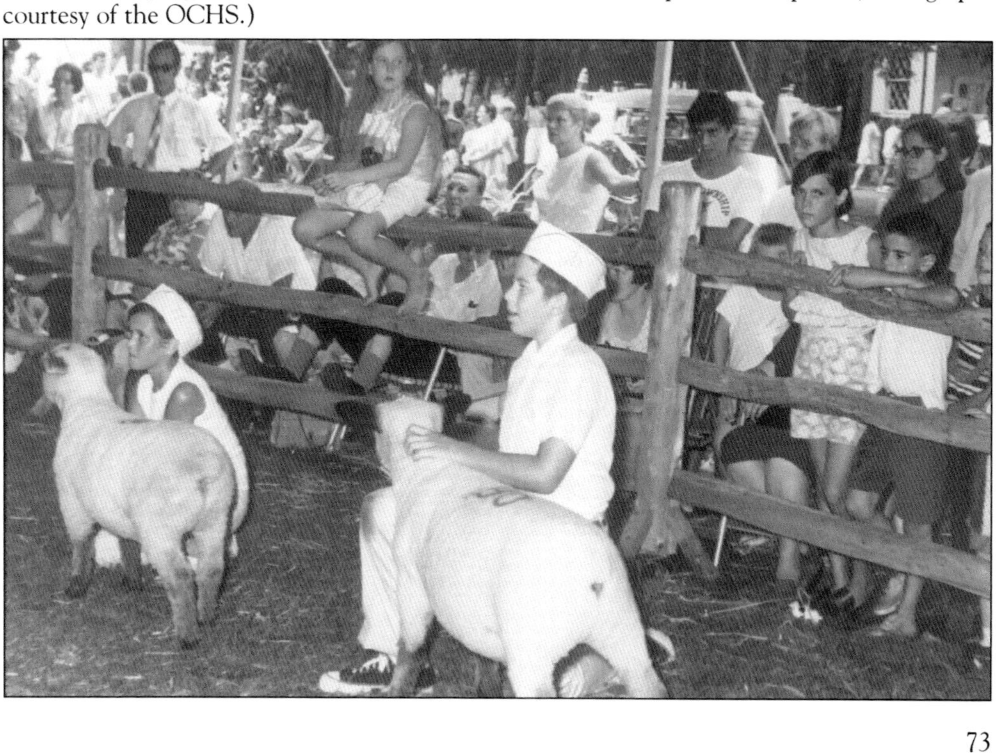

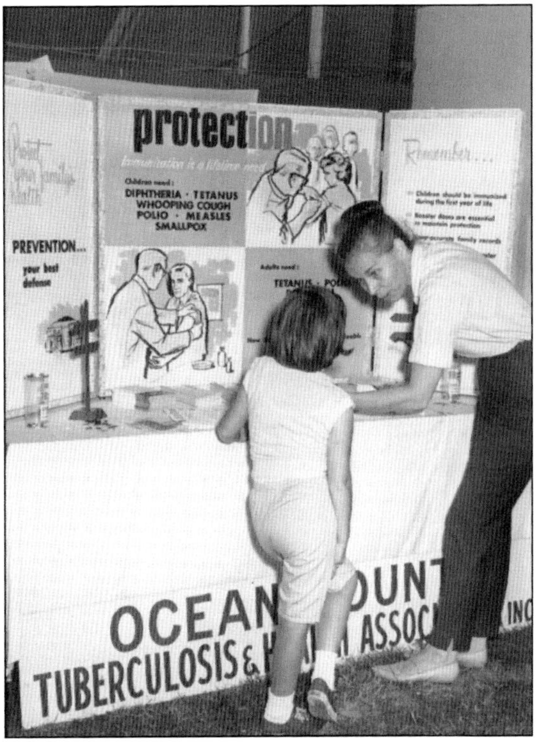

Elizabeth Ann Grant answers a young fair patron's question at the Ocean County Tuberculosis and Health Association's exhibit at the fair, c. 1960. (Photograph courtesy of the OCHS.)

A trip to the fair would not be complete without getting sketched. Fairgoers wait in line for their turn in the chair, while others snack on lollipops and enjoy the artwork. (Photograph courtesy of the OCHS.)

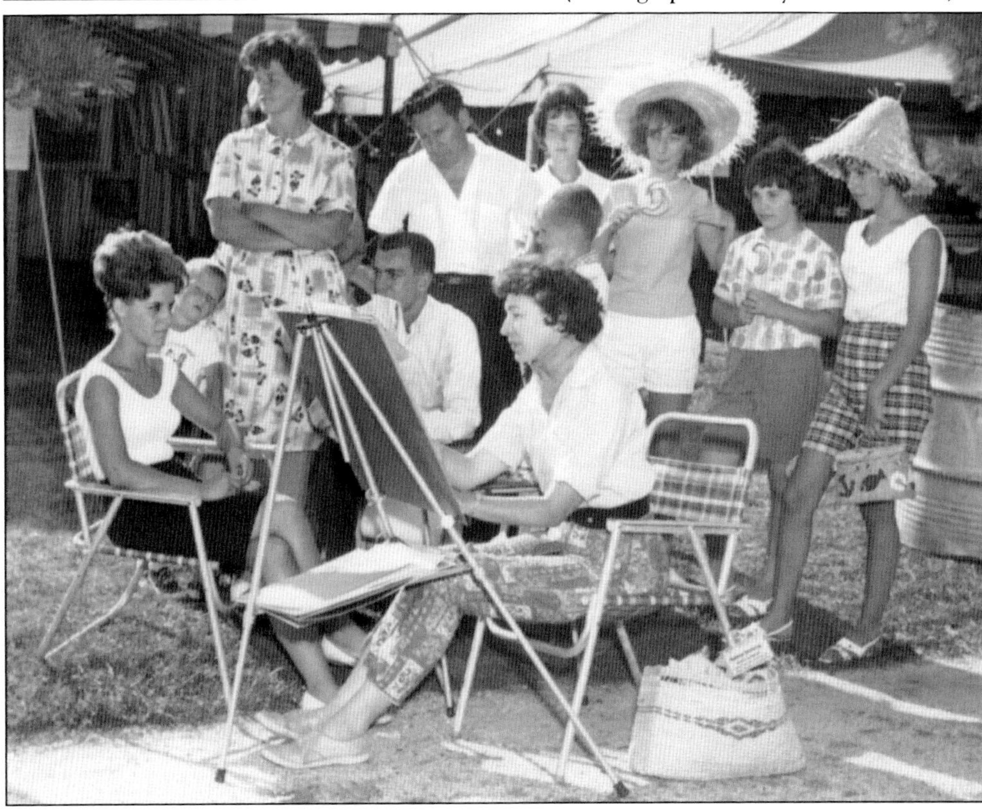

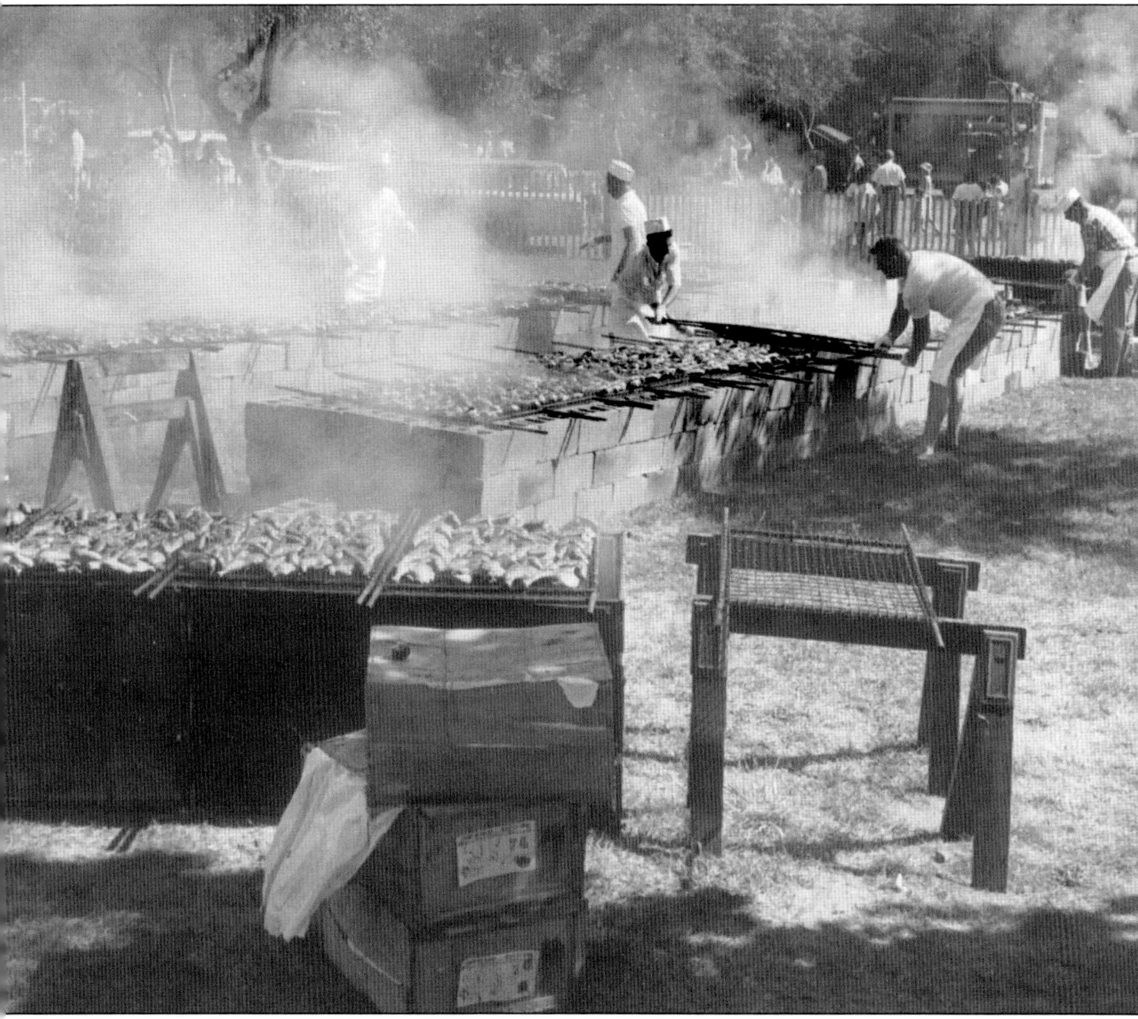

Cooks at the Ocean County Fair turn over the racks of chicken cooking on the barbecue pit. Every year cooks prepared barbecued chicken dinners and sold them later in the day, around 4:00 or 5:00 p.m., to hungry fairgoers. The chickens were obtained from several of Lakewood's many poultry farms. (Photograph by A.H. Graf, courtesy of the OCHS.)

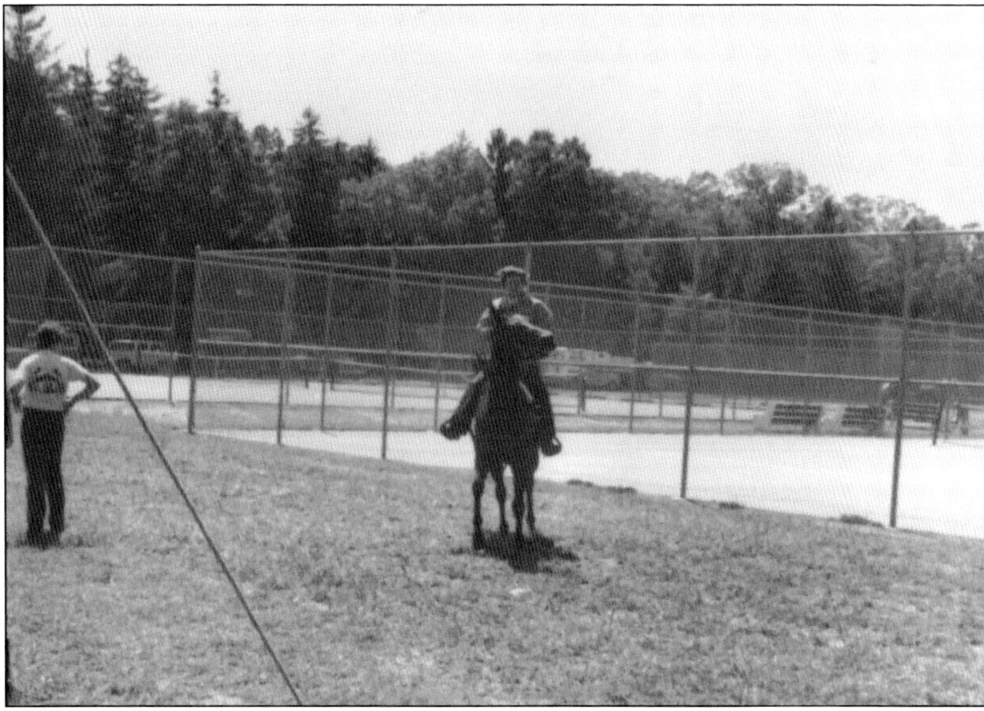

Horses were a big attraction at the Ocean County Fair. This rider is trying hard to get his horse under control and ready to be shown to the crowd, as onlookers observe the actions of the stubborn horse. (Photograph courtesy of the OCHS.)

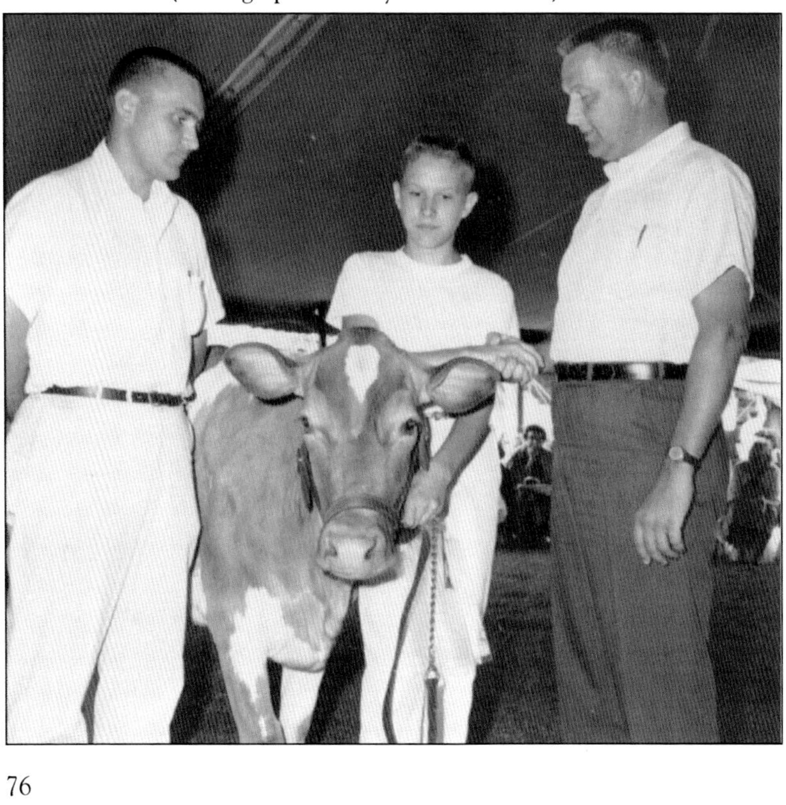

This young gentleman is congratulated for his prize-winning cow at one of the 4-H livestock tents at the Ocean County Fair. (Photograph courtesy of the OCHS.)

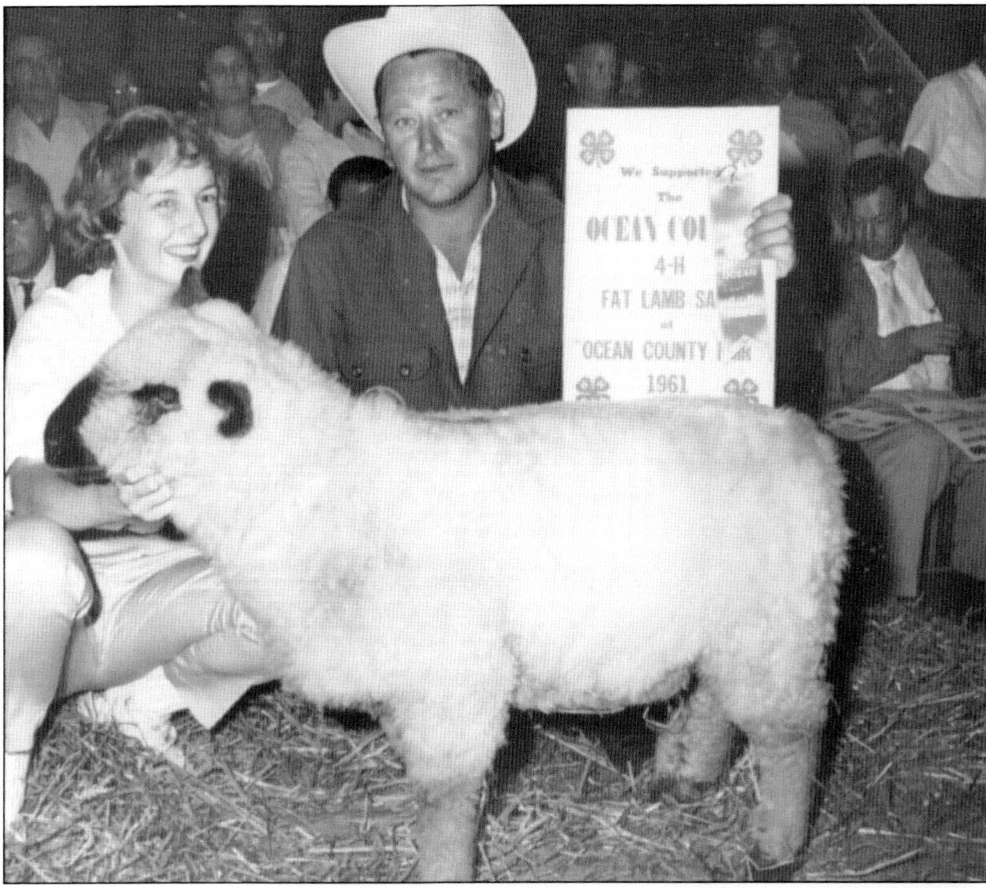

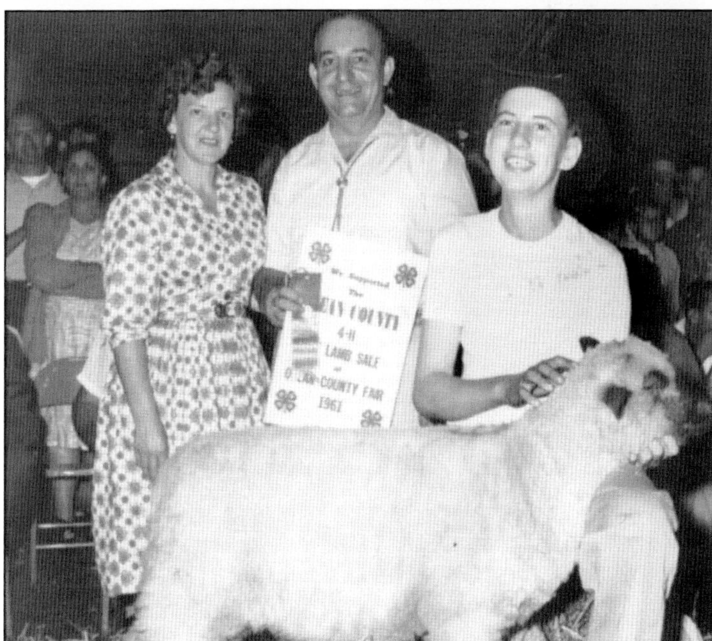

Contestants pose for pictures with their victorious animals. These animals were the award winners of the Ocean County Fair's 4-H Fat Lamb Sale of 1961. (Photographs courtesy of the OCHS.)

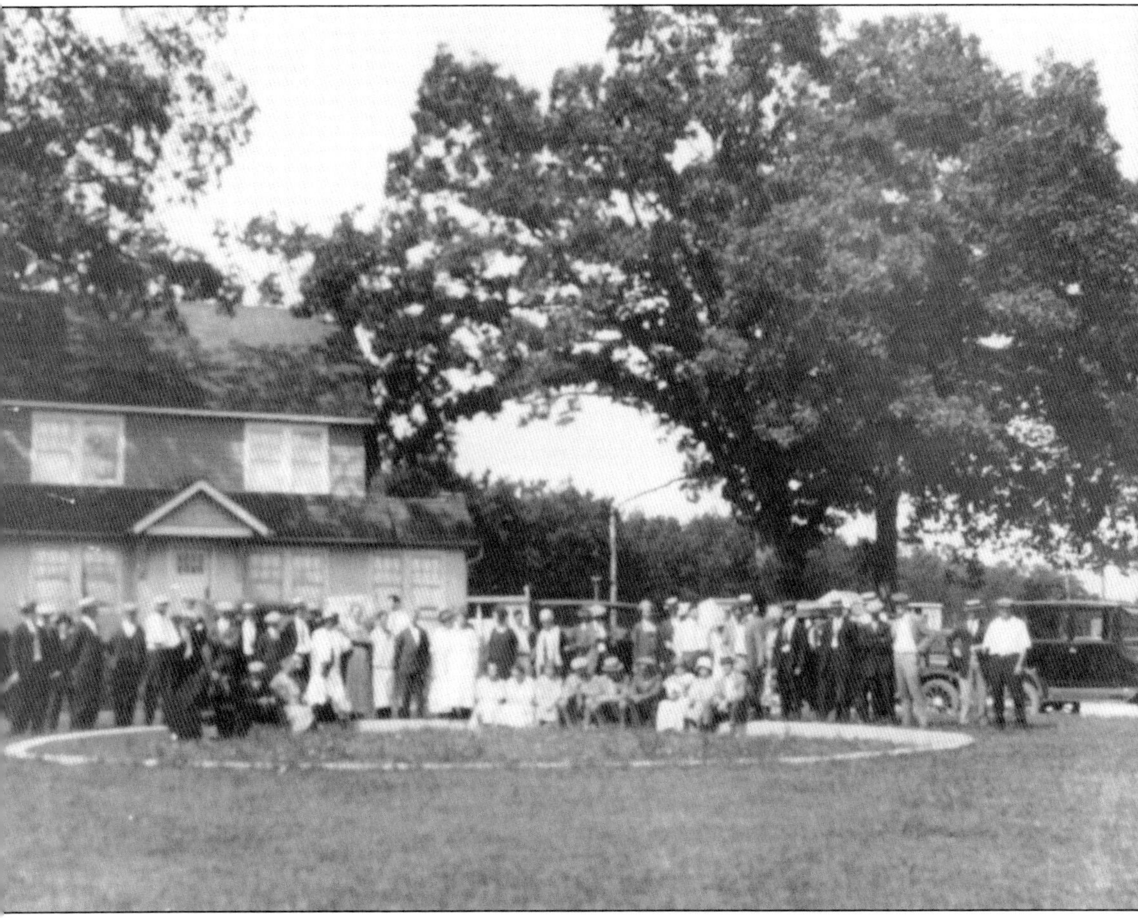

This is a group portrait of the Ocean County Poultry Club at the poultry farm of Martin Schubkegel. The farm was on the border of Lakewood and Jackson Townships and consisted of more than 10,000 egg-laying birds. (Photograph courtesy of the OCHS.)

Three

Law Enforcement

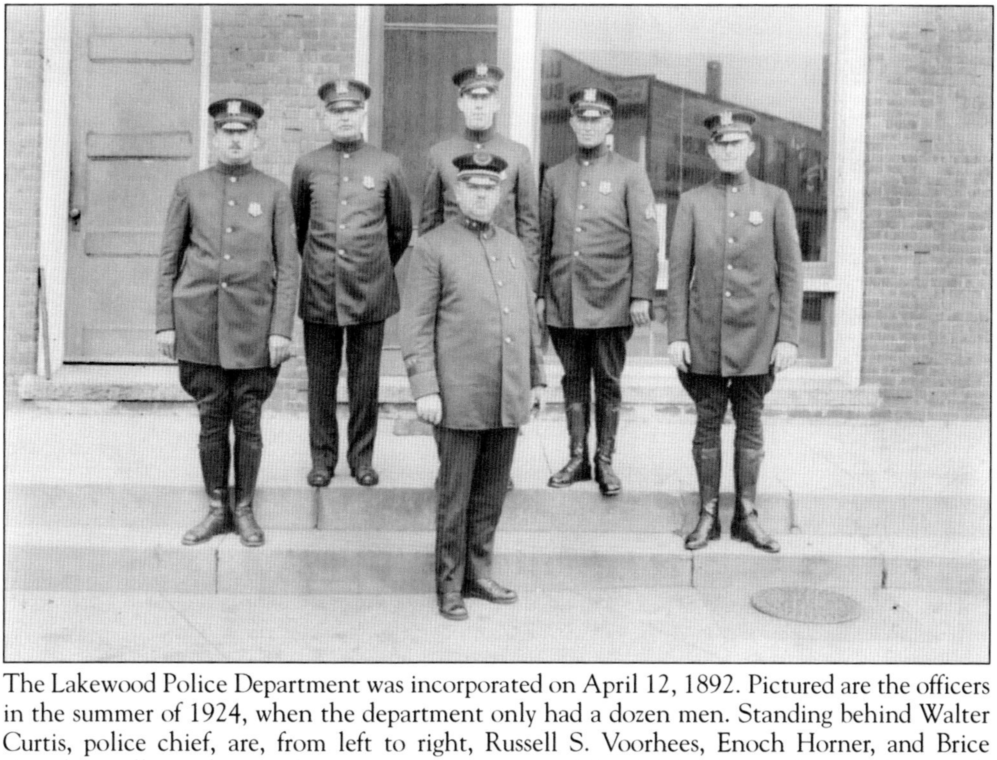

The Lakewood Police Department was incorporated on April 12, 1892. Pictured are the officers in the summer of 1924, when the department only had a dozen men. Standing behind Walter Curtis, police chief, are, from left to right, Russell S. Voorhees, Enoch Horner, and Brice Evernham, all patrolmen; John C. Soden, sergeant; and Waldo Merrit, patrolman. (Photograph courtesy of the OCHS.)

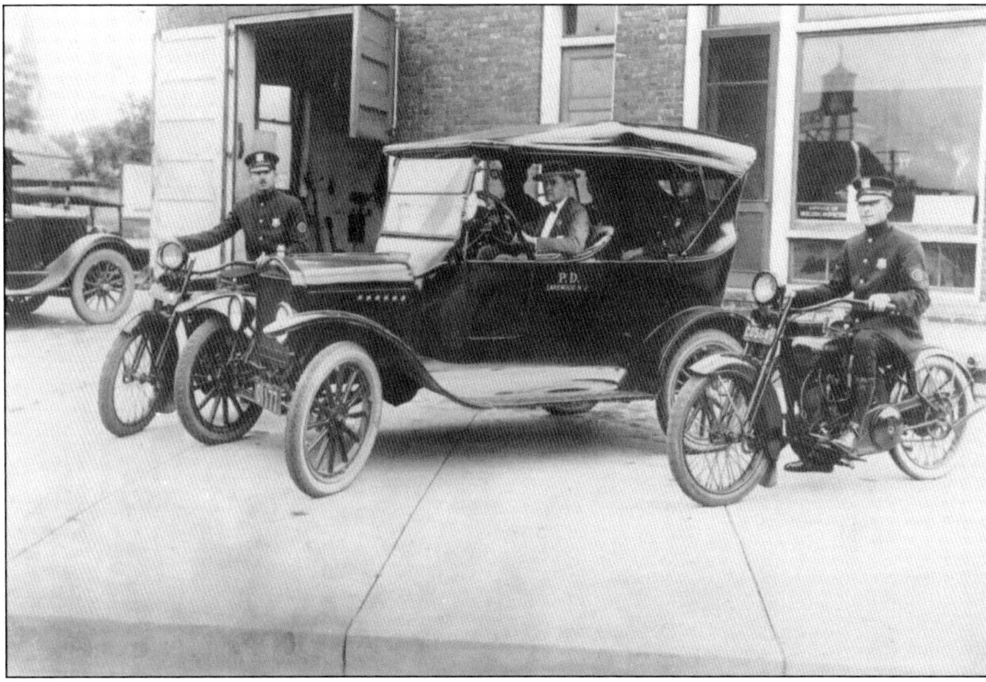

Pictured is part of the Lakewood Police Department's 1924 motorized group. Arthur R. Smock, head of the Lakewood Police Committee, gets comfortable behind the wheel of a brand new Ford police car. Chief Walter A. Curtis sits behind Smock, and officers Russel Voorhees and Waldo Merritt try the new Harley Davidson motorcycles. (Photograph courtesy of the OCHS.)

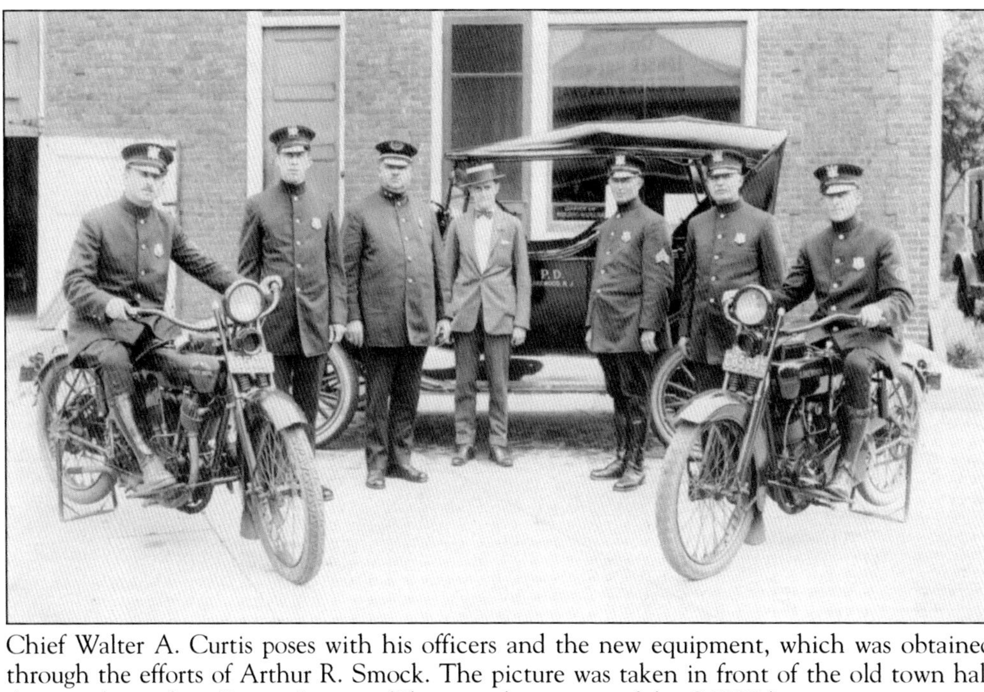

Chief Walter A. Curtis poses with his officers and the new equipment, which was obtained through the efforts of Arthur R. Smock. The picture was taken in front of the old town hall that was located on Ocean Avenue. (Photograph courtesy of the OCHS.)

The first police chief of Lakewood was Charles W. Crane, who was followed by Chief Beebe, Charles Norcross, and Walter A. Curtis, shown in 1924. (Photograph courtesy of the OCHS.)

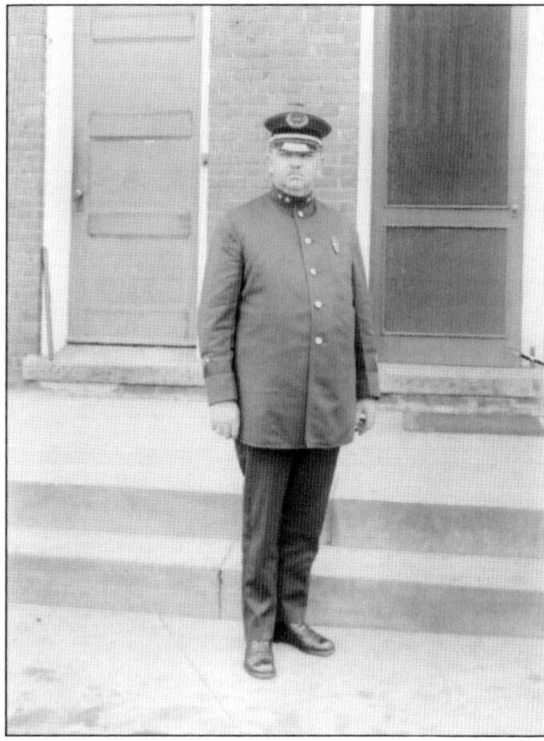

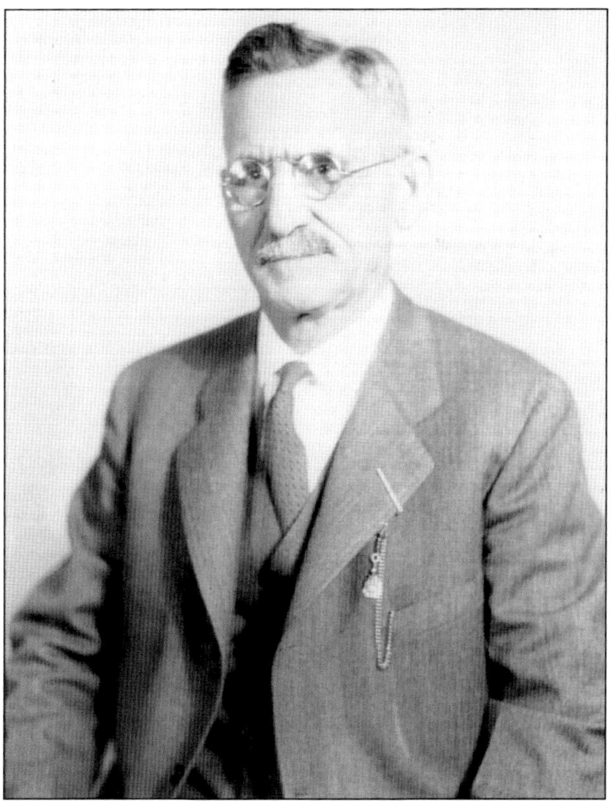

Joseph Holman entered the law enforcement field at age 25 by accepting a job as special officer at the Laurel-in-the-Pines hotel. In 1921, he was elected sheriff of Ocean County and spent much of his career raiding stills and controlling illegal slot machines within Lakewood, as well as the rest of Ocean County. (Photograph courtesy of the OCHS.)

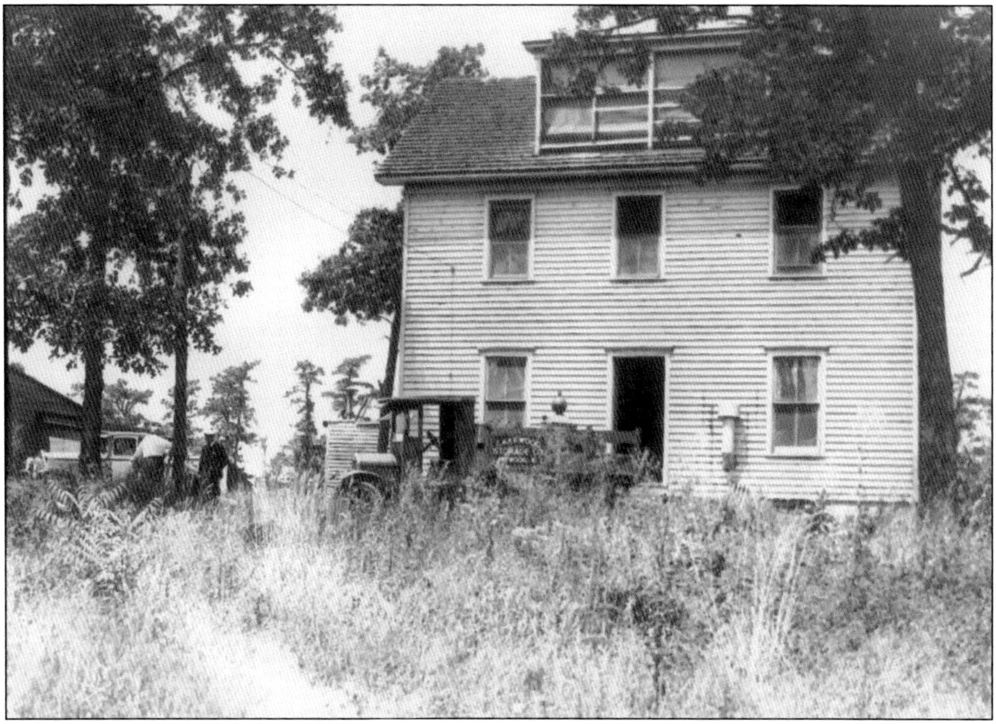

During Prohibition, the Ocean County Sheriffs Department was busy enforcing the Volsted Act, which prohibited the manufacturing, transportation, and selling of alcohol. Houses, such as the one above that is about to be raided, hid illegal stills. Much to the disappointment of the unidentified man below, alcohol found on the property had to be discarded. (Photographs by F.W. Tupper, courtesy of the OCHS.)

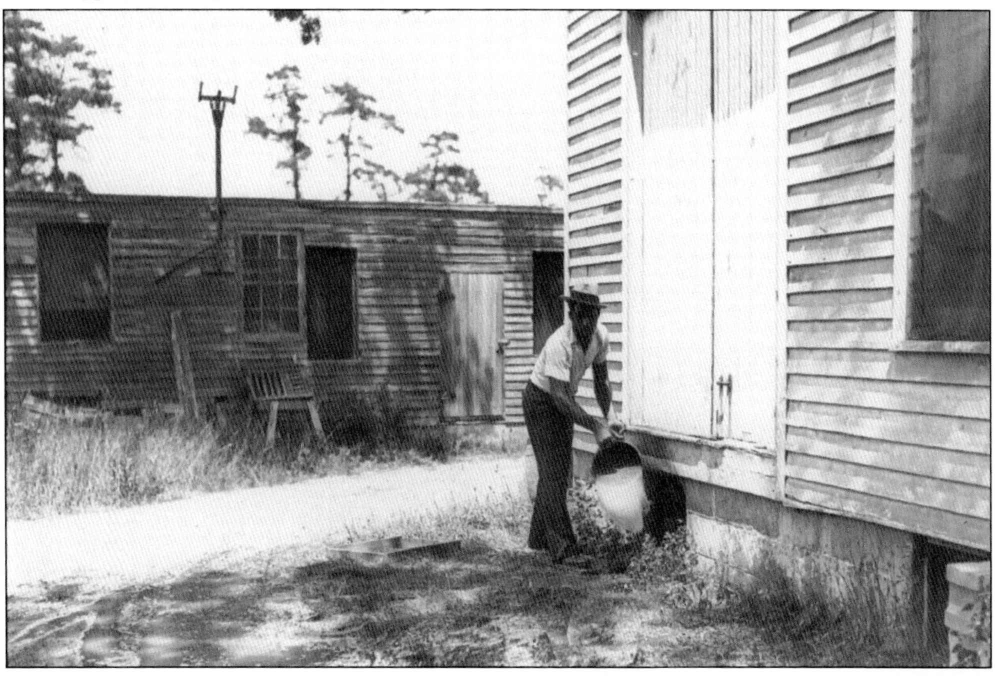

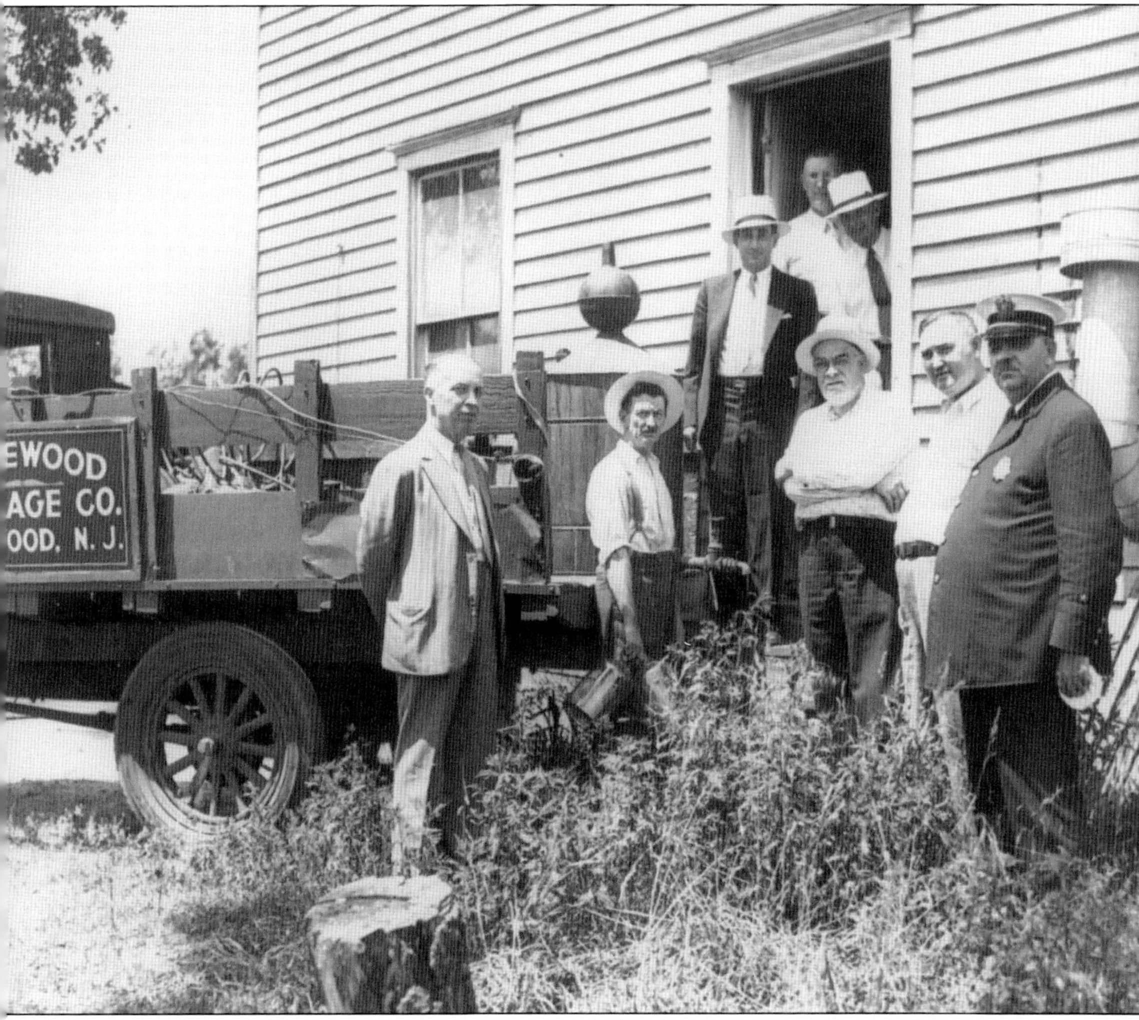

Members of the Lakewood Police Department and the Ocean County Sheriffs Department inspect an illegal still. Chief Walter A. Curtis, far right, and others coordinate the effort to confiscate the bootlegged alcohol. A truck from the Lakewood Storage Company was used to haul off the illegal contraband. (Photograph by F.W. Tupper, courtesy of the OCHS.)

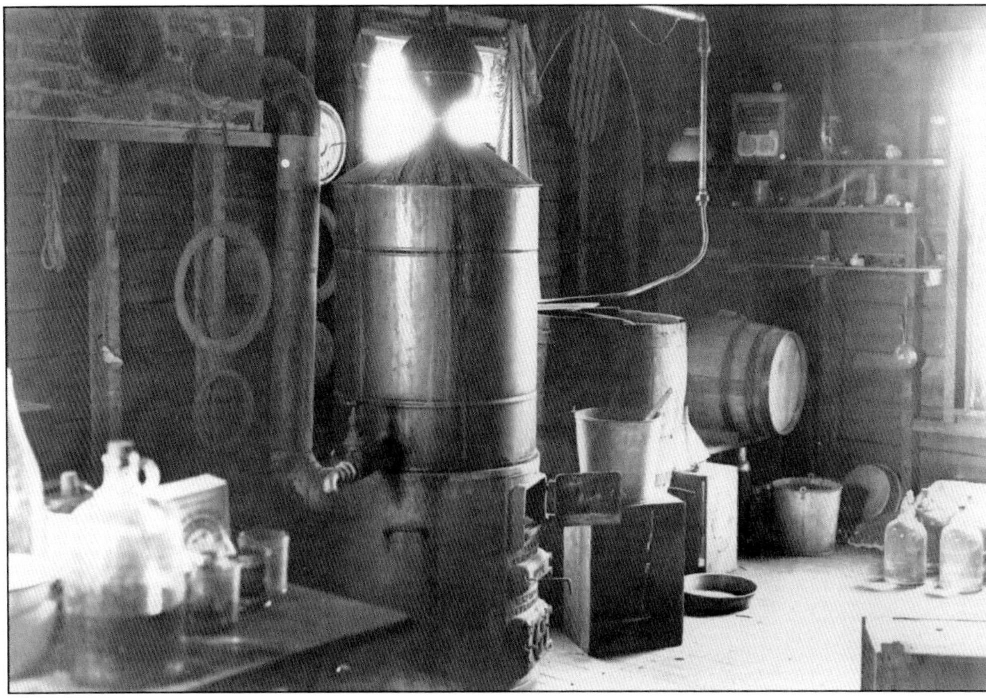

These pictures show the inside of a building that housed an illegal still. The still and laboratory pictured above were used to test and make bootlegged alcohol, which was then sold for an enormous profit. The loading room below is filled with jugs of moonshine, waiting to be packed into boxes and placed in a vehicle for delivery—had the Lakewood Police Department not raided the still. (Photographs by F.W. Tupper, courtesy of the OCHS.)

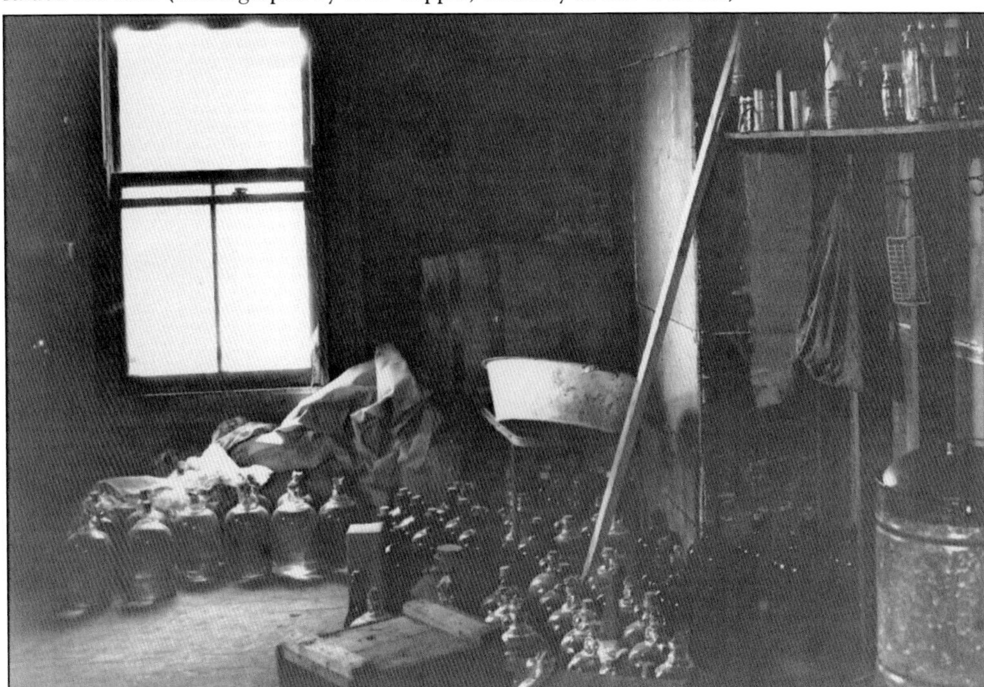

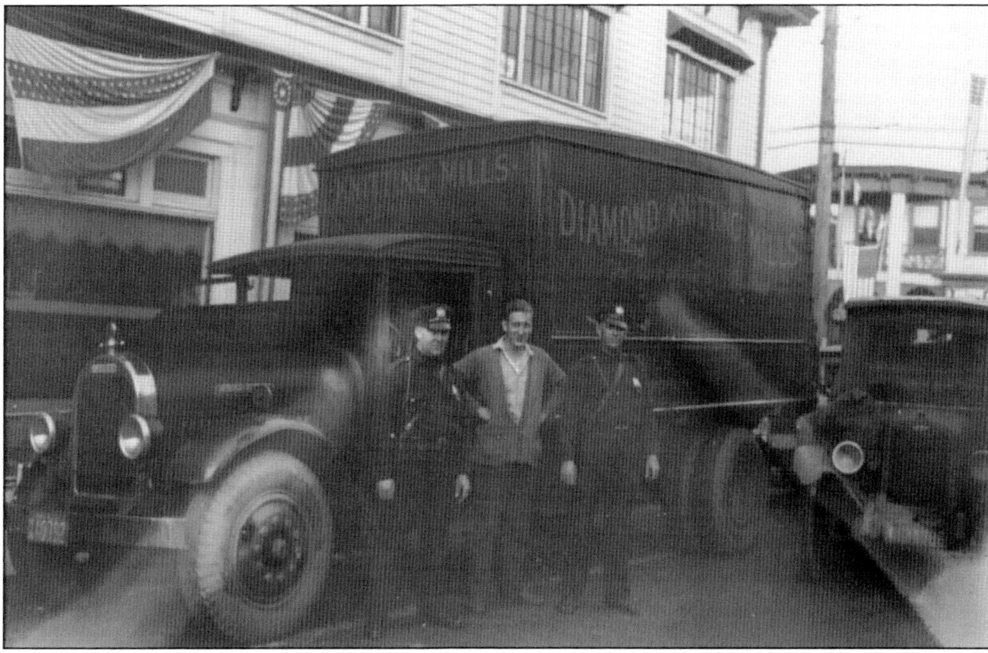

Officers Smith and Justice stopped this Diamond Knitting Mills truck for a simple traffic violation during the summer of 1930. Upon inspection, bootlegged alcohol was found and seized. Between the two officers is the embarrassed truck driver. (Photograph courtesy of the OCHS.)

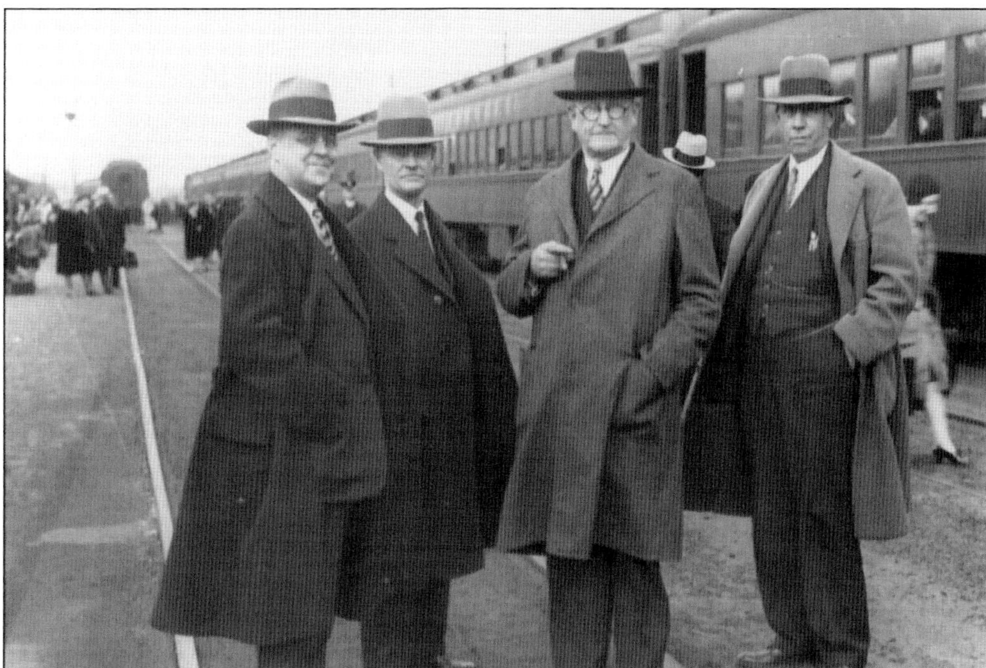

This picture was taken on February 2, 1930, at the Lakewood Train Station outside of the Blue Comet. The gentleman holding the cigar is Sen. Dwight Murrow. Murrow was an advocate for the abolition of prohibition. (Photograph courtesy of the OCHS.)

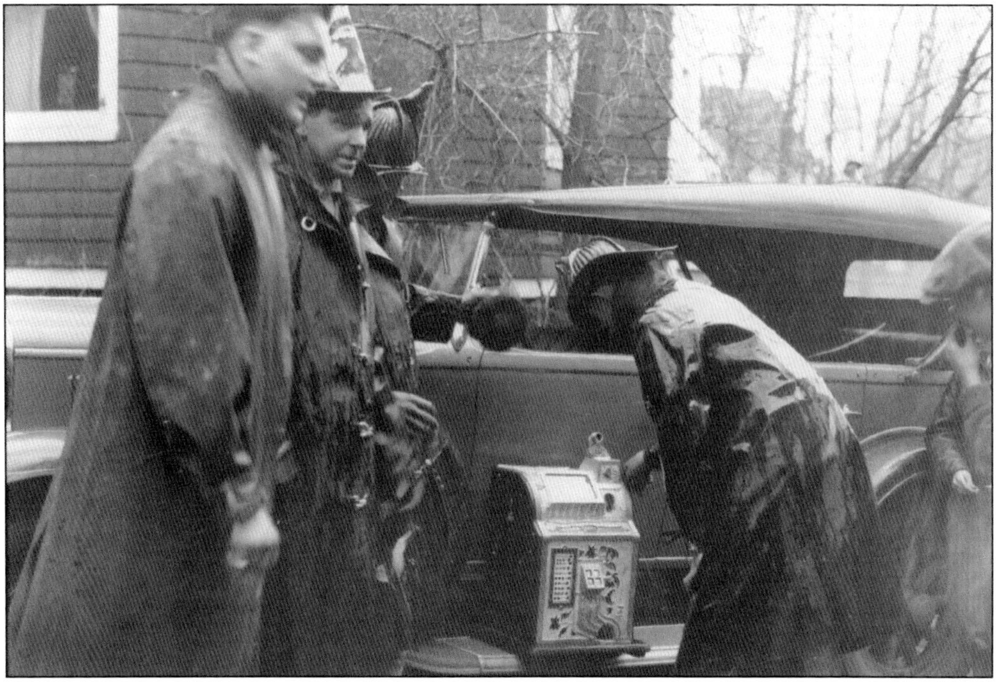

Members of Lakewood Fire Company No. 4 seize an illegal slot machine that had been found after exploring the aftermath of the Hotel Traymore fire on April 16, 1930. The *New York Evening Globe* reported that there were illegal gambling houses in Lakewood run by professional gamblers who were expelled from New York City by city law enforcement agents. (Photograph courtesy of the OCHS.)

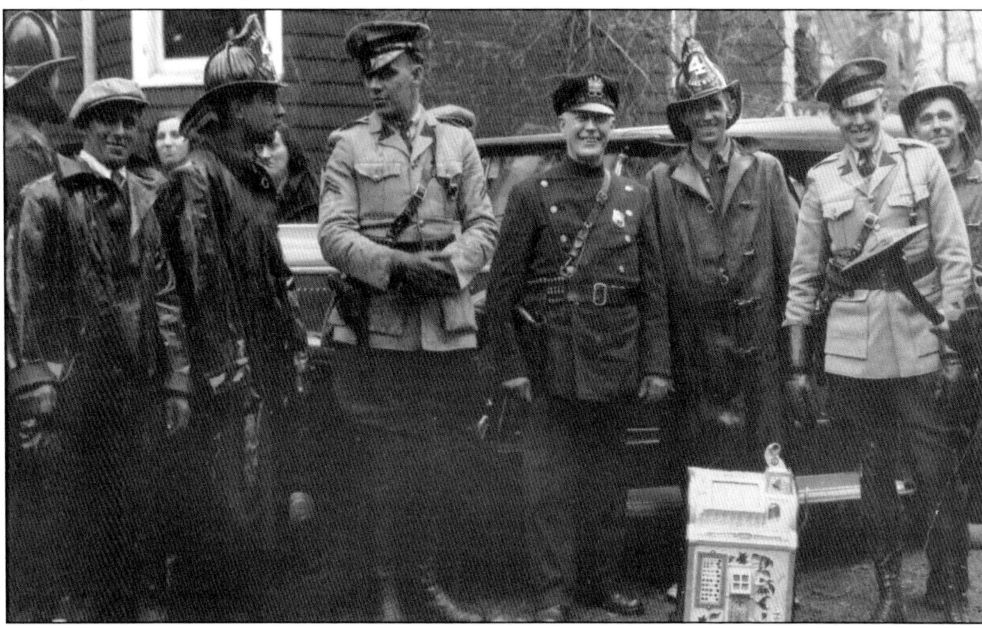

Members of the Lakewood Police Department, the New Jersey State Police, and several companies of the Lakewood Fire Department pose for a picture with the illegal slot machine seized following the Hotel Traymore fire. (Photograph courtesy of the OCHS.)

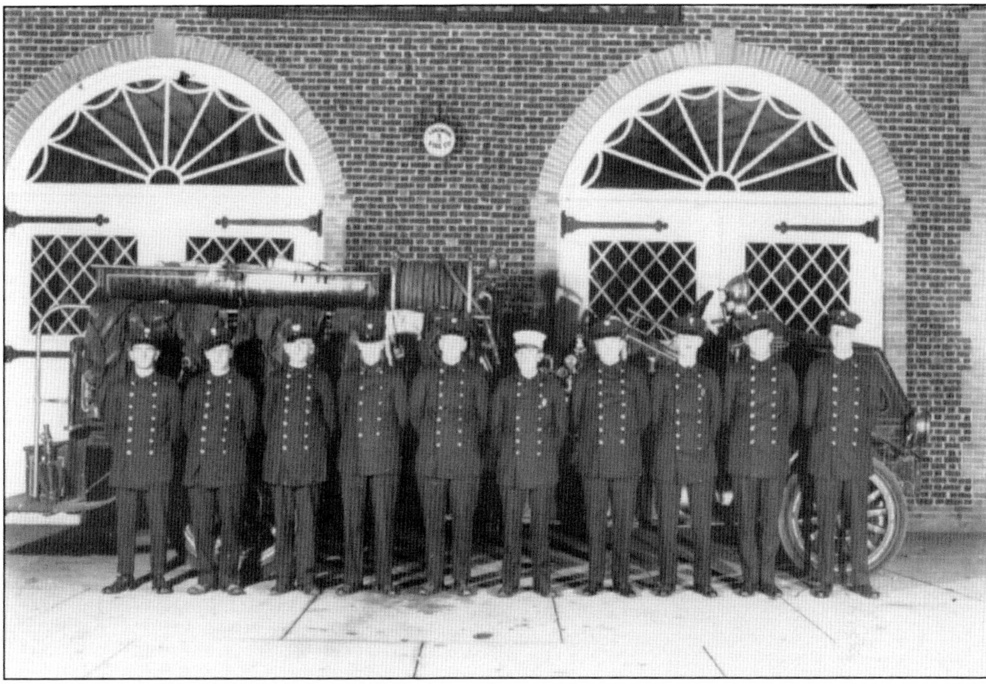

The Lakewood Fire Department was incorporated in the late 1800s. The earliest vehicles used by the department were horse-drawn wagons. The team of horses had to be secured through local liveries. The Lakewood Fire Company had its first meeting on Main Street inside the store of James H. Todd. The pictures on this page feature two of the Lakewood Fire Companies in October 1929. The Lakewood Fire Department's Company No. 1 and its ten members are pictured above; below is the Lakewood Hook and Ladder Company. (Photographs courtesy of the OCHS.)

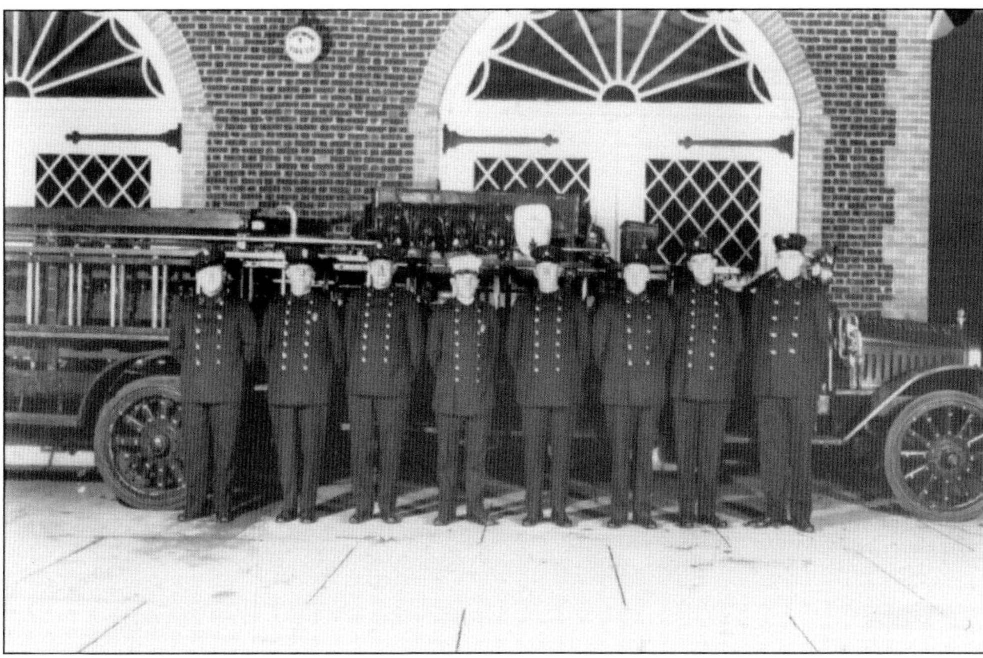

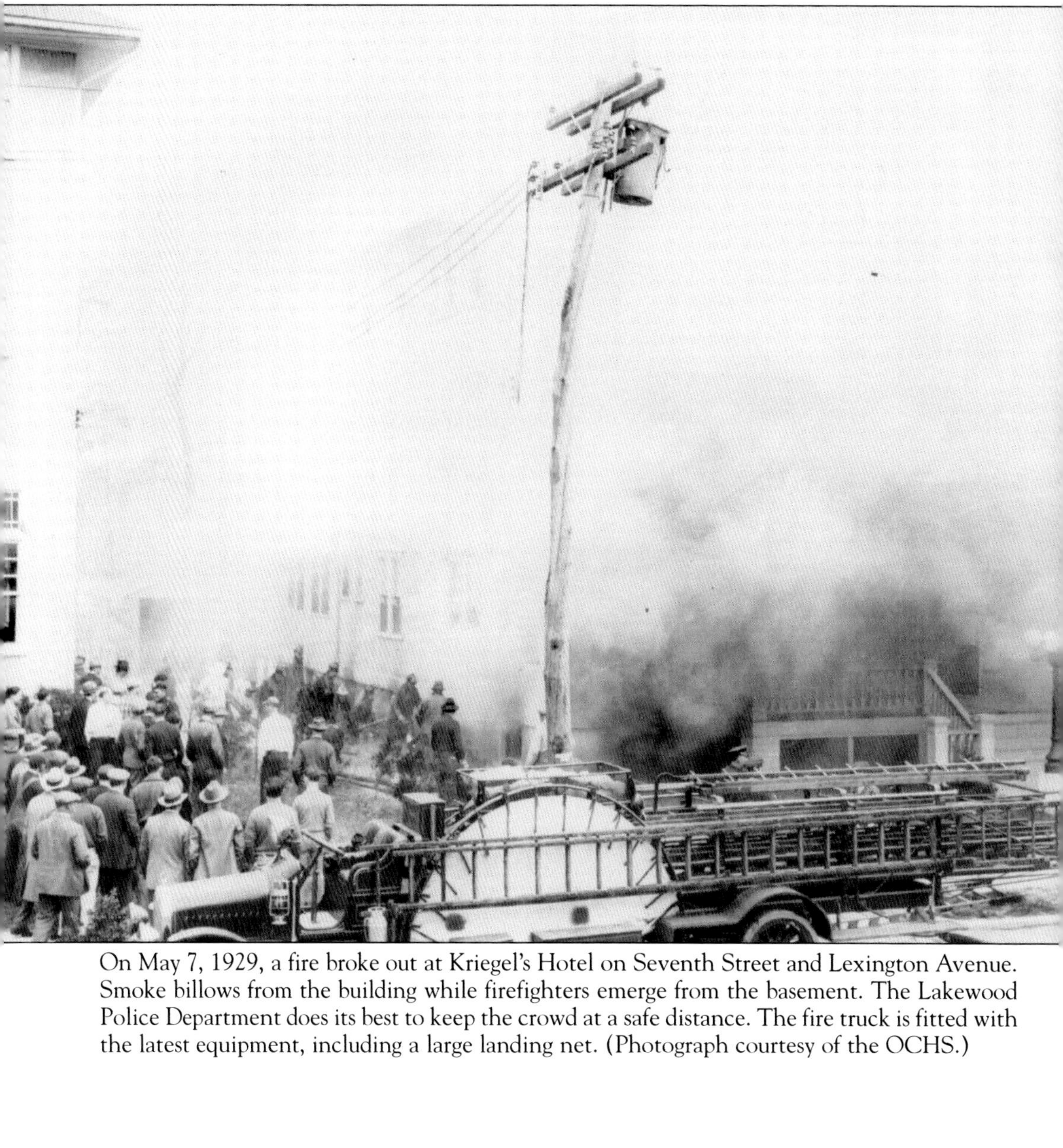

On May 7, 1929, a fire broke out at Kriegel's Hotel on Seventh Street and Lexington Avenue. Smoke billows from the building while firefighters emerge from the basement. The Lakewood Police Department does its best to keep the crowd at a safe distance. The fire truck is fitted with the latest equipment, including a large landing net. (Photograph courtesy of the OCHS.)

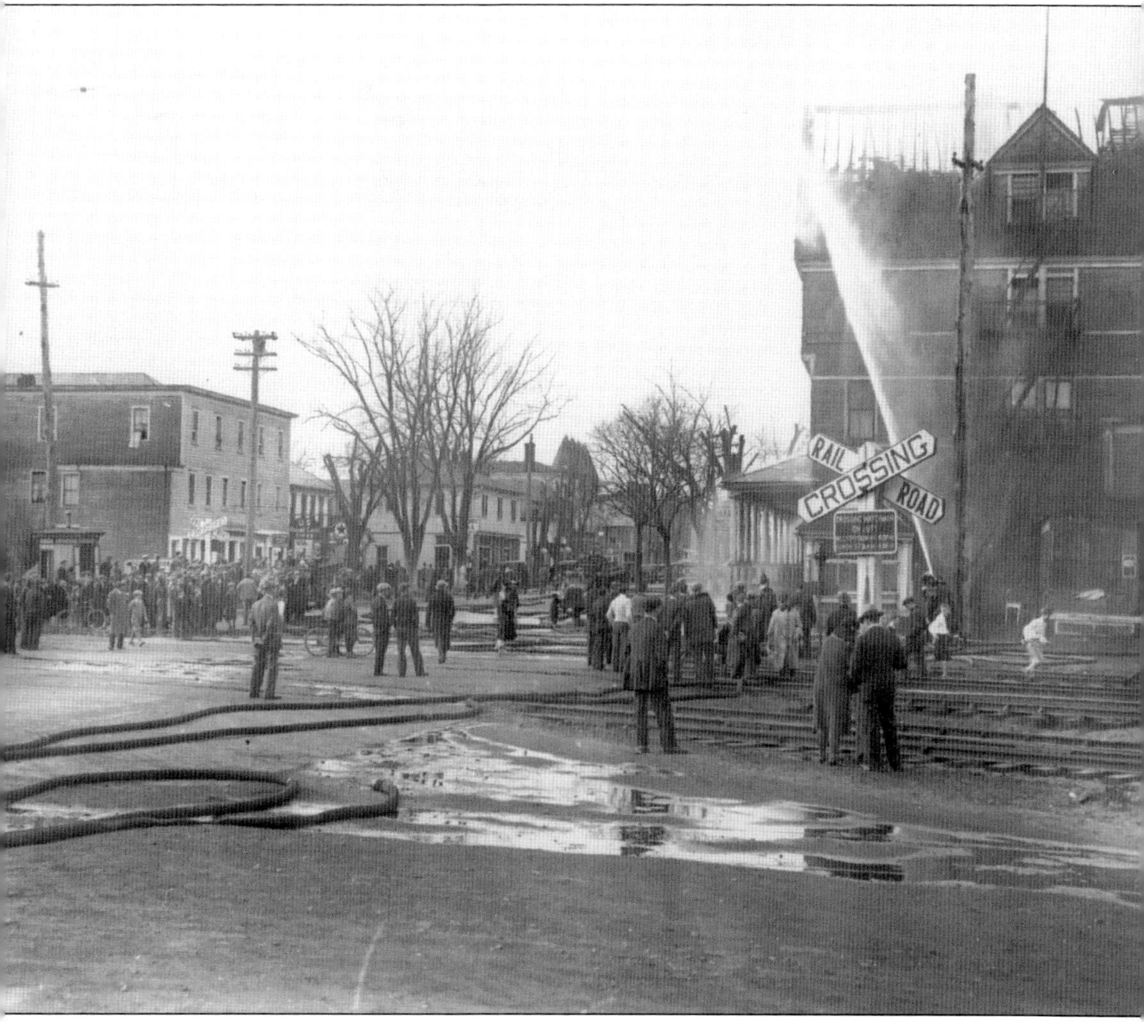

The Lexington Hotel, one of the first hotels in Lakewood to stay open year-round, smolders as two Lakewood firefighters spray water on the damaged roof. A large crowd gathers on the corner of Main Street and Lexington Avenue to observe the incident. (Photograph courtesy of the OCHS.)

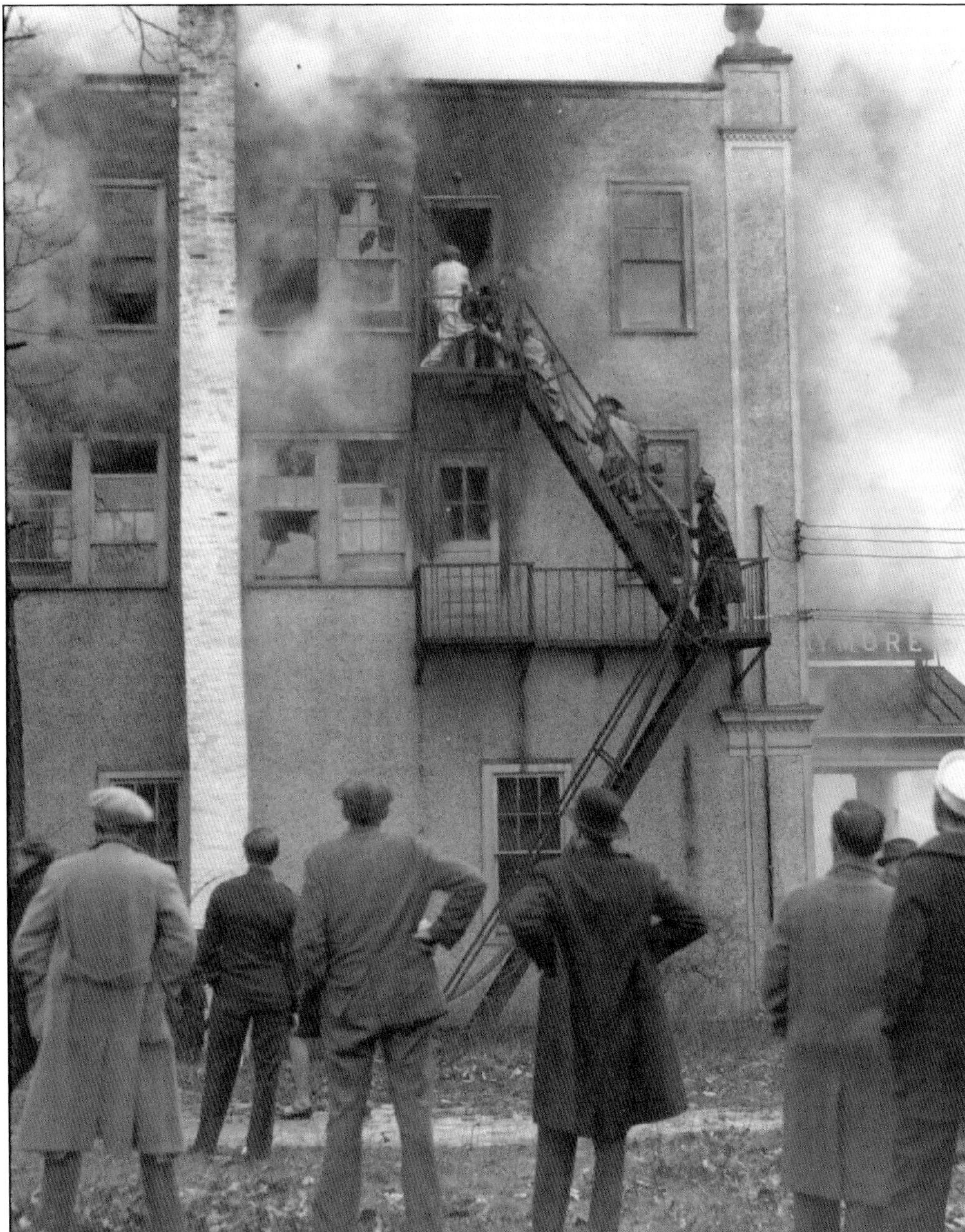

Hotel Traymore was ravaged by fire on April 16, 1930. This photograph captures several brave firefighters as they rush up the fire escape to battle the blaze and to search for trapped victims. Onlookers nervously observe the heroics, as smoke pours out of the upper-floor windows. (Photograph courtesy of the OCHS.)

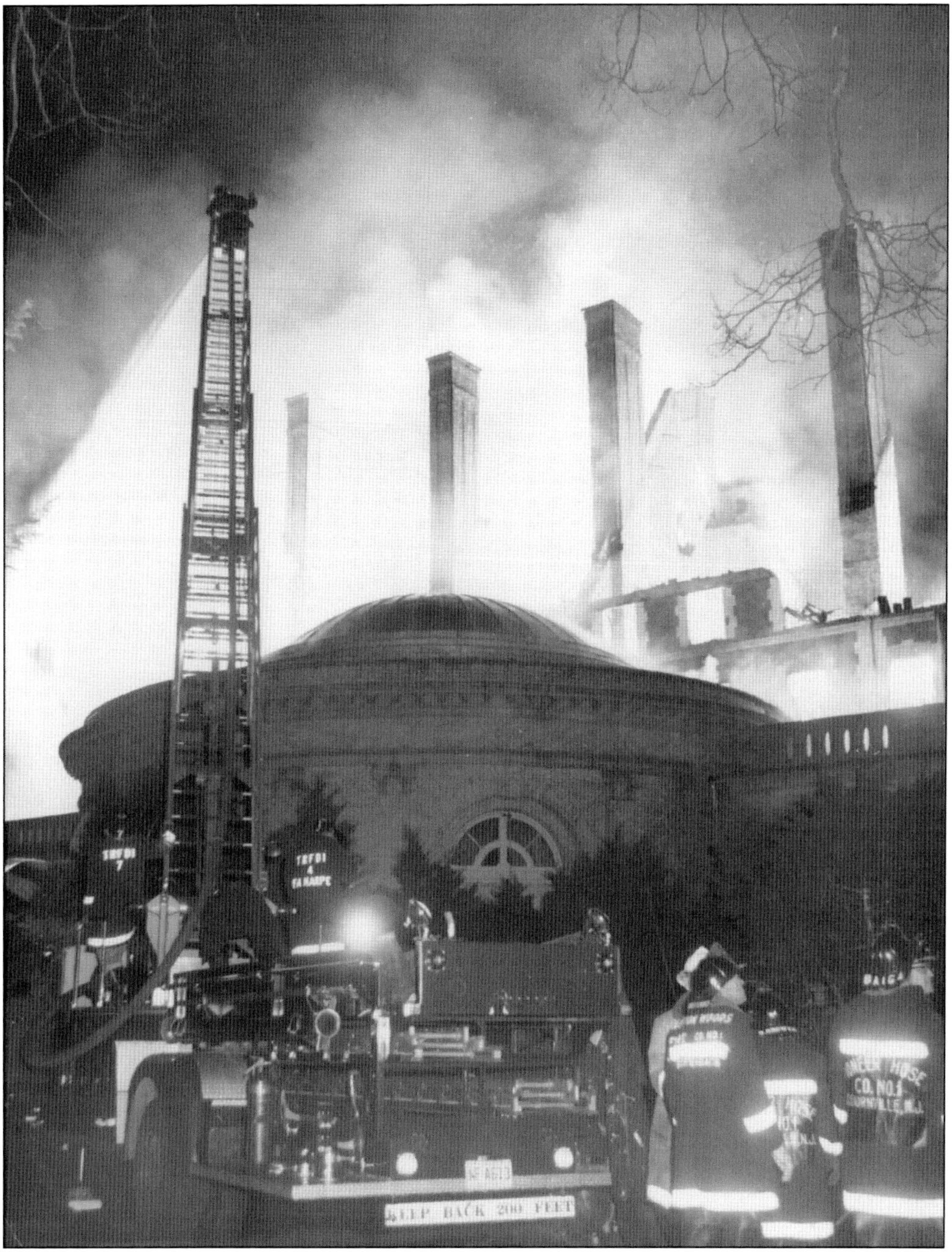

The Laurel-in-the-Pines was plagued by a series of fires over time. This fire, which started around 11:00 p.m. on March 28, 1967, seriously damaged the structure of the hotel. It took more than 500 firefighters from Lakewood and several other Ocean and Monmouth County towns to put out the fire. It is believed that arson was the cause of the fire. The chimneys of the once magnificent building were the only things spared. (Photograph by R. Steele, courtesy of the OCHS.)

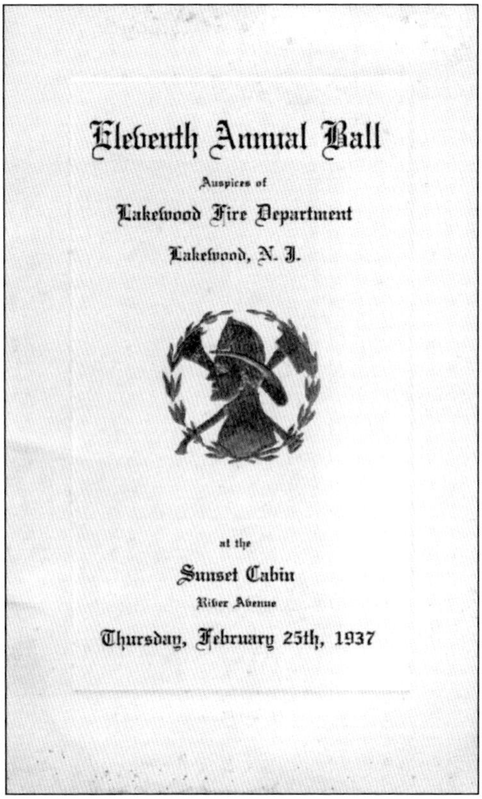

Eleventh Annual Ball

Auspices of

Lakewood Fire Department

Lakewood, N. J.

at the

Sunset Cabin

River Avenue

Thursday, February 25th, 1937

This is the cover of the program booklet for the 11th annual ball held to benefit the Lakewood Fire Department. The event took place at the Sunset Cabin on Route 9 on February 25, 1937. The program included 19 fox trots, 2 tangos, 1 waltz, and 1 rumba.

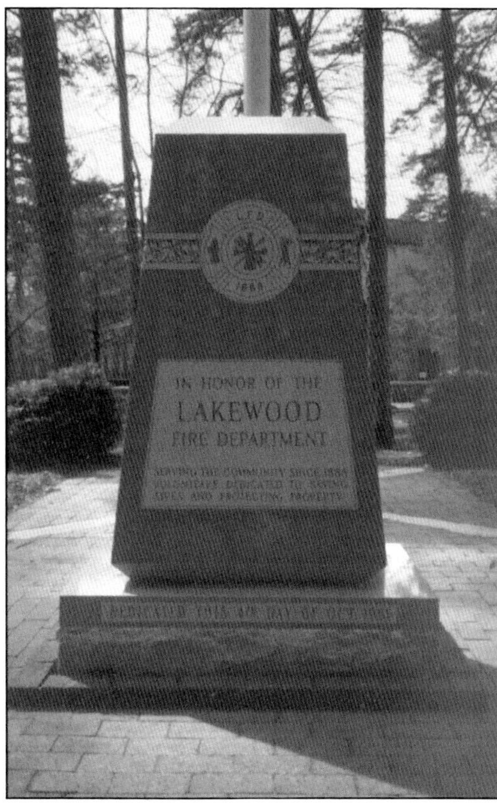

This monument was built to honor the heroic deeds of the Lakewood Fire Department over the years. The monument was dedicated at a ceremony in Pine Park on October 4, 1981. (Photograph courtesy of Jill Katus.)

Four

LODGING

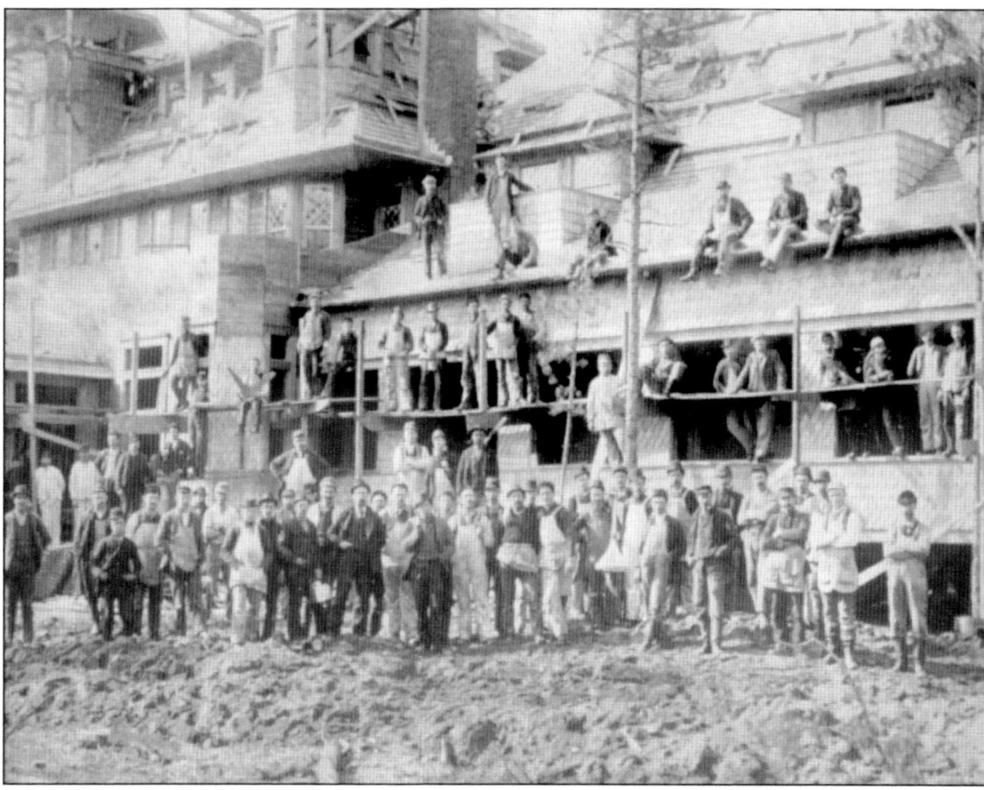

An article published in the *New Jersey Courier* on October 2, 1902, describes Lakewood and its winter resort as a "Place remote from the whirl of the city where quietness reigns, the hotels are marvelously kept and every contrivance is at hand for the convenience and comfort of the guest." This picture is of the Lakewood Casino Hotel during its construction phase. The hotel was located in South Lakewood in the vicinity of Cross Street. (Photograph courtesy of Al Platt.)

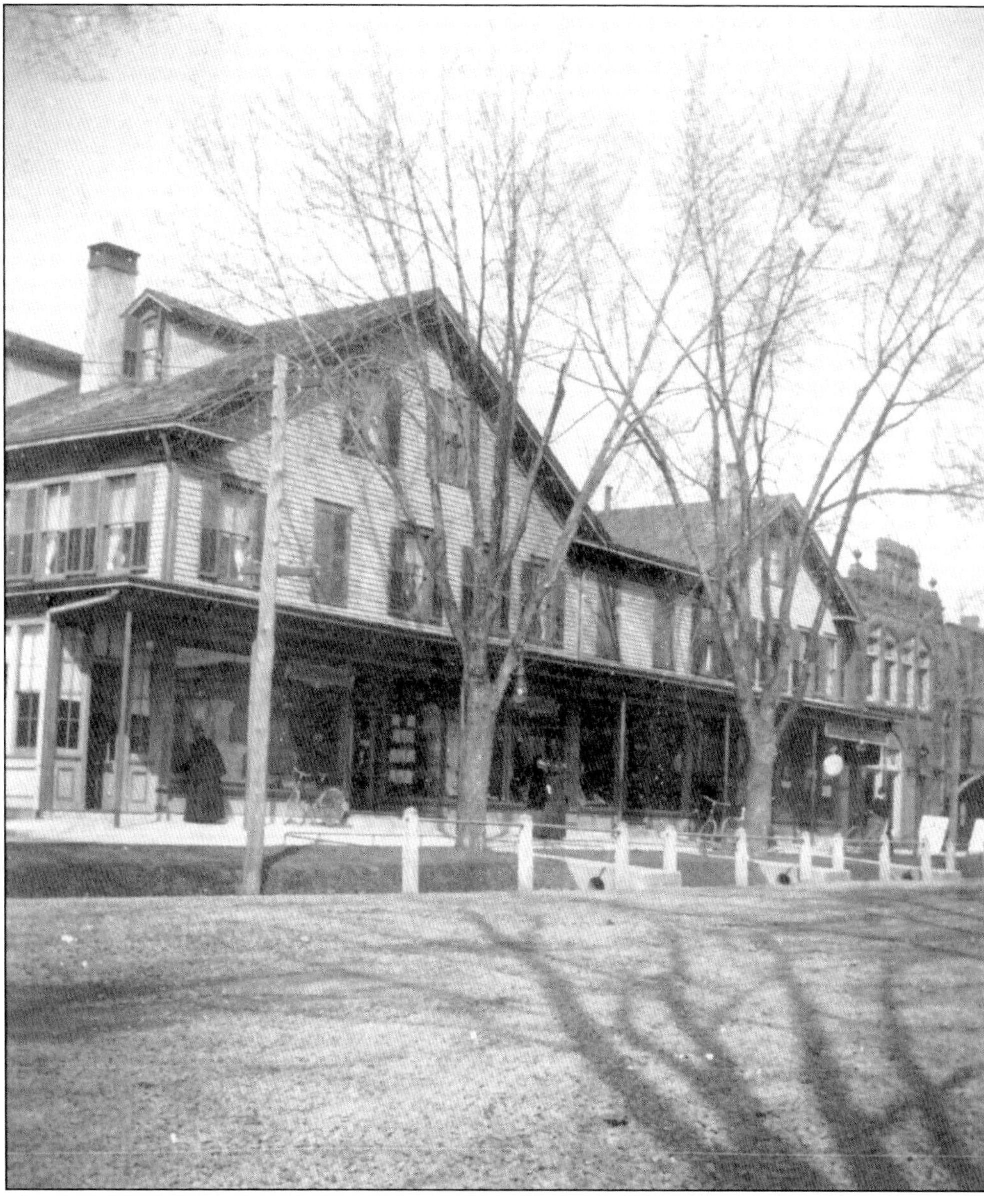

The building that housed the Hotel Carasaljo was constructed in 1867. The hotel was located on the north side of Main Street. It had a capacity to accommodate close to 80 patrons. The hotel was mostly used as a hall for special events, but its rooms were rented from time to time. Room rates at the hotel were $2.50 and up per day and $15 and up per week. The hotel was demolished in 1973. (Photograph courtesy of the OCHS.)

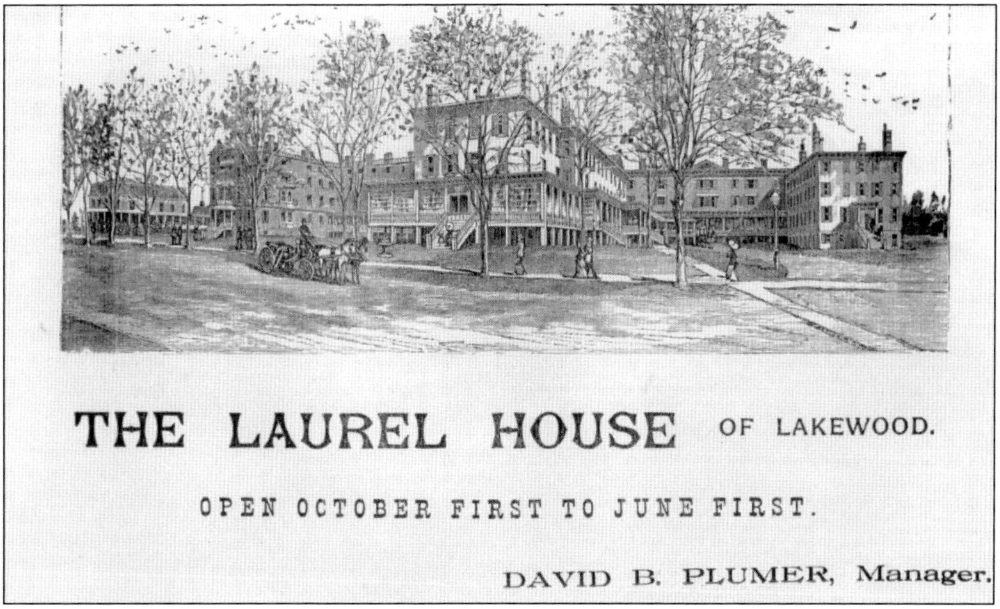

The structure that was known as the Laurel House was built in 1865 on Main Street between Clifton and Lexington Avenues. The original name for the building was the Bricksburg House; the original use was as a tavern, tended by Robert Estell. When the building was expanded in 1880, the name was changed to the Laurel House. The hotel grew over the years and in 1900, it consisted of close to 300 rooms. This structure represents the start of the great hotel resort industry in Lakewood.

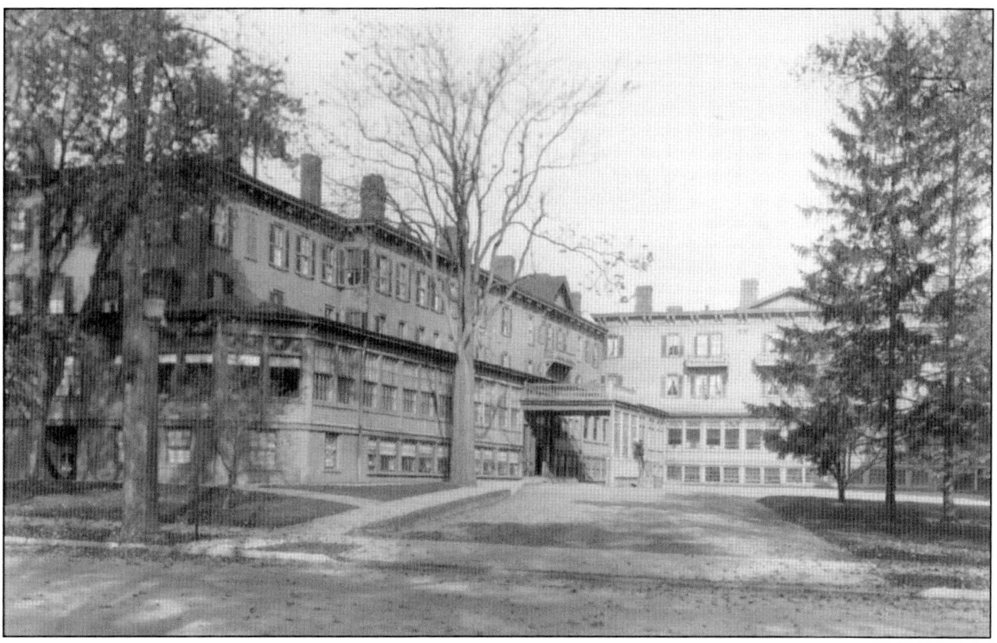

An article in the *Asbury Park Sunday Press* in 1933 praised the Laurel House by saying that it was the social center of town during Lakewood's early resort days. Some of the prominent names that could be found on the hotel registry included Rudyard Kipling, Oliver Wendell Holmes, and Mark Twain. (Photograph courtesy of the OCHS.)

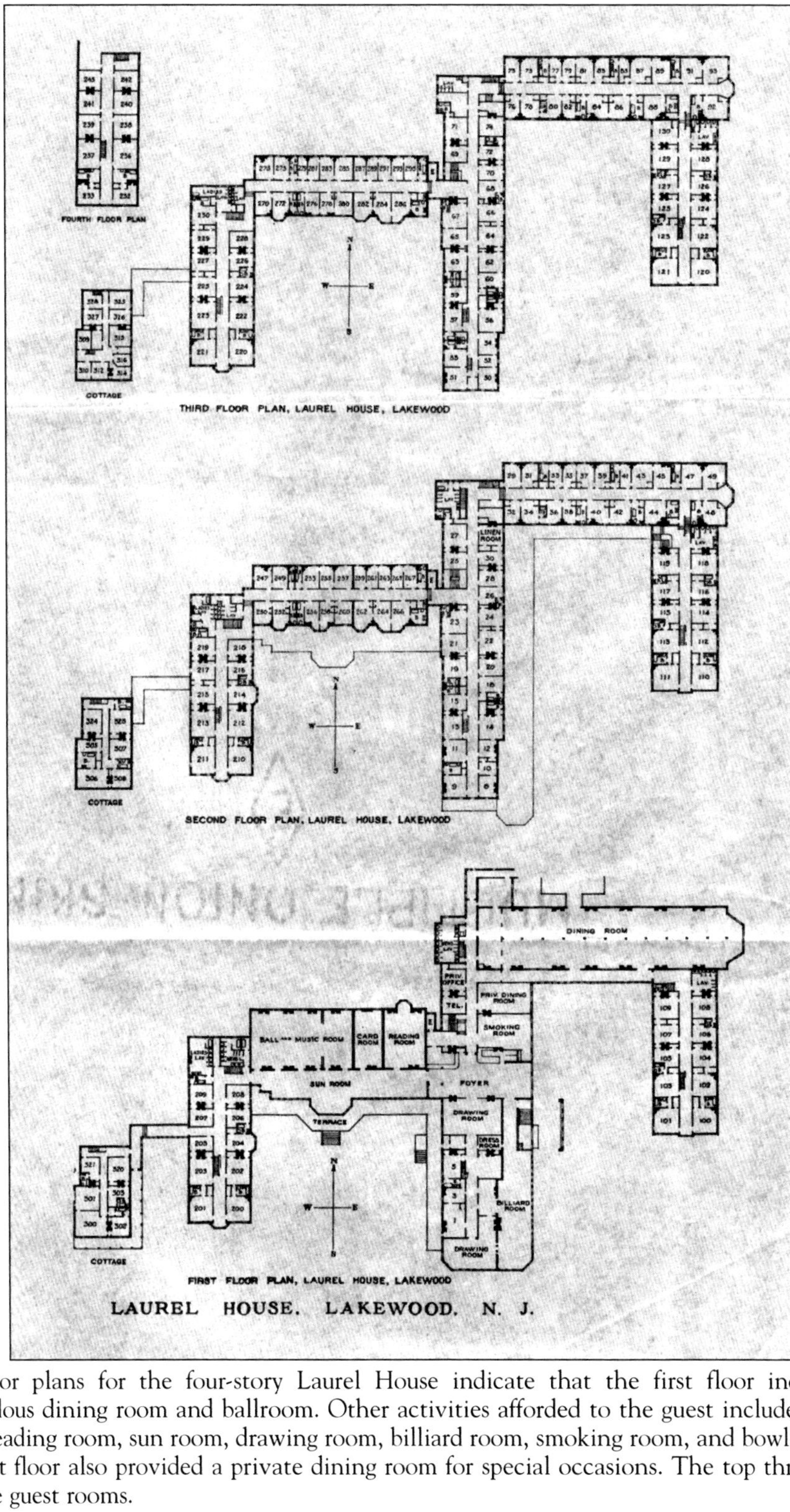

The floor plans for the four-story Laurel House indicate that the first floor included a tremendous dining room and ballroom. Other activities afforded to the guest included a card room, reading room, sun room, drawing room, billiard room, smoking room, and bowling alley. The first floor also provided a private dining room for special occasions. The top three floors held the guest rooms.

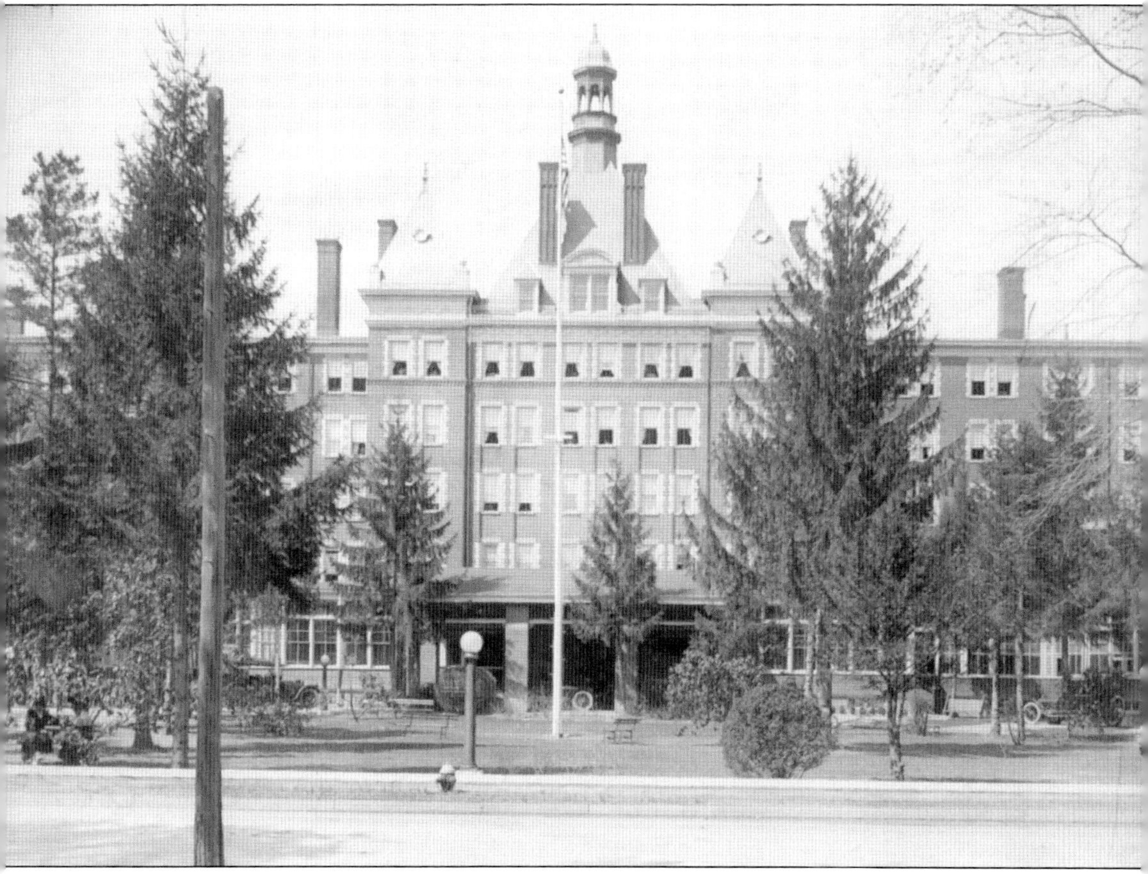

The Lakewood Hotel was the largest hotel in town. The structure was erected in 1891 at a cost of nearly $1 million. The hotel had the capacity to host close to 700 guests. An advertisement for the resort exclaimed, "The Lakewood Hotel has all the luxuries of the city and all of the attractions of the country . . . It has the finest water cure and electric baths on the American Continent, modeled after the famous Charcoat Institutions at Paris." During World War I, the government took over the building and turned it into U.S. Army Hospital No. 9. (Photograph courtesy of the OCHS.)

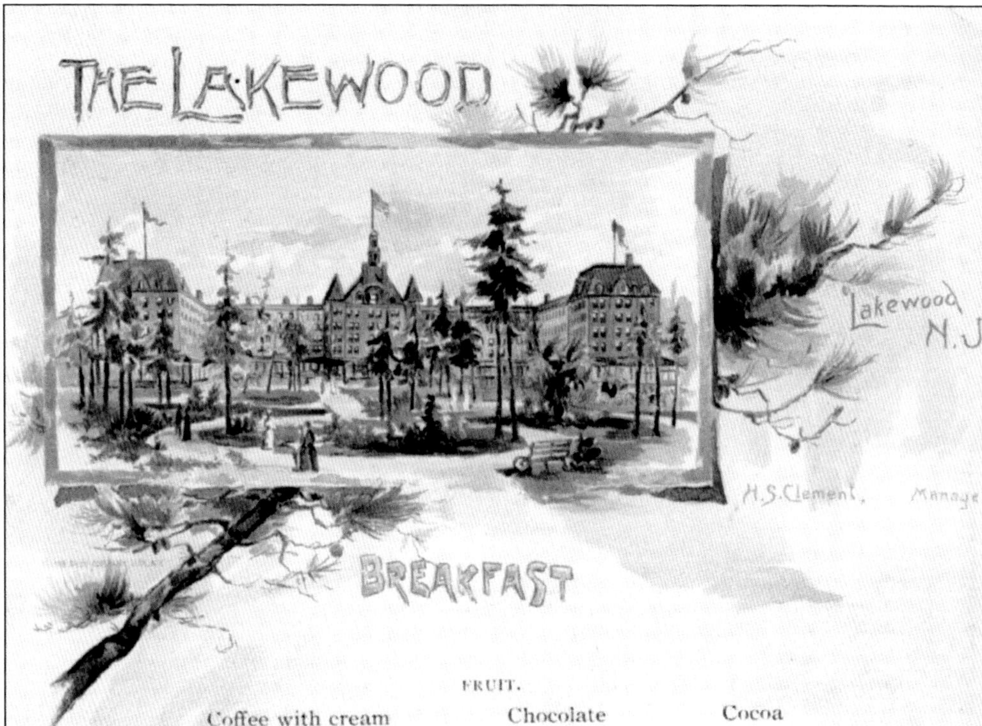

FRUIT.

Coffee with cream   Chocolate   Cocoa

Japan, Oolong and English breakfast Tea

Vienna rolls   Brioche French style   Wheat muffins

French Rolls   Flutes   Toast   Corn Muffins

Graham Muffins   Germain Bread   Oatmeal

Hominy with hot cream   Graham Bread   Grits   Boiled Rice

Rice Cakes   Buckwheat Cakes

Clam Broth

Shad roe maitre d'hotel   Fried Flounders   Fish Balls

Salt Mackerel   Smoked salmon   Pickedup Cod Fish

Fancy Eggs

Eggs turc   Omelette with kirsh

Eggs—Boiled,   Omelettes plain or with Parsley,   Onions,   Ham,   Kidney

Plain Scrambled   Scrambled with smoked beef

Poached eggs on toast   Fried with Ham or Bacon

Broiled Chicken

Kidney Sautè   Broiled Calf's Liver   Bacon   Ham

Sirloin Steak   Lamb Chops

Deerfoot farm sausage

Ribs of Beef   Corn Beef

This breakfast menu from the Lakewood Hotel is dated Saturday, April 4, 1891. (Courtesy of the OCHS.)

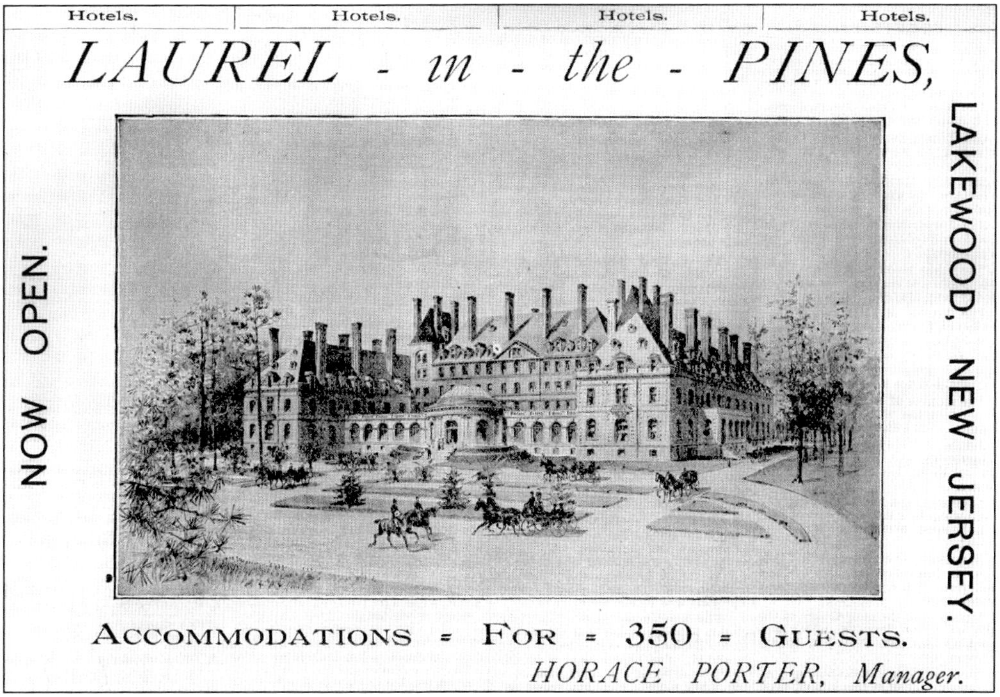

This was an advertisement for the Laurel-in-the-Pines Hotel, which stood regally among the pine trees on North Lake Drive across from Lake Carasaljo. At the time of this advertisement, the hotel had the accommodations to serve 350 guests.

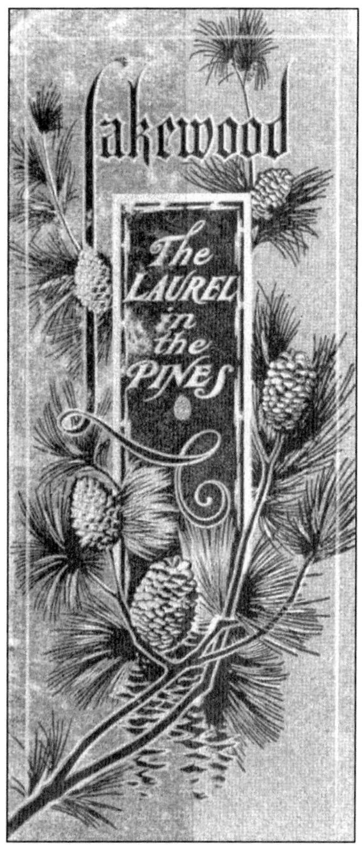

This is the cover page of an early brochure for the Laurel-in-the-Pines Hotel. (Courtesy of the OCHS.)

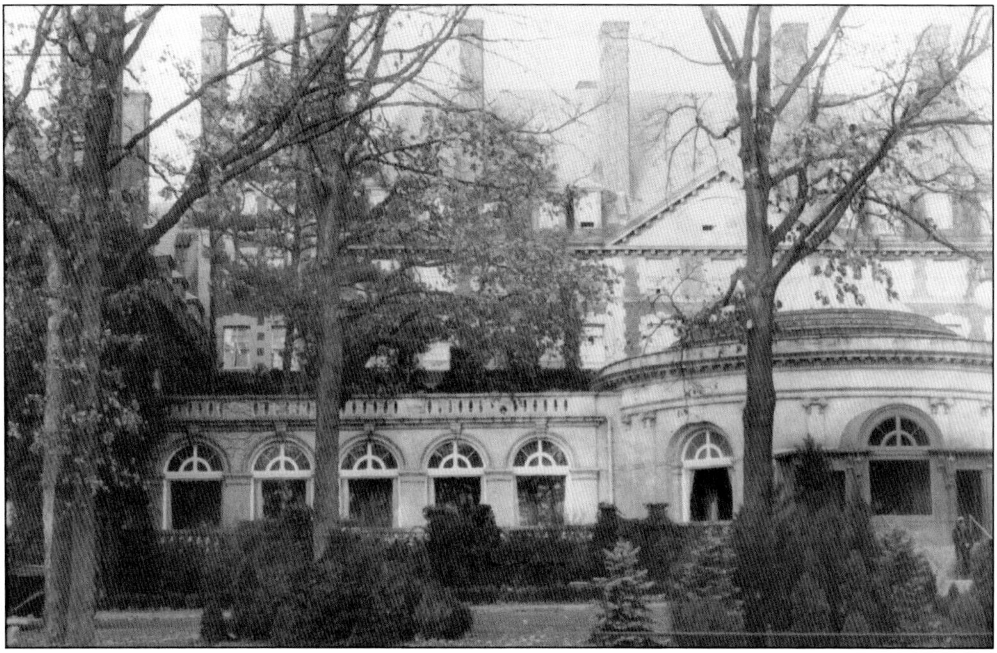

The Laurel-in-the-Pines Hotel had a construction cost of close to $500,000. It opened its doors for business less than a week before Christmas of 1891. The most noticeable characteristic of the hotel was the copper rotunda situated over the entrance of the building. (Photograph courtesy of the OCHS.)

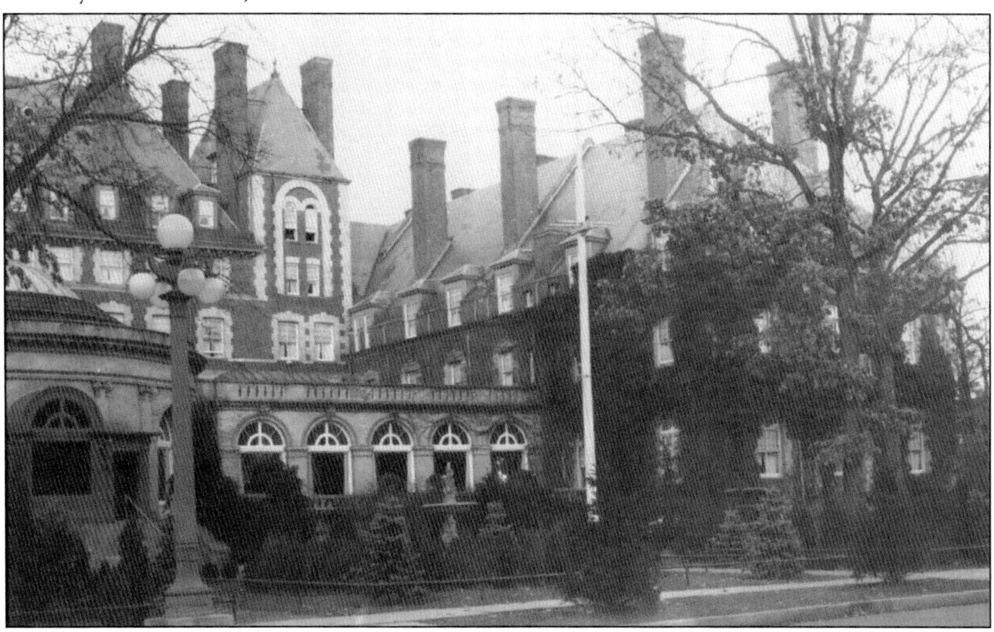

The Laurel-in-the-Pines consisted of four floors and had a capacity to entertain nearly 500 guests. An advertisement for the hotel boasted that the most used and admired room in the hotel was the Palm Room. The advertisement read, "Through whole glass roof shines down on a sparkling fountain of hundreds of luxuriant palms, which is an ideal spot for rest and quiet." (Photograph courtesy of the OCHS.)

This advertisement for the Mirror Room at the Laurel-in-the-Pines featured Howard Woods and His Orchestra and announced comedian Henny Youngman, one of the well-known entertainers who frequented the hotel spotlight.

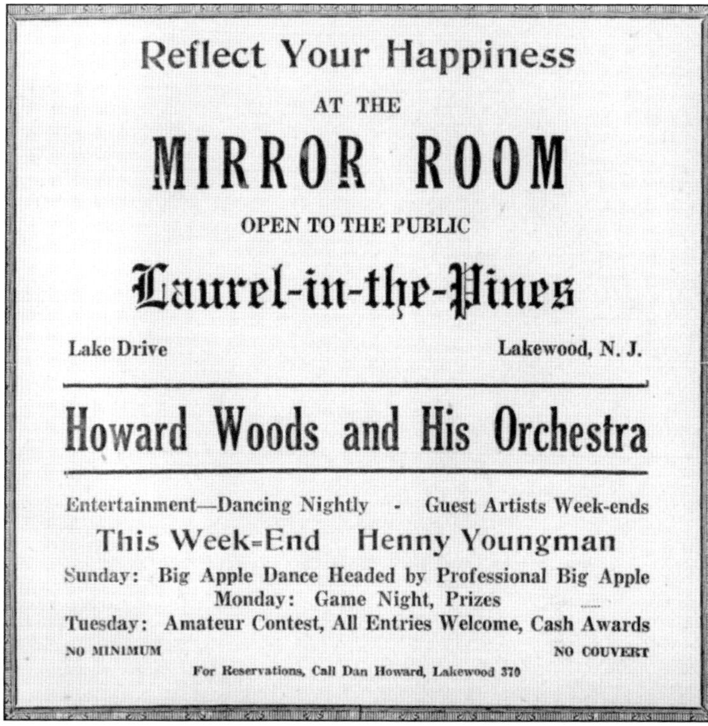

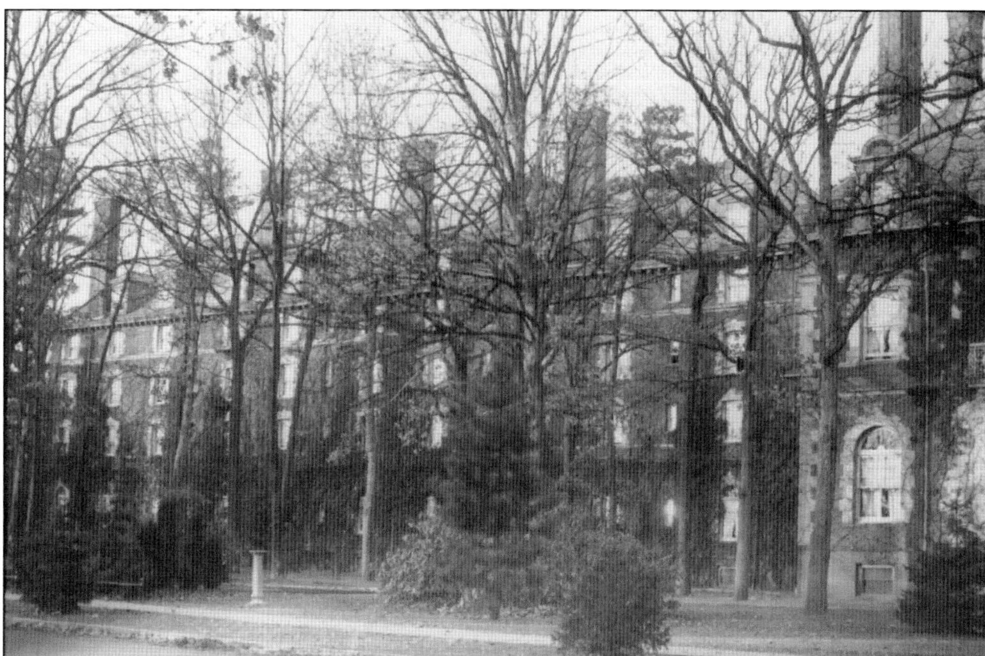

This photograph shows the vastness of the exterior of the Laurel-in-the-Pines Hotel. The interior of the building featured an artesian well that reached nearly 400 feet into the ground to supply its guest with pure drinking water. The hotel also housed a plant that generated steam heat and electric power for the convenience of its patrons. (Photograph courtesy of the OCHS.)

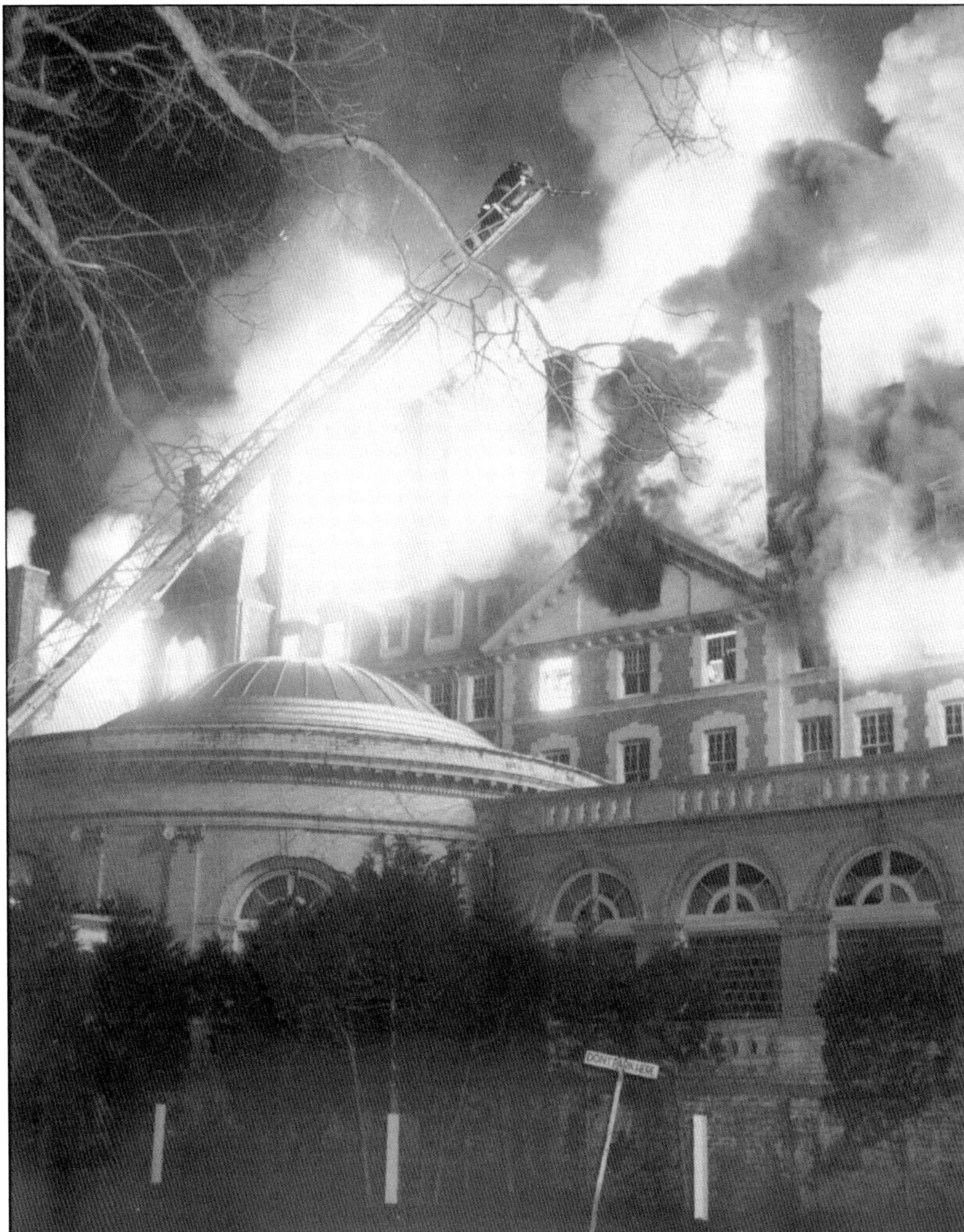

The Laurel-in-the-Pines, like many of the grand hotels in Lakewood, fell victim to fire. The blaze that destroyed the hotel was deemed suspicious, since eight different fires were found burning in different parts of the hotel when the fire department arrived. Like many of the old historic structures in Lakewood, the remnants of the destroyed hotel were cleared to make room for town houses and apartments. (Photograph by R. Steele, courtesy of the OCHS.)

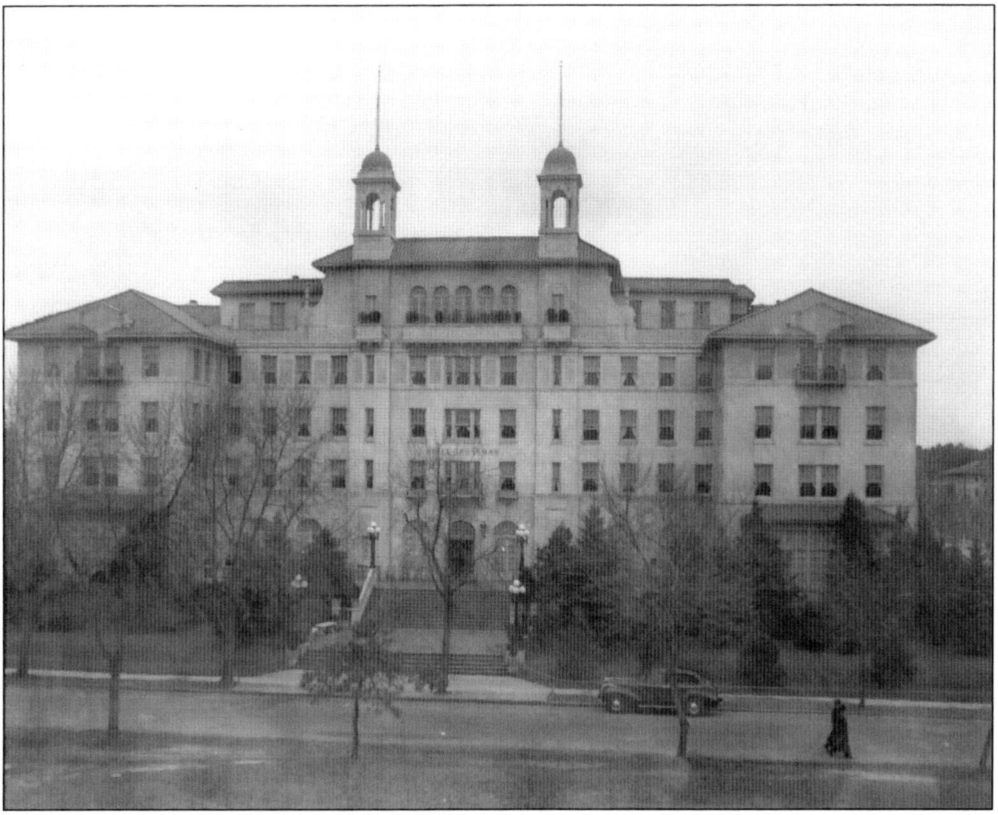

The Hotel Grossman, constructed in 1920, was located on Eighth Street and Madison Avenue. The original name of the structure was Hotel Elisberg. The Hotel Grossman could service close to 400 guests. The hotel was destroyed by fire during the autumn of 1955. (Photograph by F.W. Tupper, courtesy of the OCHS.)

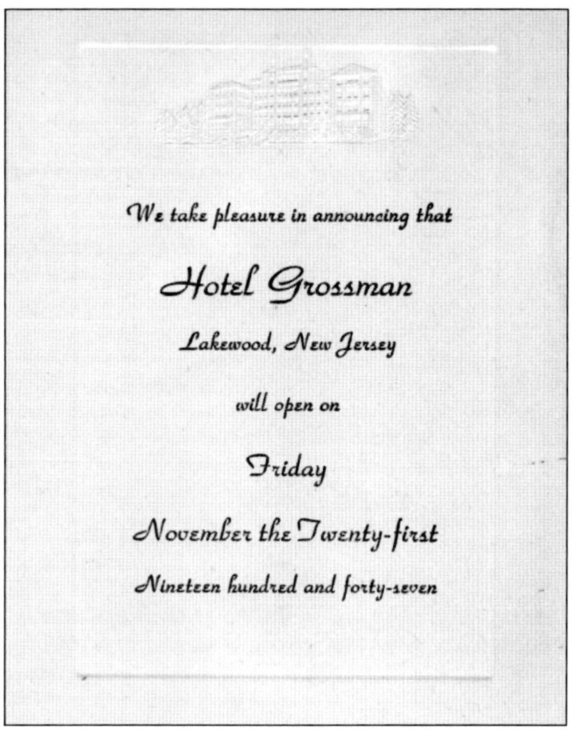

We take pleasure in announcing that

Hotel Grossman

Lakewood, New Jersey

will open on

Friday

November the Twenty-first

Nineteen hundred and forty-seven

This announcement was sent out to notify prospective guests that the Hotel Grossman would open for the 1947 season on Friday, November 21.

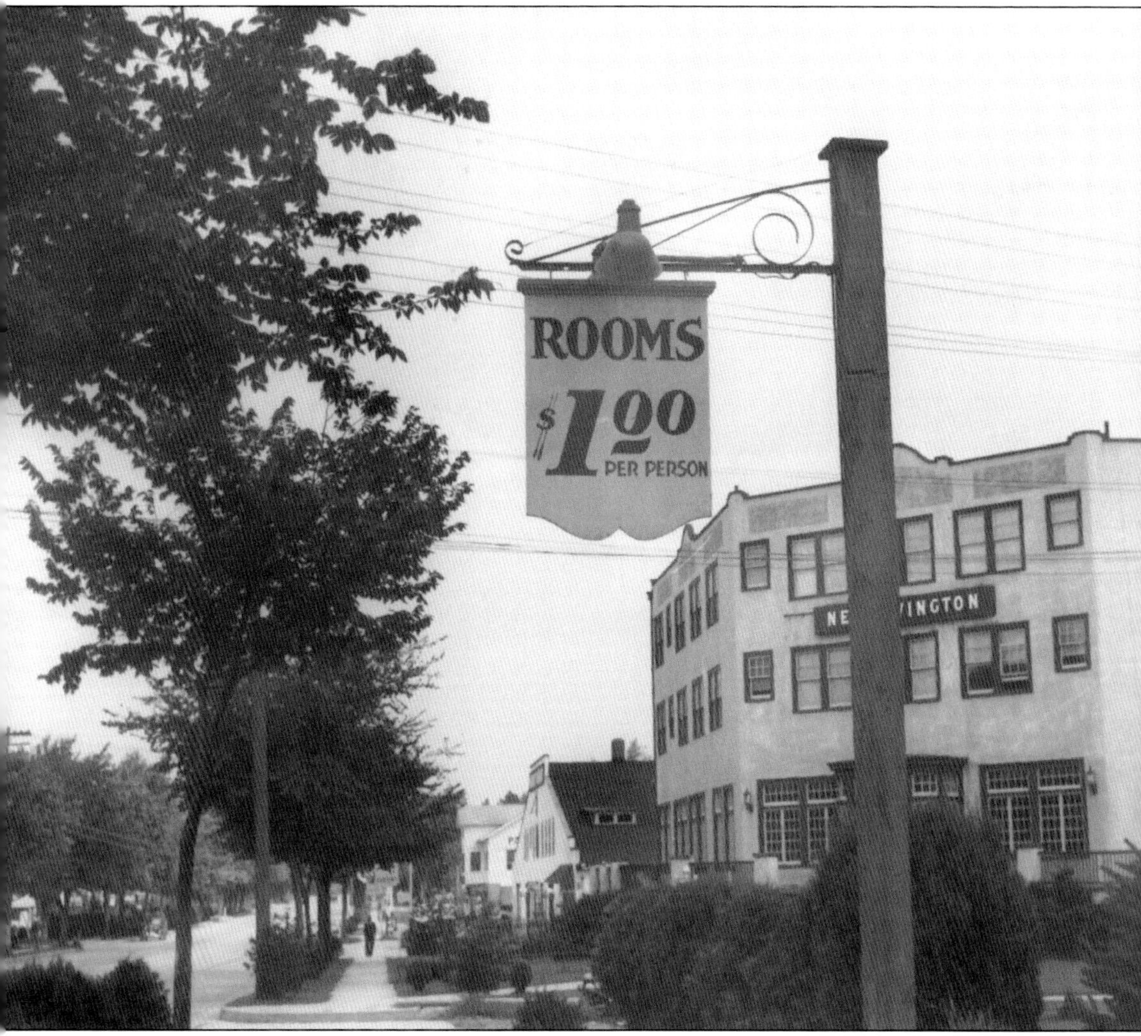

A sign advertises rooms for $1 per person at the New Irvington Hotel during the fall of 1937. The building is located on Madison Avenue and Ninth Street. The New Irvington was a member of the Hotel Association of Lakewood. In 1960, the hotel had the capacity to accommodate 400 patrons. (Photograph by F.W. Tupper, courtesy of the OCHS.)

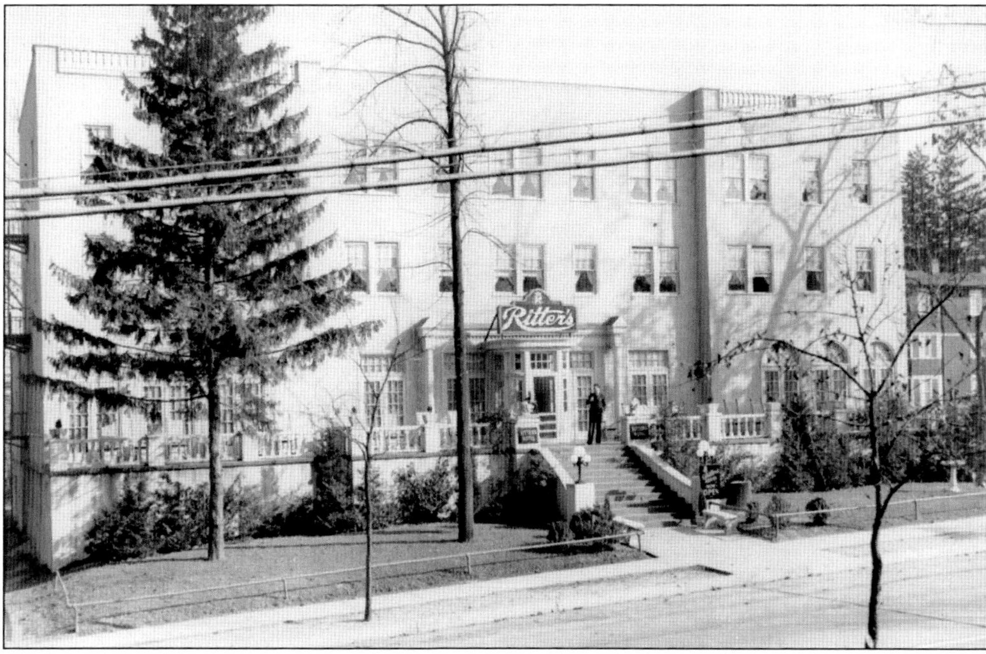

Ritter's Hotel (above) was located at 605 Madison Avenue and Sixth Street. The building was named Hotel Claridge (below) previous to the name change to Ritter's. The hotel could accommodate close to 150 guests and boasted some of the best cuisine in town. Max Lefkowitz and his wife managed the hotel. (Photographs by F.W. Tupper, courtesy of the OCHS.)

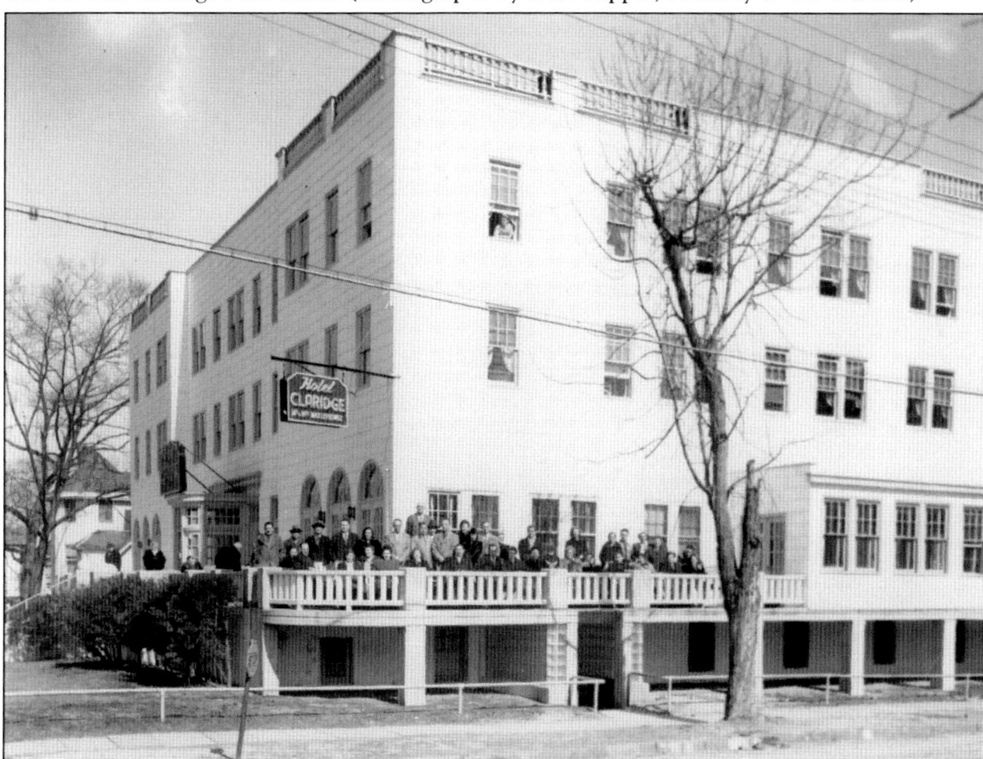

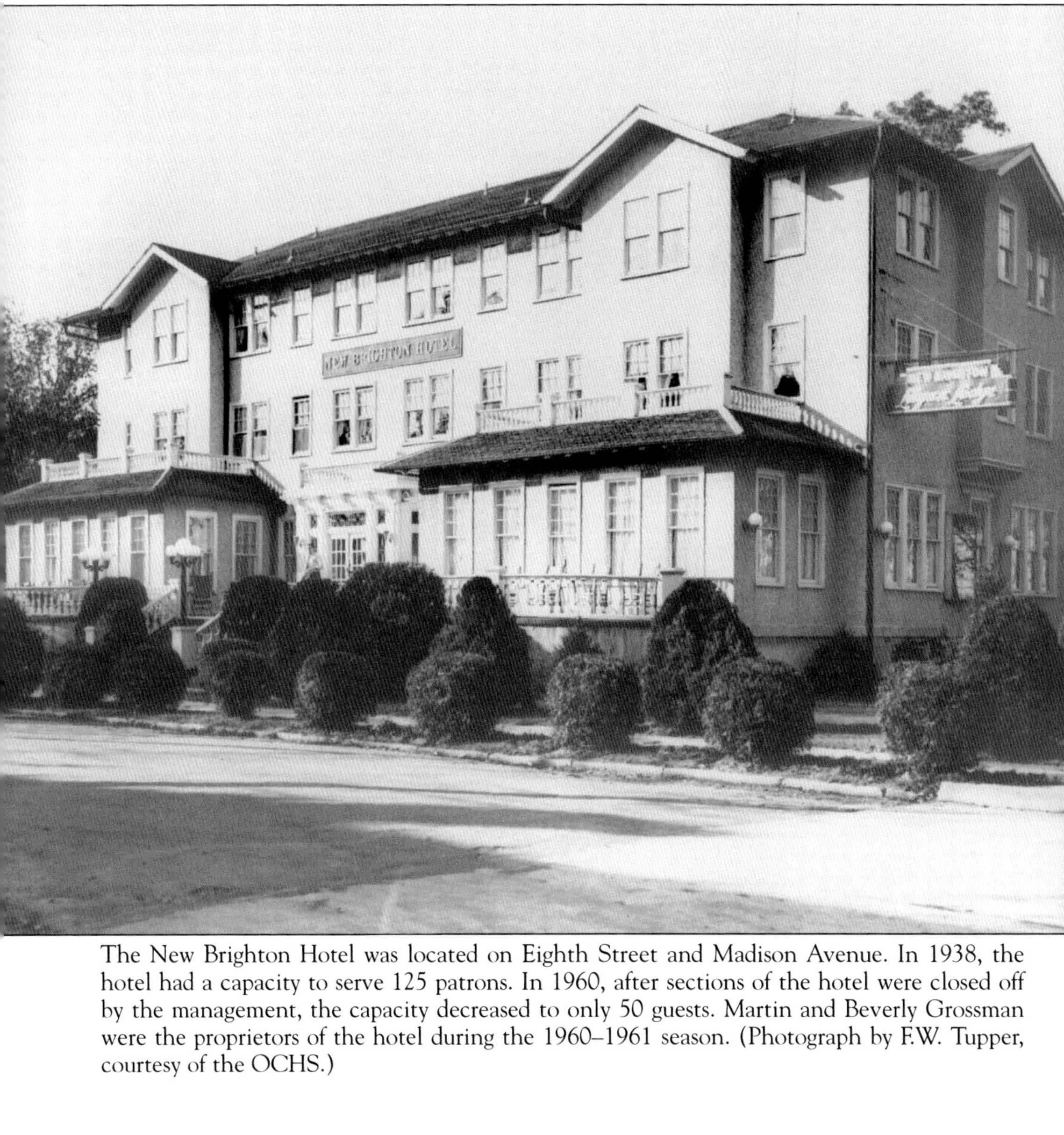

The New Brighton Hotel was located on Eighth Street and Madison Avenue. In 1938, the hotel had a capacity to serve 125 patrons. In 1960, after sections of the hotel were closed off by the management, the capacity decreased to only 50 guests. Martin and Beverly Grossman were the proprietors of the hotel during the 1960–1961 season. (Photograph by F.W. Tupper, courtesy of the OCHS.)

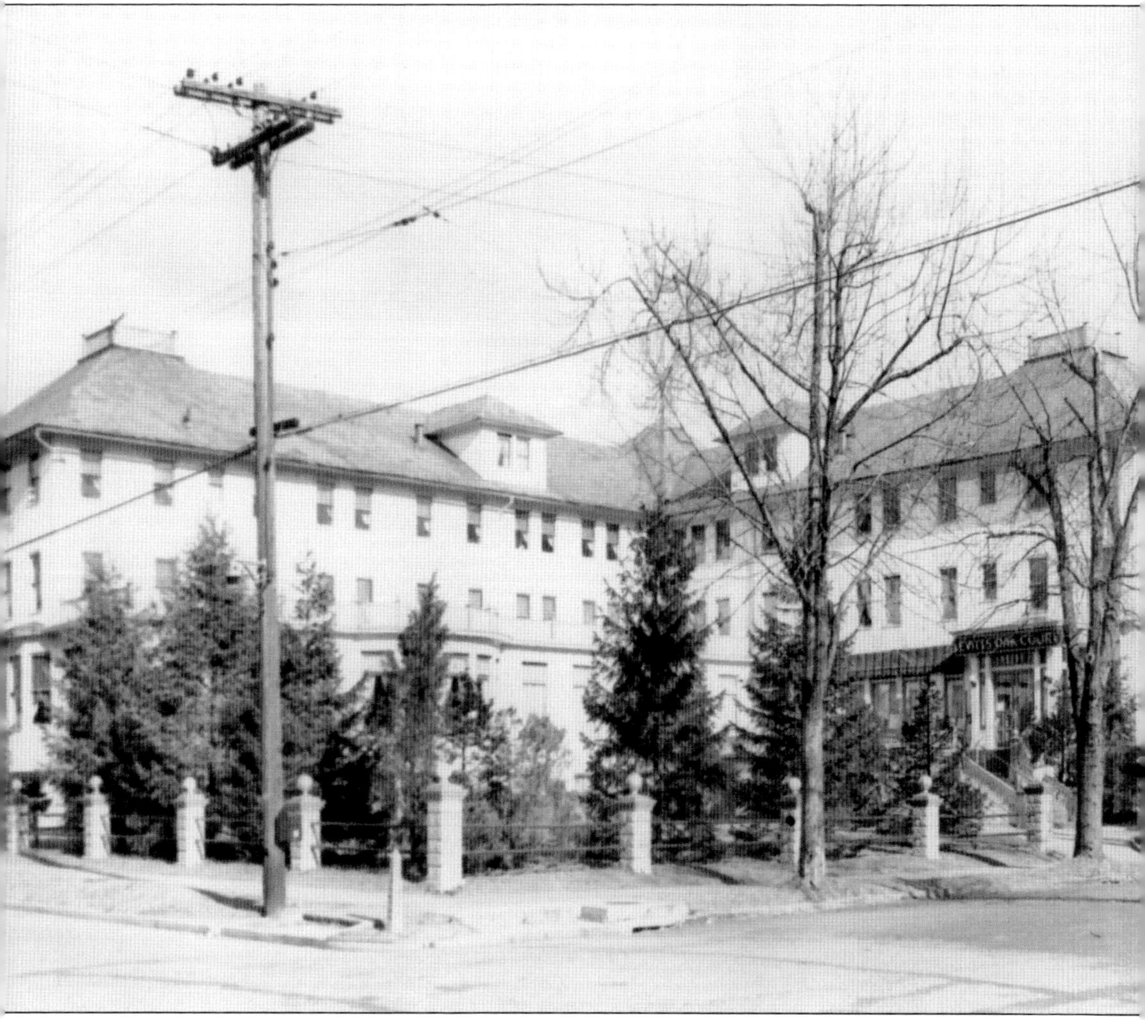

Oak Court was constructed *c.* 1900. The hotel was located on Lexington Avenue and Third Street. Like most of the Lakewood hotels, the capacity of Oak Court decreased over time. In 1901, the hotel could accommodate up to 200 guests and in 1960, it could hold slightly over 100. The most notable feature of Oak Court was its famous Sun Parlor, which was over 100 feet long. Oak Court was razed and cleared during the 1970s. (Photograph by F.W. Tupper, courtesy of the OCHS.)

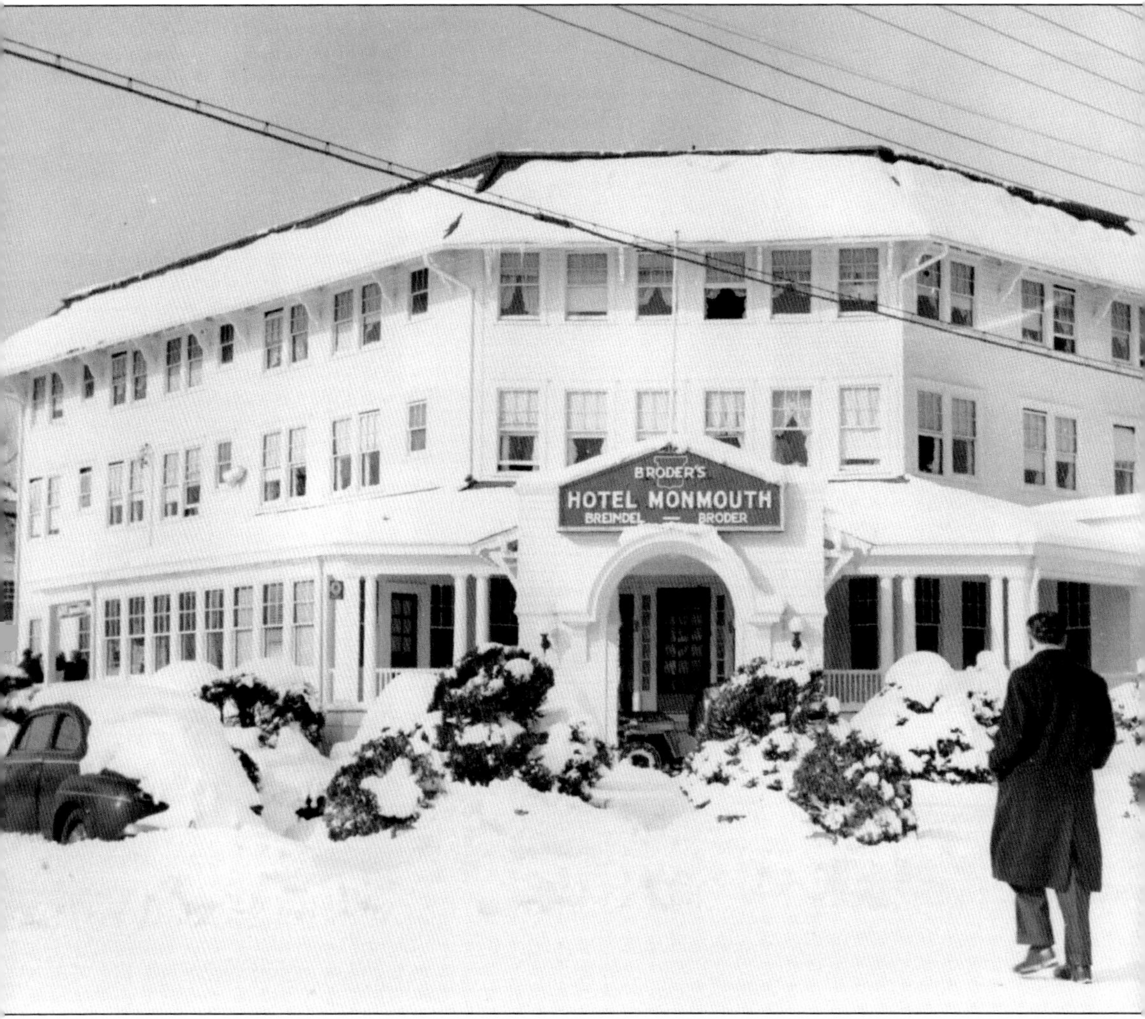

A patron of the Hotel Monmouth tracks through the winter scenery in hopes of warming up inside the building's lobby. The Hotel Monmouth was located on the corner of Monmouth Avenue and Seventh Street. The Breindel and Broder families were serving as proprietors when this picture of the hotel was taken. (Photograph by F.W. Tupper, courtesy of the OCHS.)

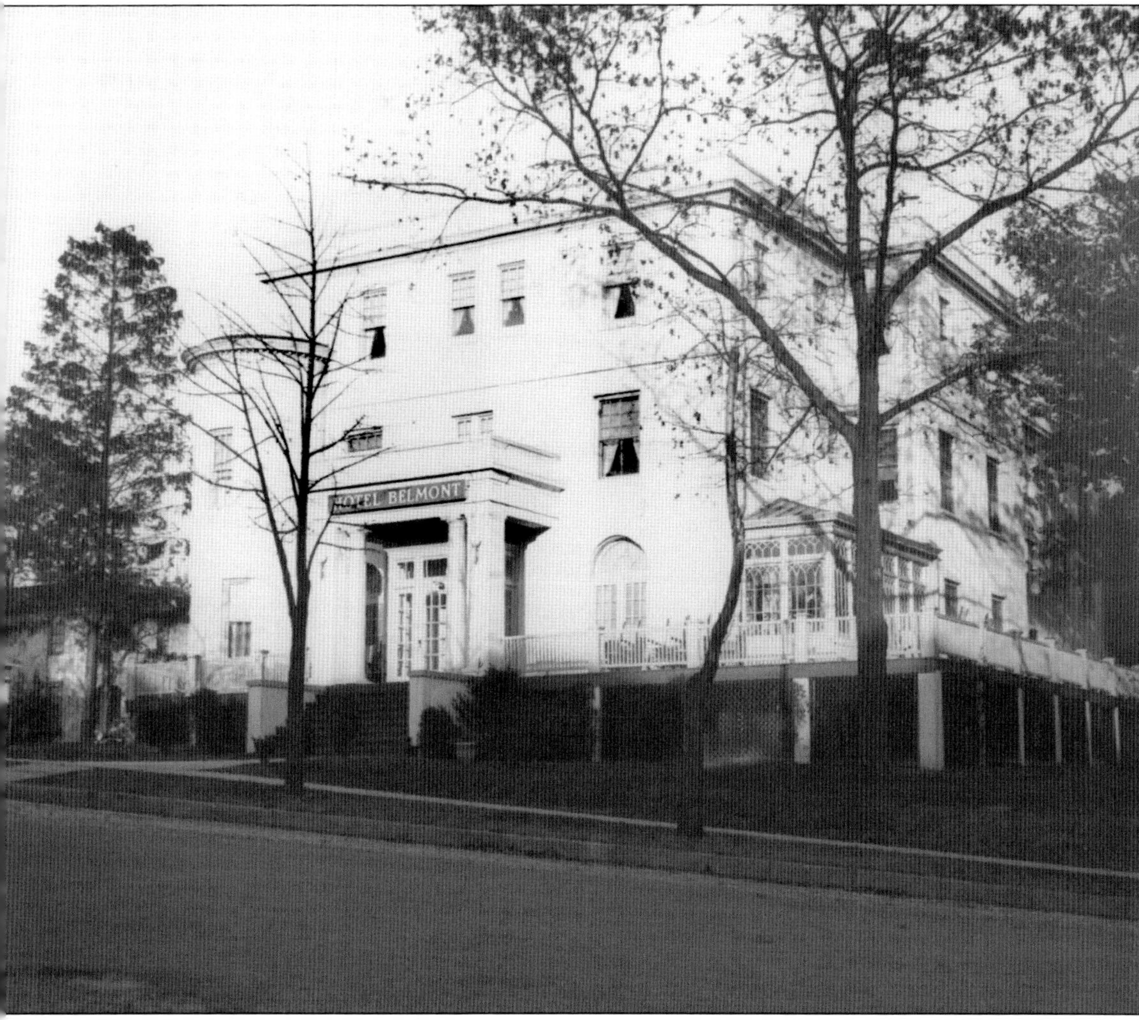

The Hotel Belmont overlooked the aesthetically pleasing scenery of Forest Avenue and Sixth Street. The building's peaceful location made it a prime resting spot for those looking for a quiet getaway. Many famous entertainers, including comedian Jerry Lewis, frequented the Hotel Belmont. (Photograph courtesy of the OCHS.)

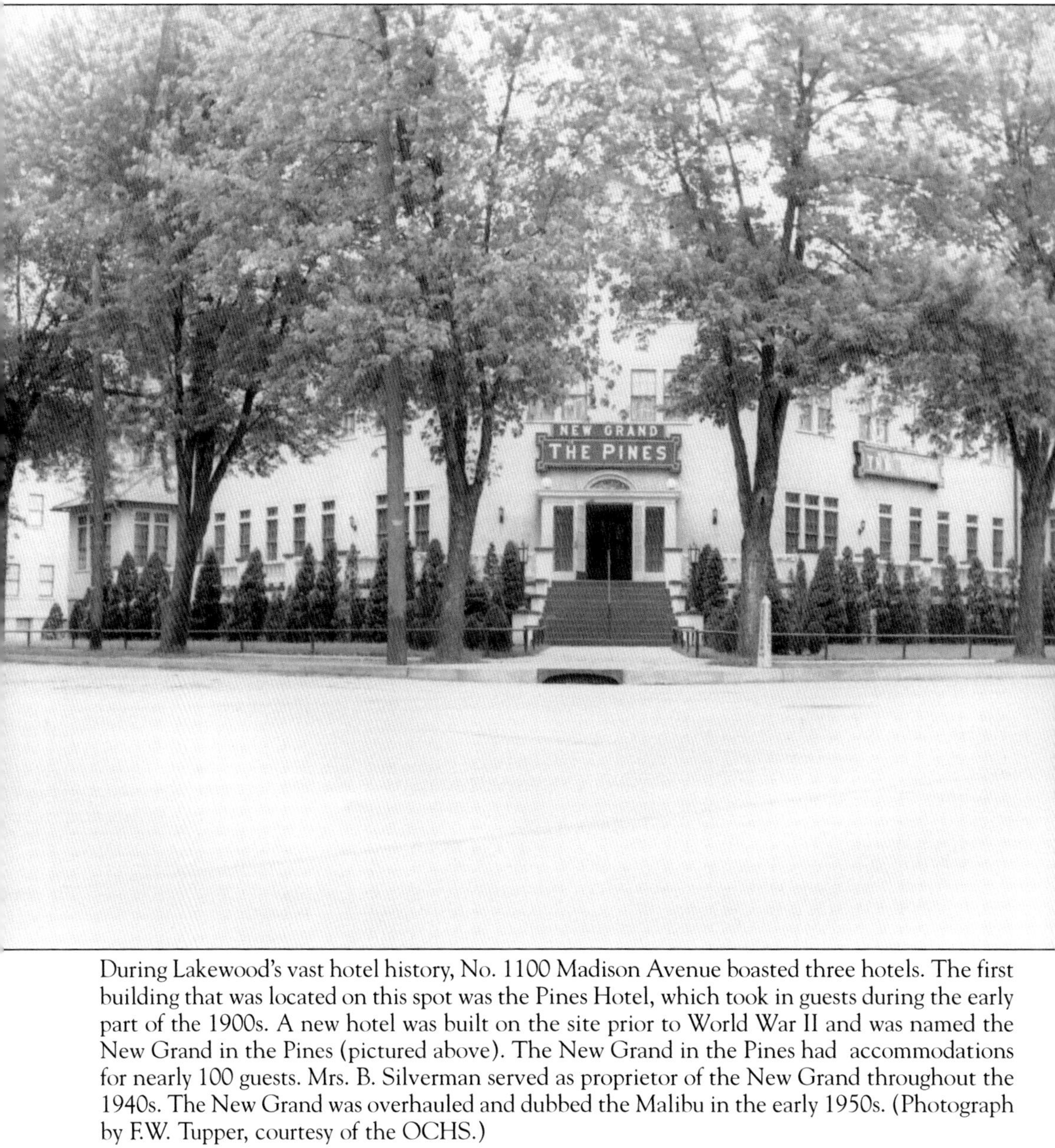

During Lakewood's vast hotel history, No. 1100 Madison Avenue boasted three hotels. The first building that was located on this spot was the Pines Hotel, which took in guests during the early part of the 1900s. A new hotel was built on the site prior to World War II and was named the New Grand in the Pines (pictured above). The New Grand in the Pines had accommodations for nearly 100 guests. Mrs. B. Silverman served as proprietor of the New Grand throughout the 1940s. The New Grand was overhauled and dubbed the Malibu in the early 1950s. (Photograph by F.W. Tupper, courtesy of the OCHS.)

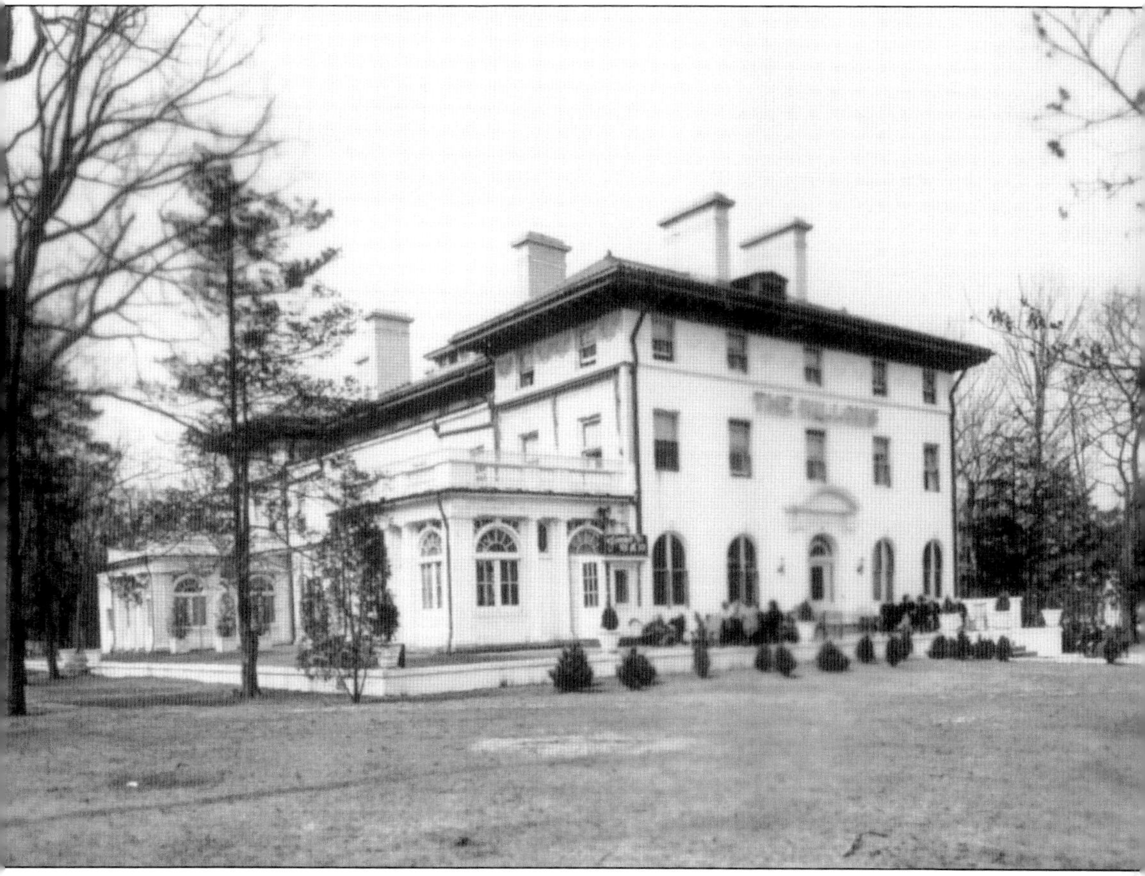

The Willows was located on Forest Avenue and Eighth Street. Before it became a hotel, the structure was the private home of the Willock family, who had made their fortune in the Pittsburgh steel industry. Milton Cohen and Sylvia Bakst managed the hotel, which in 1960 had the capacity to hold up to 300 guests. (Photograph courtesy of the OCHS.)

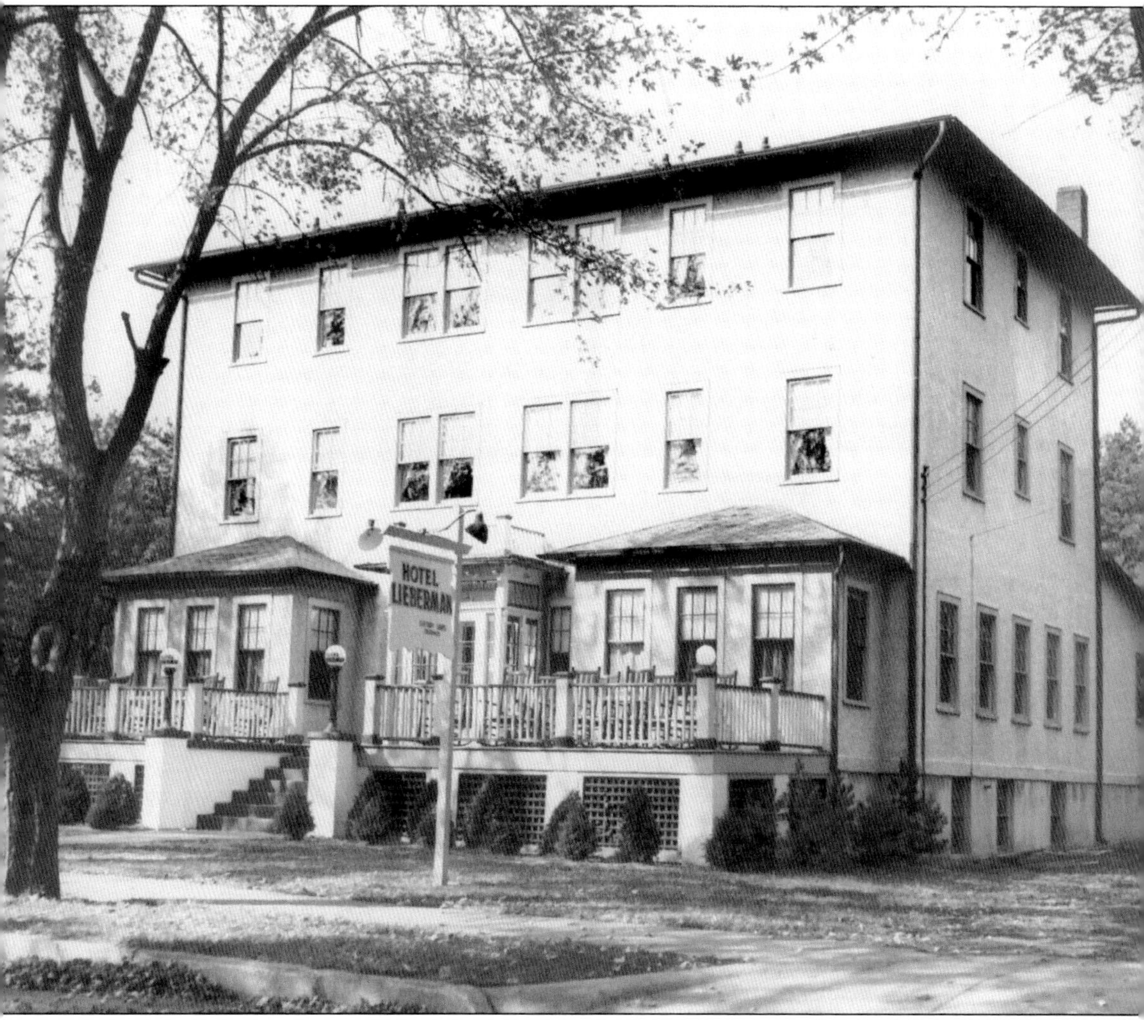

This picture of the Hotel Lieberman was taken during the autumn of 1936. The hotel was located on Madison Avenue and Ninth Street. In the mid-1930s, it had the capacity to hold 75 guests. Some 25 years later, *c.* 1960, the hotel expanded to accommodate up to 100 guests. (Photograph by F.W. Tupper, courtesy of the OCHS.)

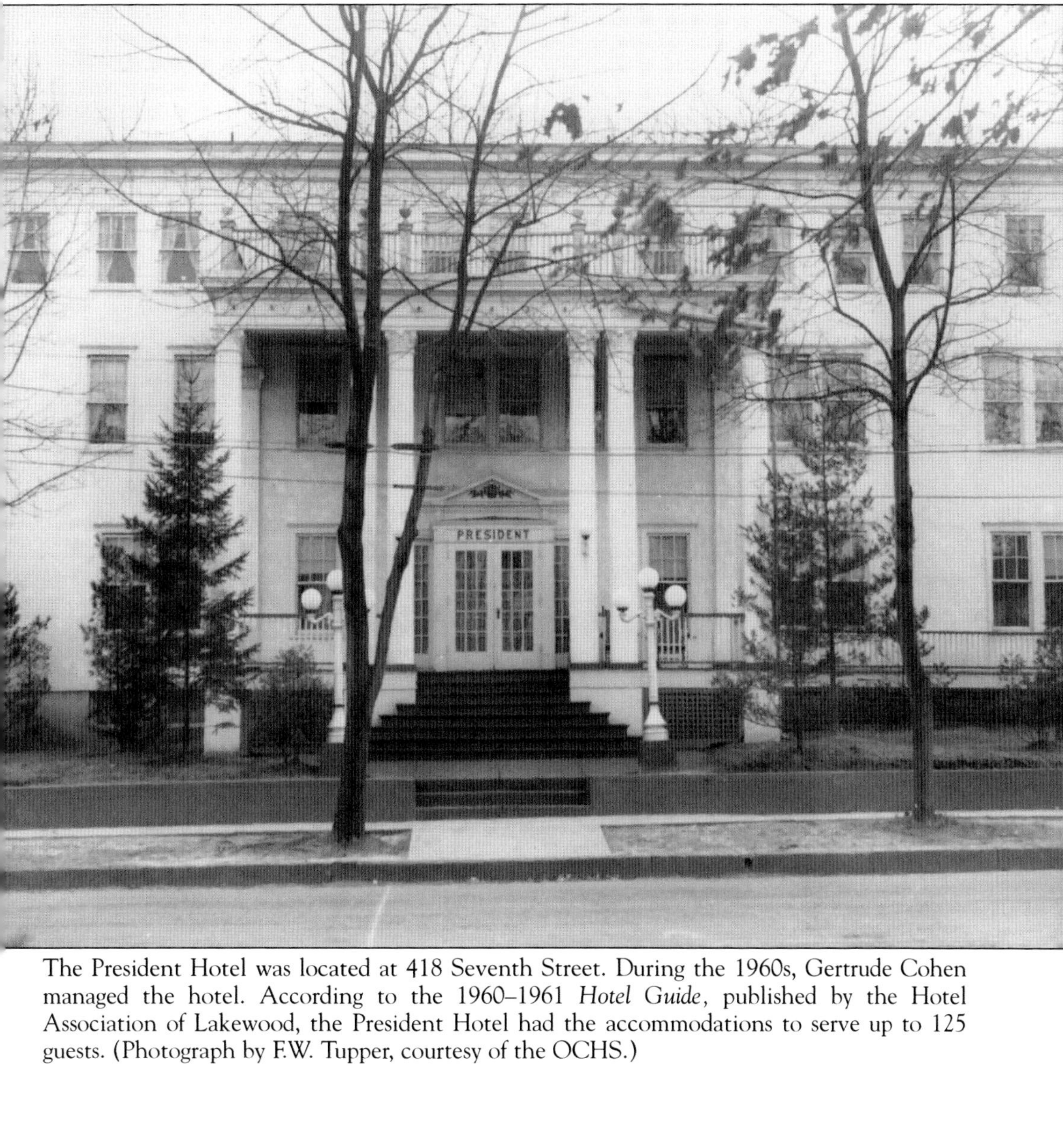

The President Hotel was located at 418 Seventh Street. During the 1960s, Gertrude Cohen managed the hotel. According to the 1960–1961 *Hotel Guide*, published by the Hotel Association of Lakewood, the President Hotel had the accommodations to serve up to 125 guests. (Photograph by F.W. Tupper, courtesy of the OCHS.)

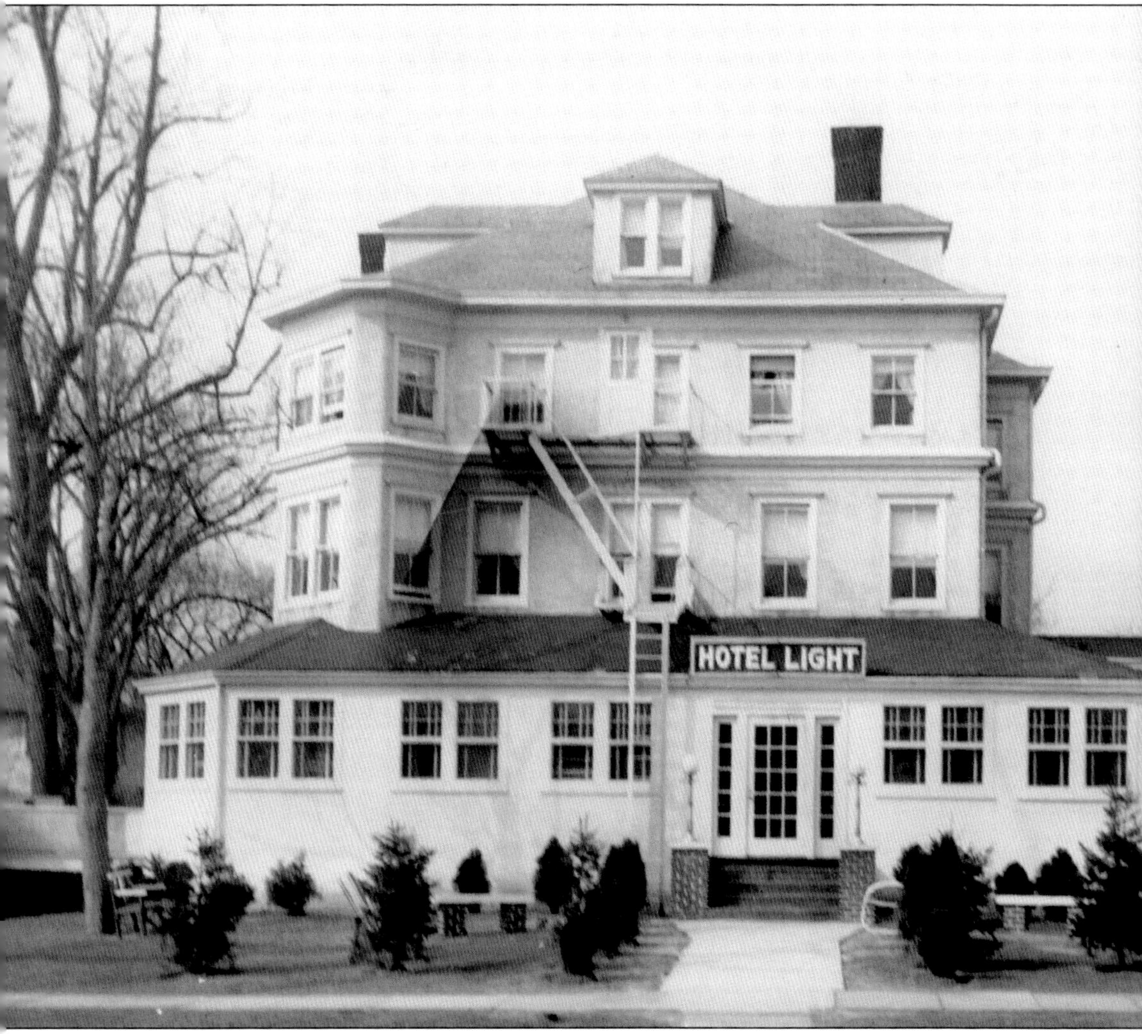

Hotel Light was located at 68 Madison Avenue. The structure, before becoming Hotel Light, was known as Lilyan Lodge. The hotel had the capacity to hold 75 patrons. (Photograph courtesy of the OCHS.)

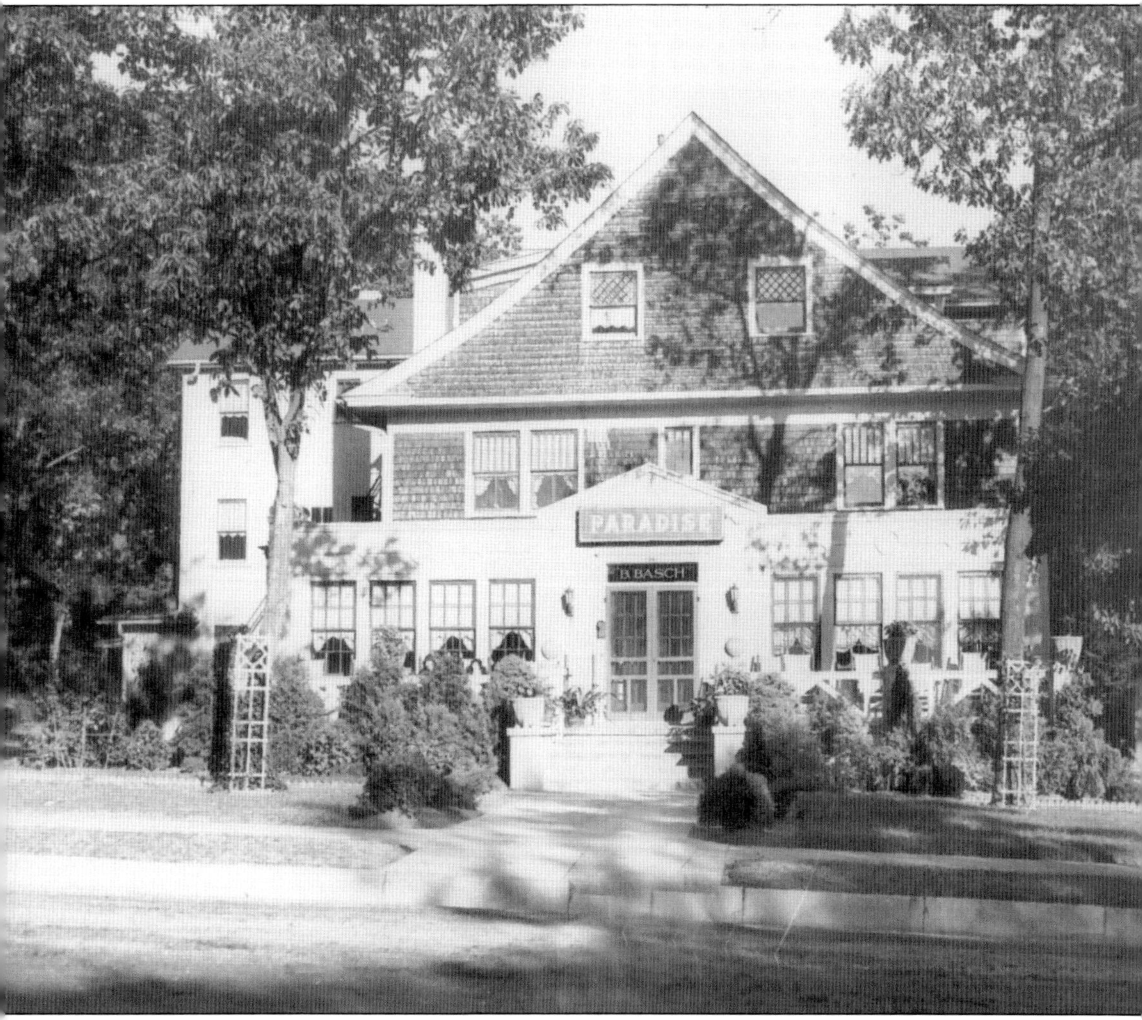

The Paradise Hotel was located at 505 Forest Avenue. B. Basch managed the facility, which had accommodations to handle close to 90 guests. (Photograph by F.W. Tupper, courtesy of the OCHS.)

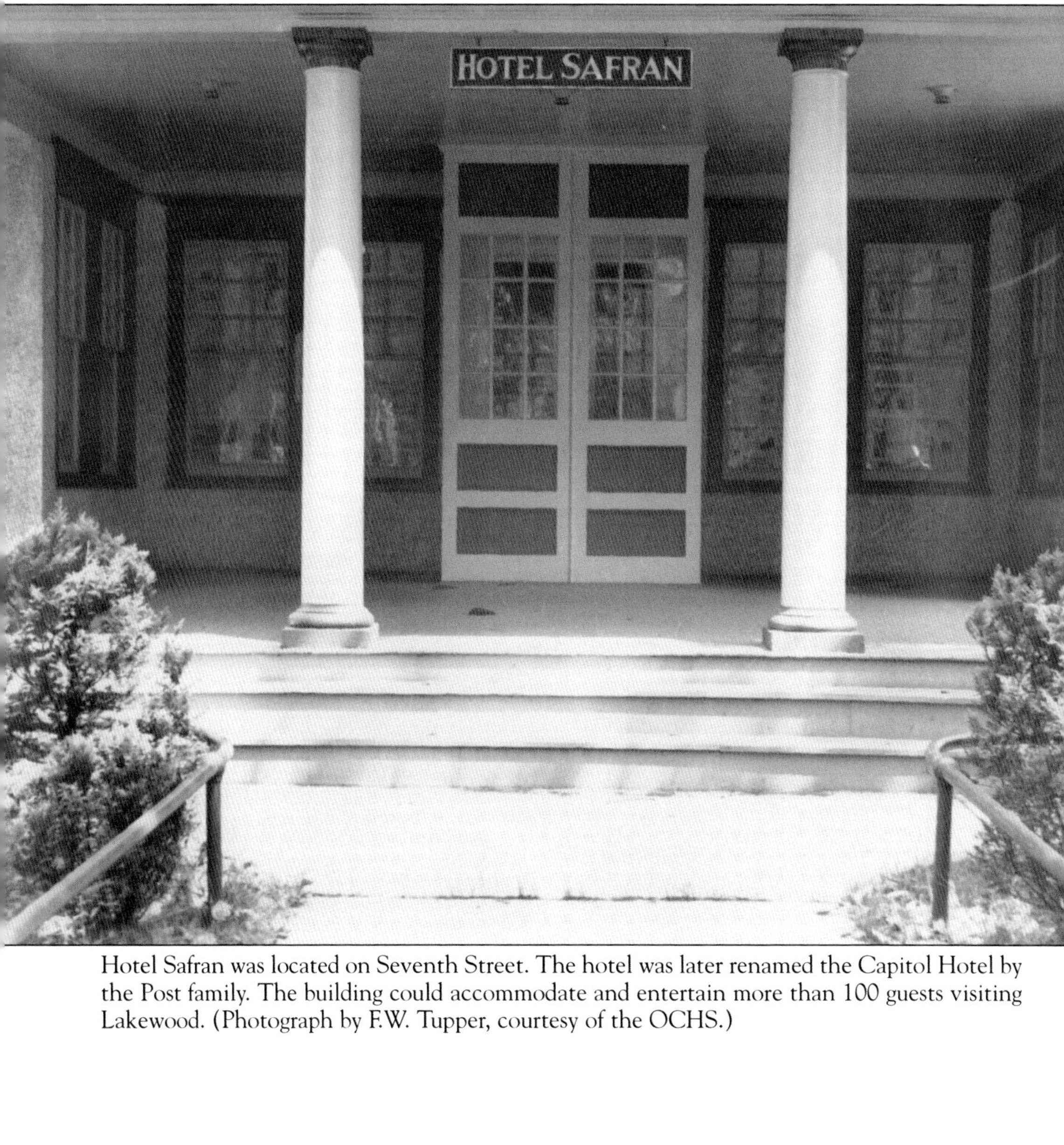

Hotel Safran was located on Seventh Street. The hotel was later renamed the Capitol Hotel by the Post family. The building could accommodate and entertain more than 100 guests visiting Lakewood. (Photograph by F.W. Tupper, courtesy of the OCHS.)

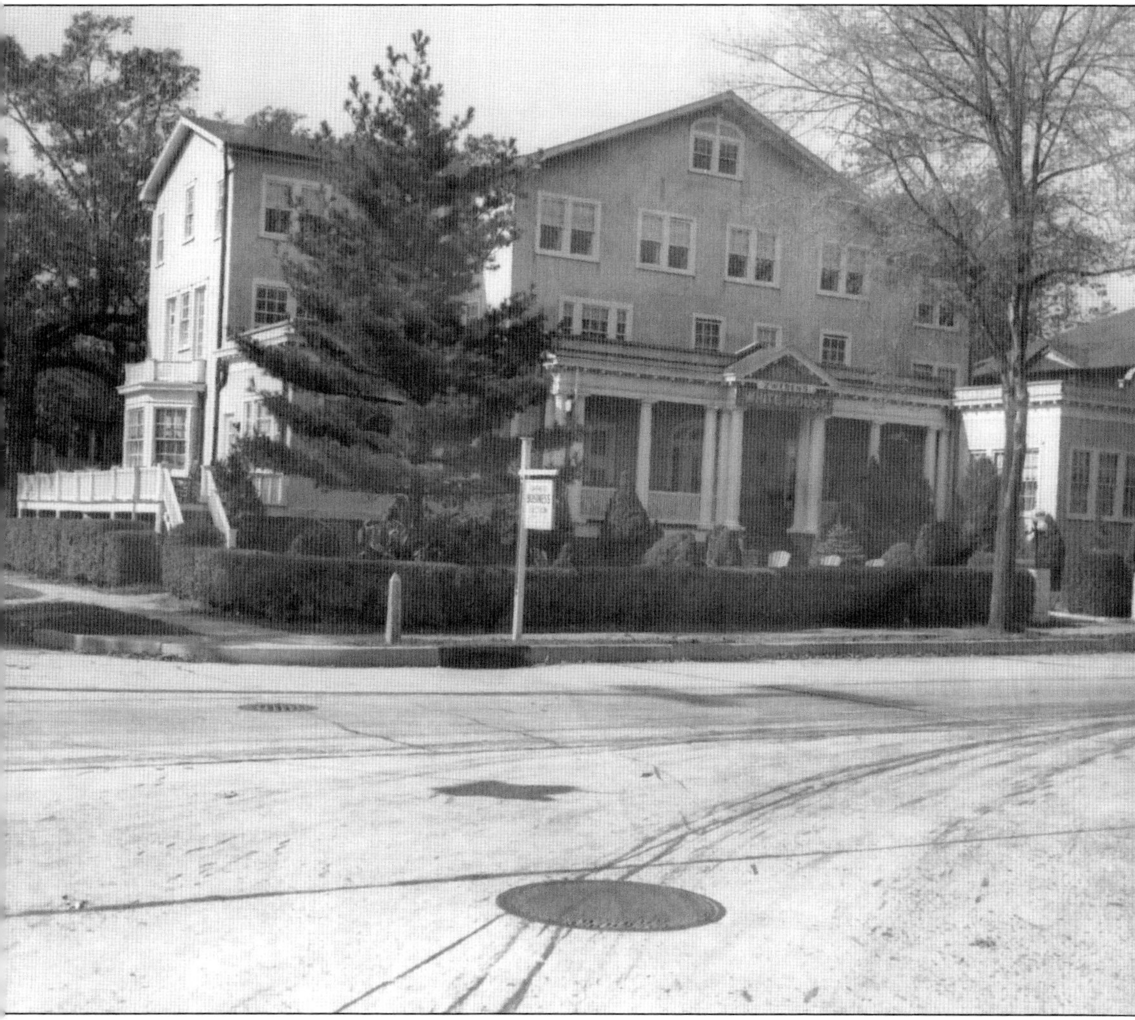

Zwebens White House was located on Madison Avenue. Sam Zweben incorporated the hotel in 1926. The White House was located within walking distance of the downtown business section of Lakewood. (Photograph by F.W. Tupper, courtesy of the OCHS.)

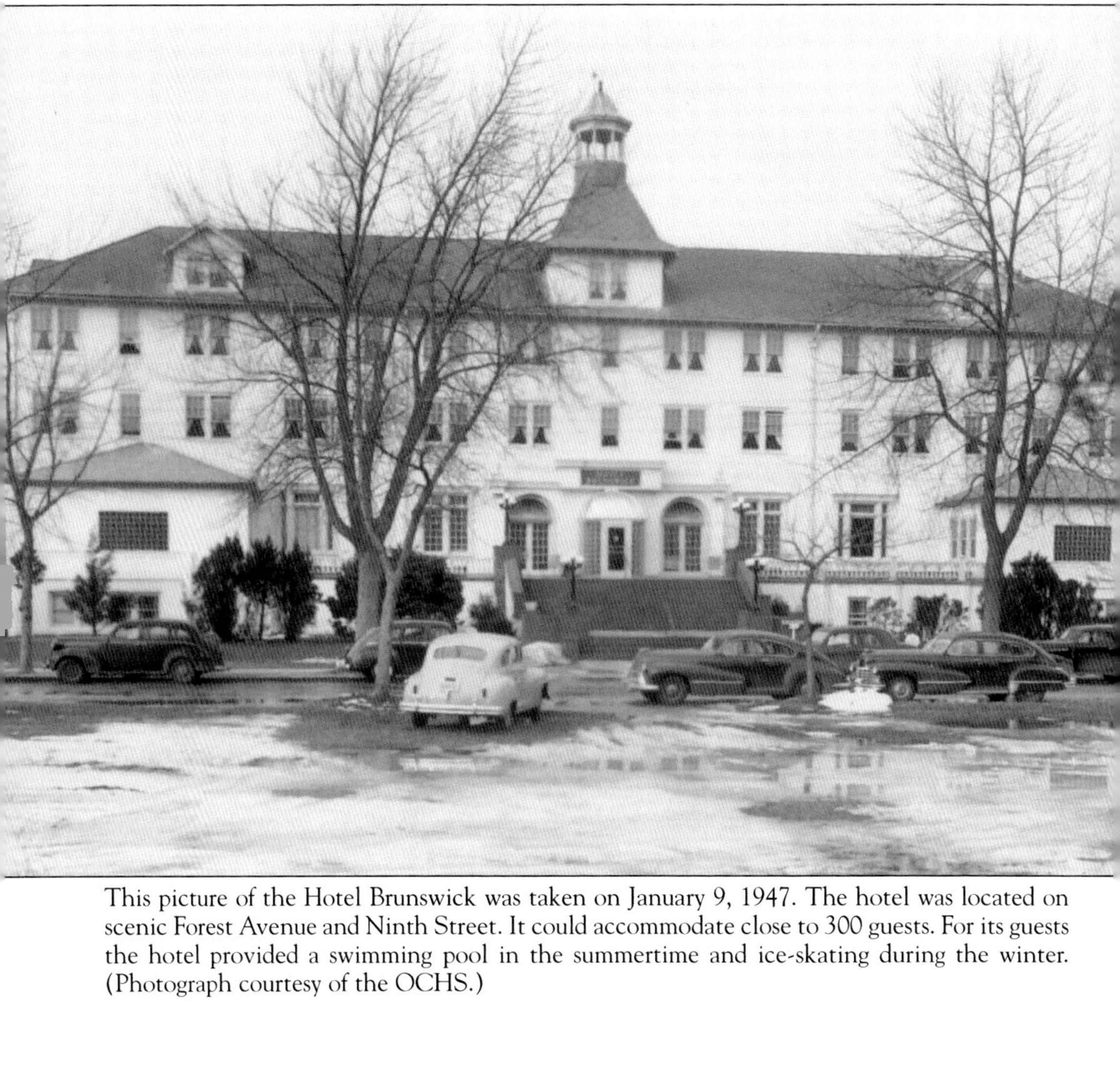

This picture of the Hotel Brunswick was taken on January 9, 1947. The hotel was located on scenic Forest Avenue and Ninth Street. It could accommodate close to 300 guests. For its guests the hotel provided a swimming pool in the summertime and ice-skating during the winter. (Photograph courtesy of the OCHS.)

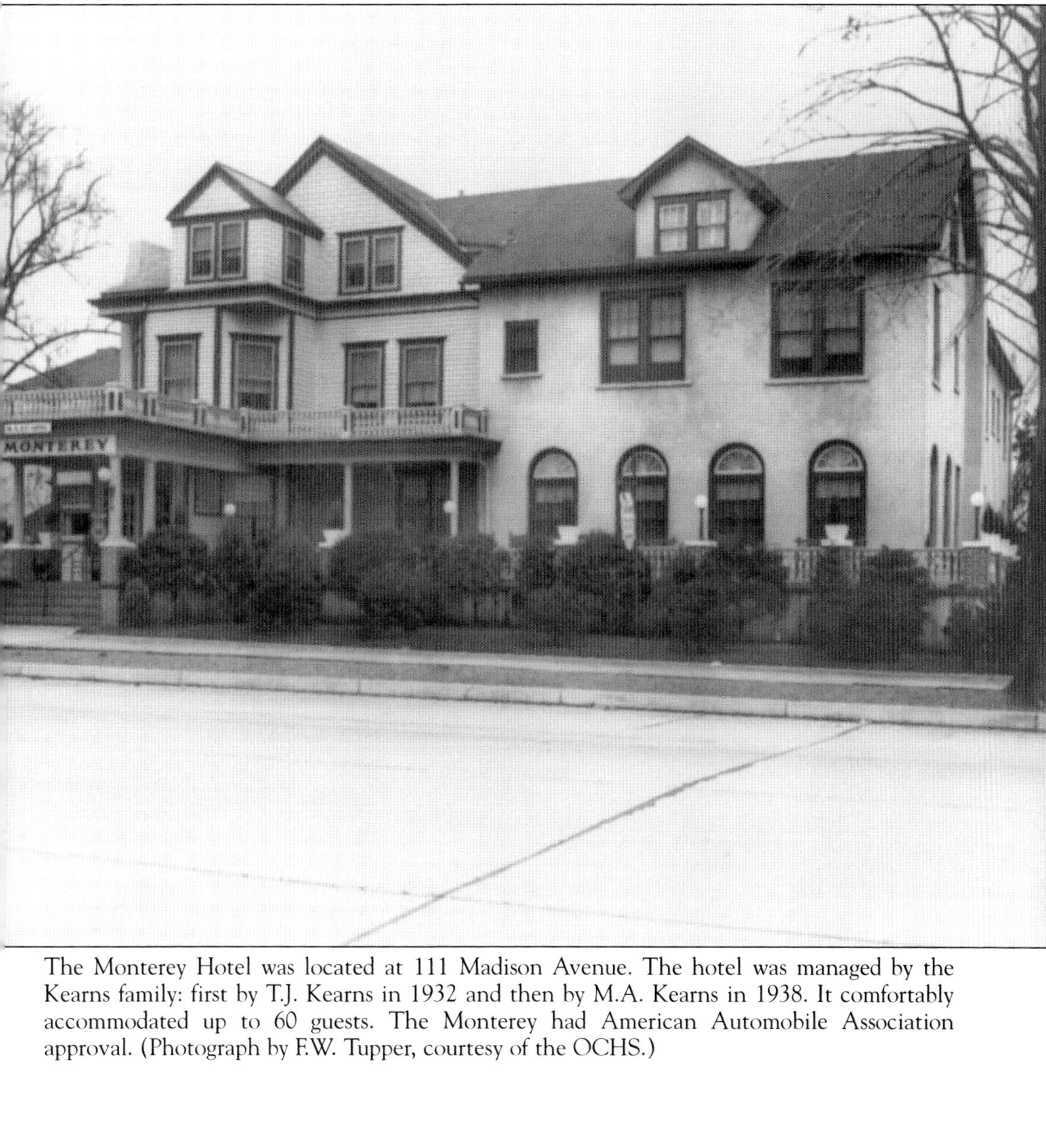

The Monterey Hotel was located at 111 Madison Avenue. The hotel was managed by the Kearns family: first by T.J. Kearns in 1932 and then by M.A. Kearns in 1938. It comfortably accommodated up to 60 guests. The Monterey had American Automobile Association approval. (Photograph by F.W. Tupper, courtesy of the OCHS.)

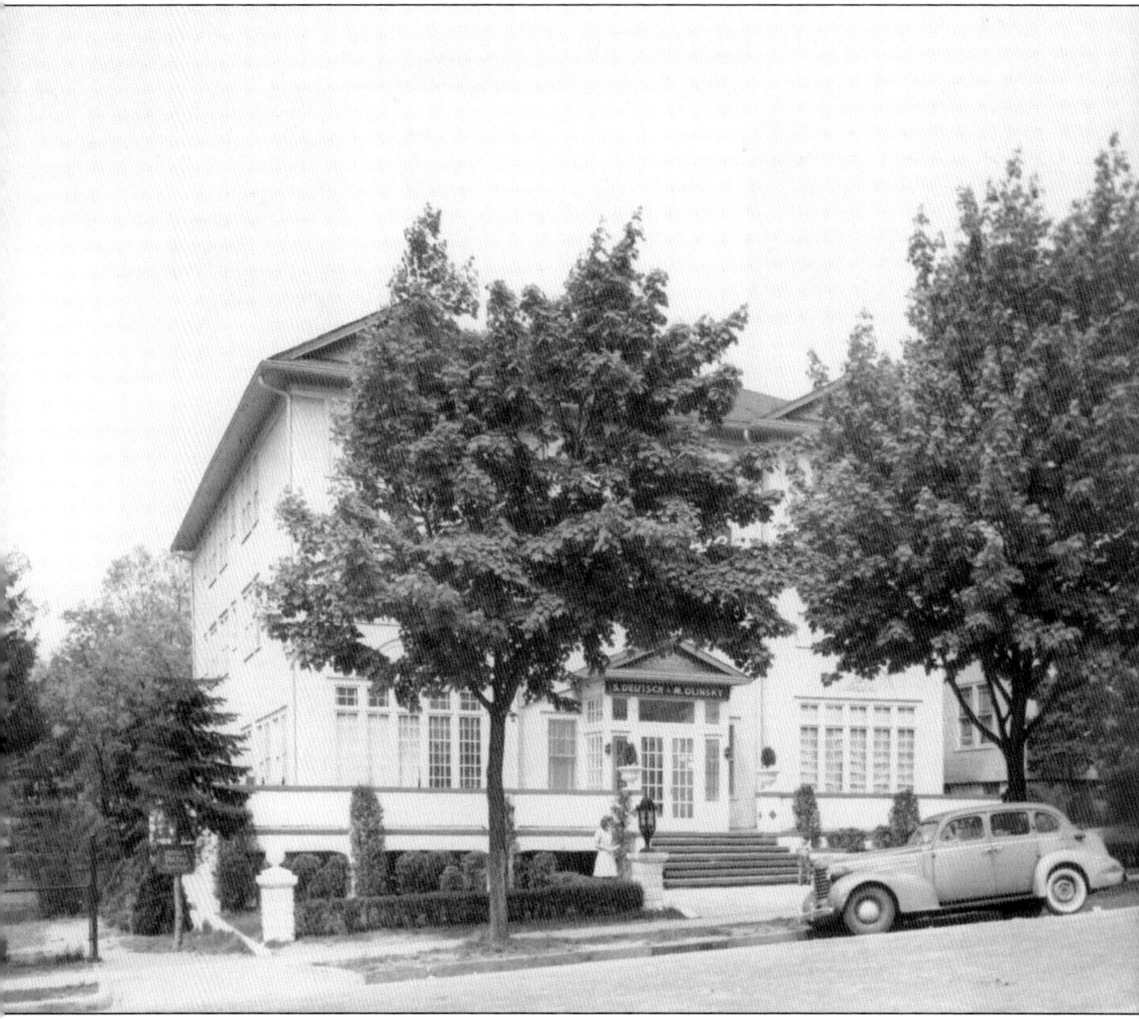

This picture of the Lilyan Lodge was taken on May 13, 1944. The building was located at 512 Forest Avenue and the corner of Fifth Street. Mr. Deutsch and Mr. Olinsky served as the proprietors of the business during 1944. The Lilyan Lodge could serve up to 100 patrons. (Photograph by F.W. Tupper, courtesy of the OCHS.)

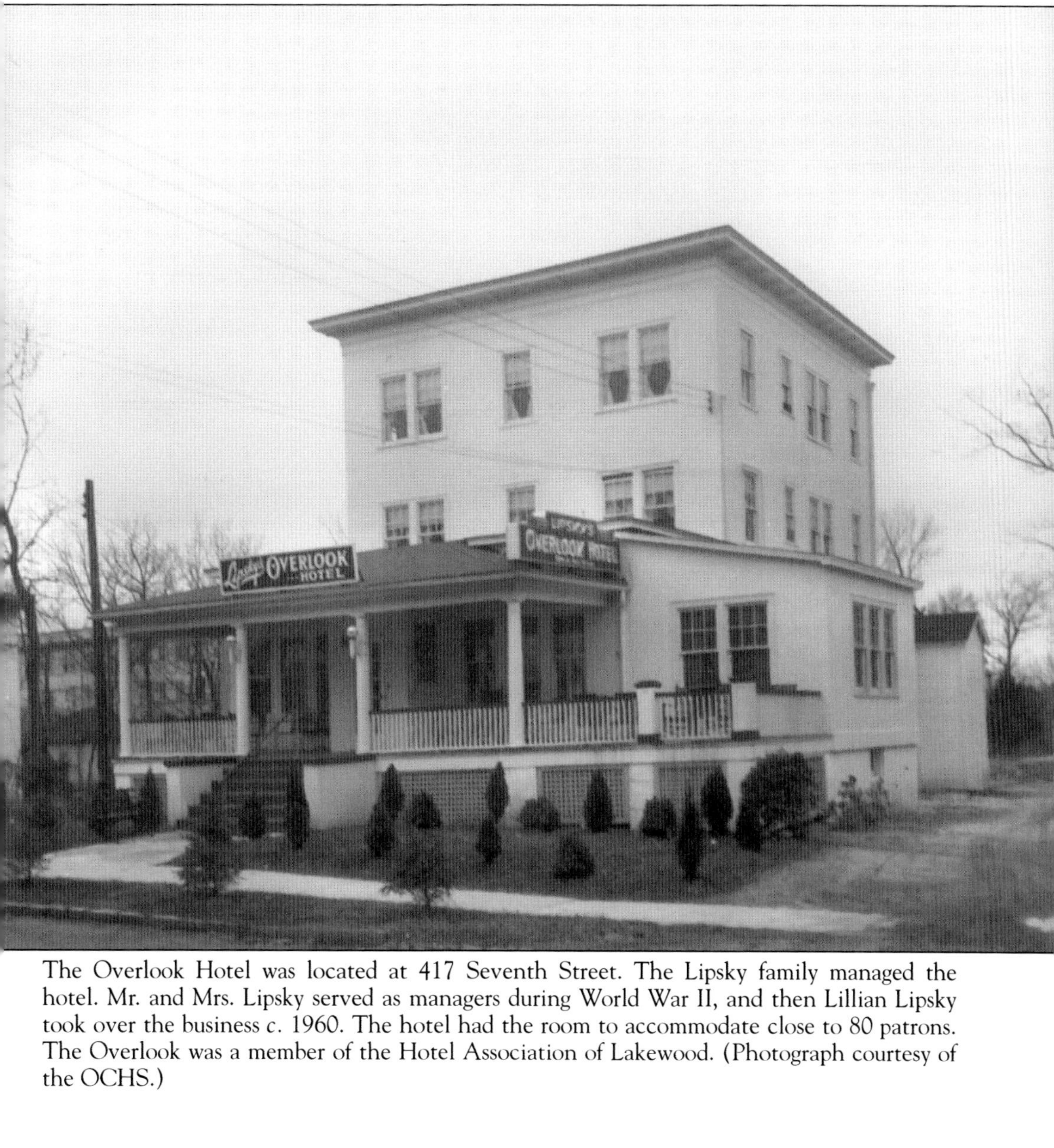

The Overlook Hotel was located at 417 Seventh Street. The Lipsky family managed the hotel. Mr. and Mrs. Lipsky served as managers during World War II, and then Lillian Lipsky took over the business c. 1960. The hotel had the room to accommodate close to 80 patrons. The Overlook was a member of the Hotel Association of Lakewood. (Photograph courtesy of the OCHS.)

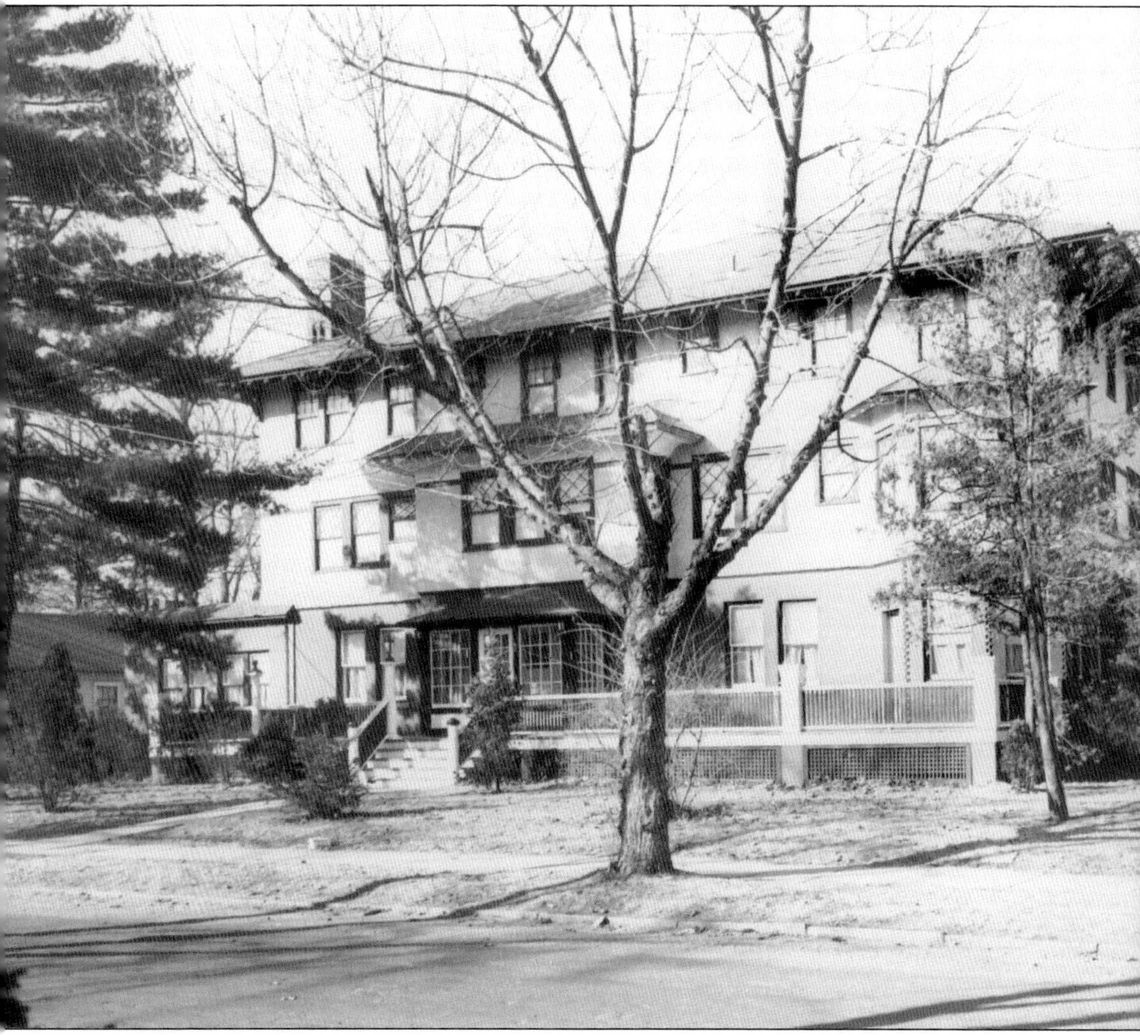

The Plaza Hotel was located on Seventh Street and Clifton Avenue. The New York Giants Baseball Club stayed at the Plaza during spring training days in town, when they played on the baseball diamonds at the Rockefeller Estate on Ocean Avenue. (Photograph by F.W. Tupper, courtesy of the OCHS.)

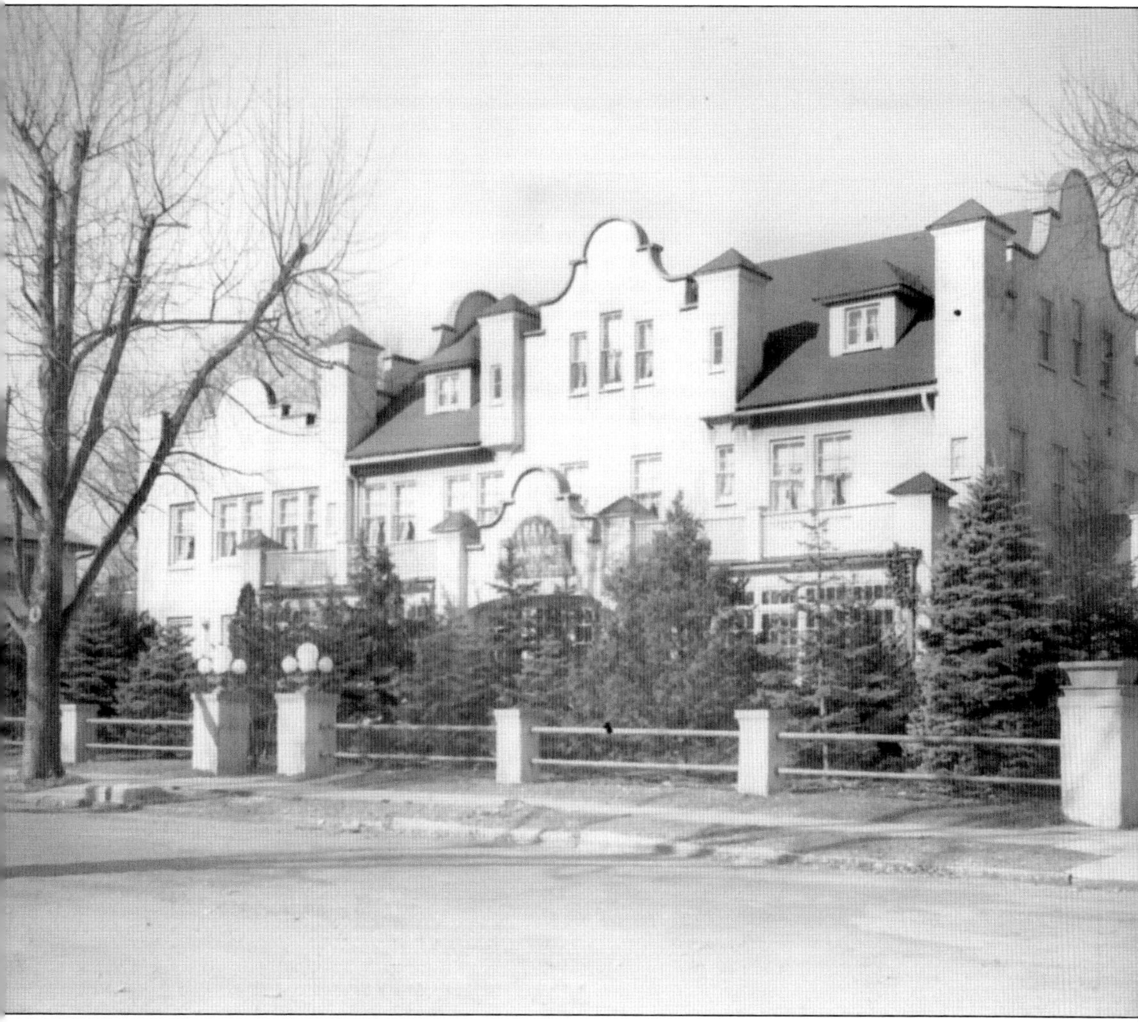

The Grand Hungarian Hotel was located on Monmouth Avenue and Third Street. The architecture of the hotel made it one of the most unique and aesthetically pleasing sites in town. (Photograph courtesy of the OCHS.)

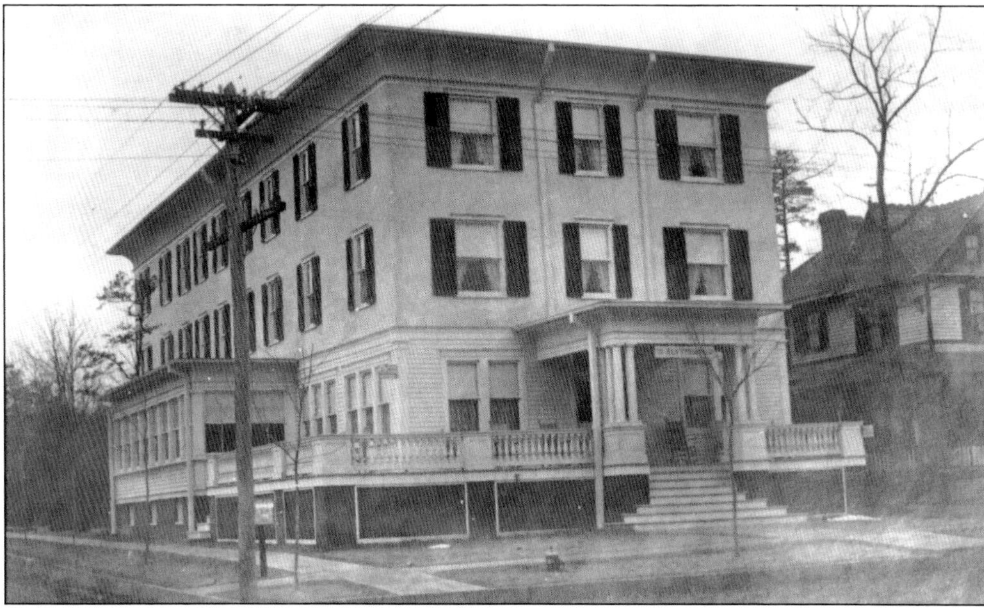

This picture of the Blythewood Hotel was taken during the summer of 1937. The Blythewood was located at 600 Monmouth Avenue and the corner of Sixth Street. The hotel had the capacity to serve up to 150 guests. (Photograph courtesy of the OCHS.)

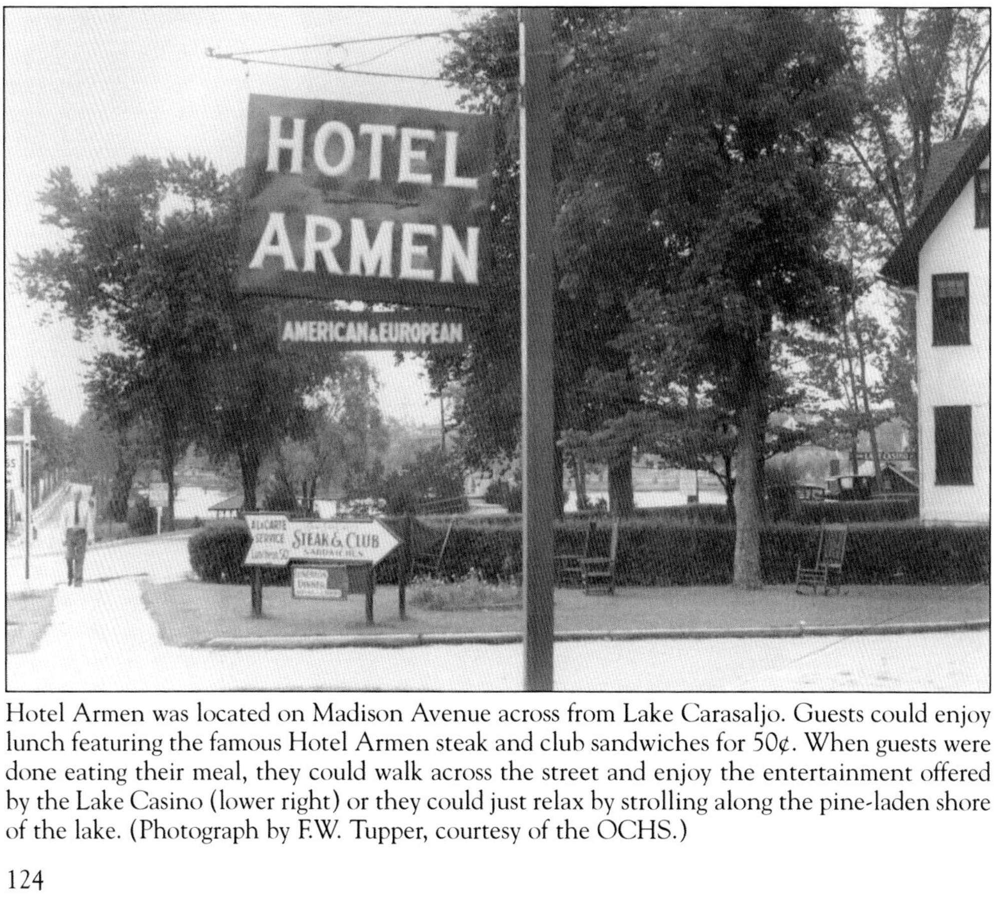

Hotel Armen was located on Madison Avenue across from Lake Carasaljo. Guests could enjoy lunch featuring the famous Hotel Armen steak and club sandwiches for 50¢. When guests were done eating their meal, they could walk across the street and enjoy the entertainment offered by the Lake Casino (lower right) or they could just relax by strolling along the pine-laden shore of the lake. (Photograph by F.W. Tupper, courtesy of the OCHS.)

Five

LAKEWOOD TODAY

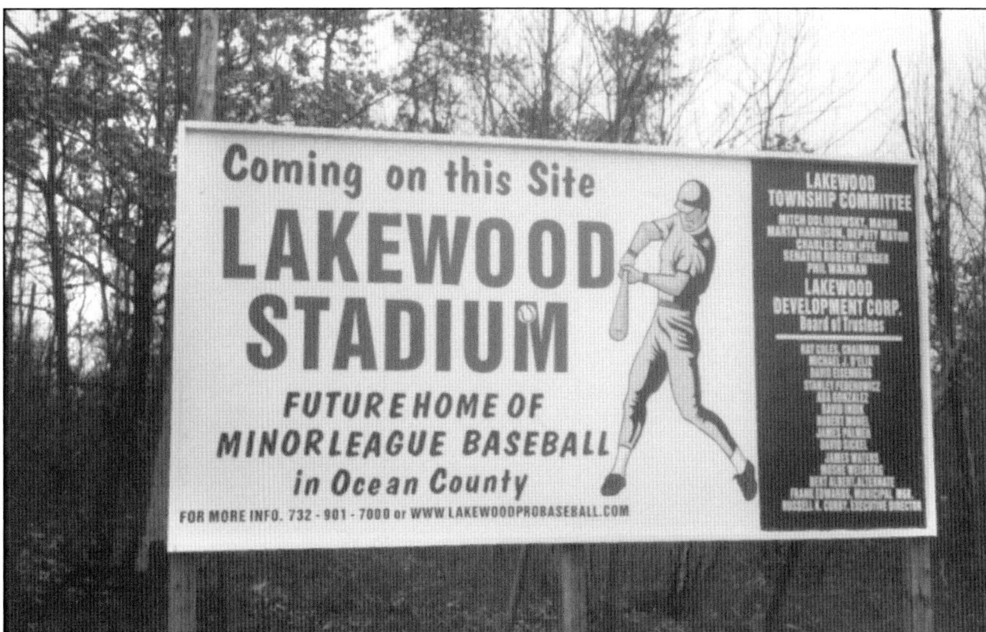

Lakewood Stadium, is scheduled to open for the spring 2001 baseball season. A $20 million facility, the stadium is to be the home of the minor league Lakewood Blueclaws. The Blueclaws, an affiliate of the Philadelphia Phillies, are slated to compete in the Single-A South Atlantic League.

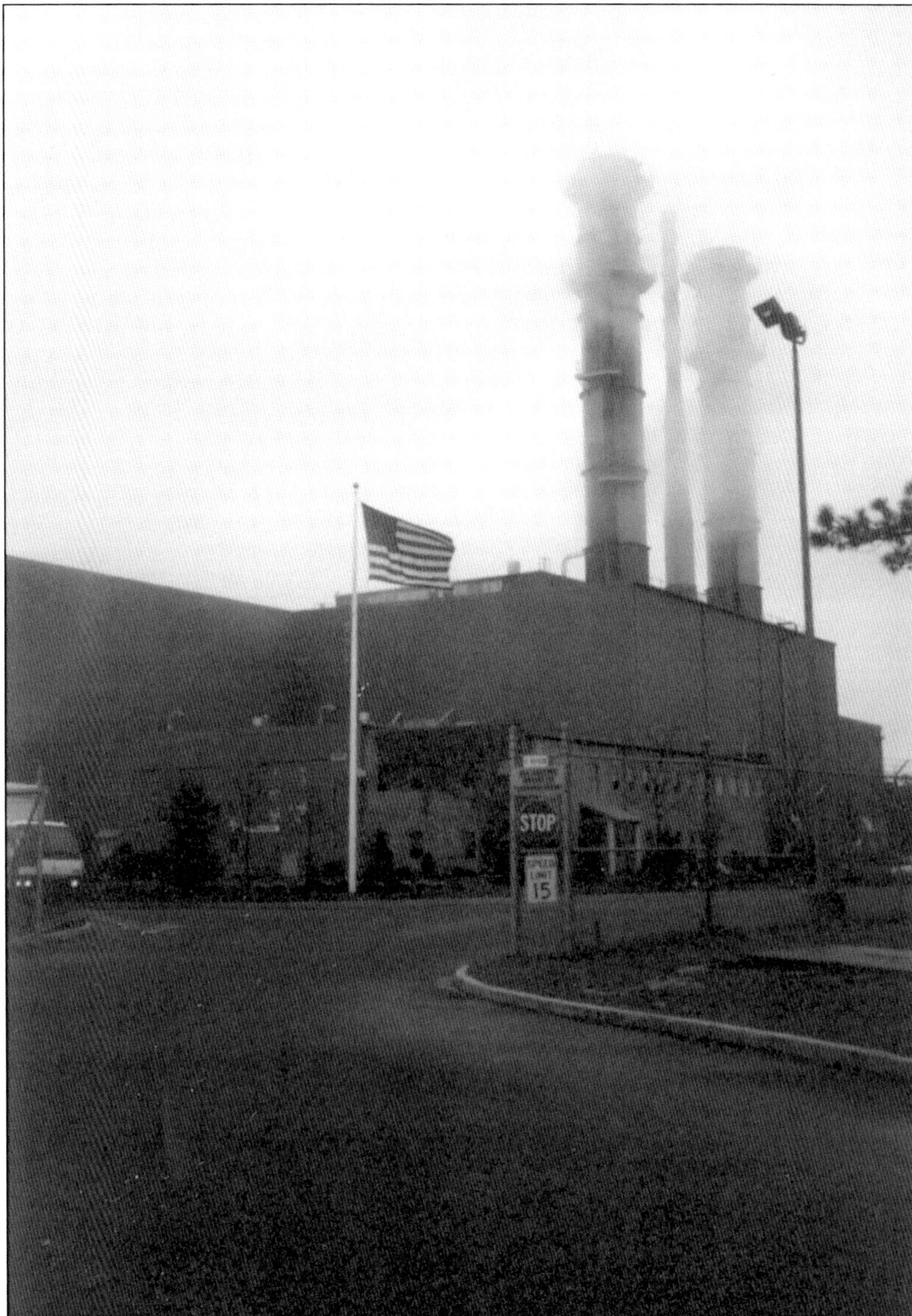

The Lakewood Cogeneration facility produces an abundant amount of electricity to power some 20,000 homes throughout the county and beyond. The facility produces steam and electricity through the use of natural gas. The plant was opened in November 1994.

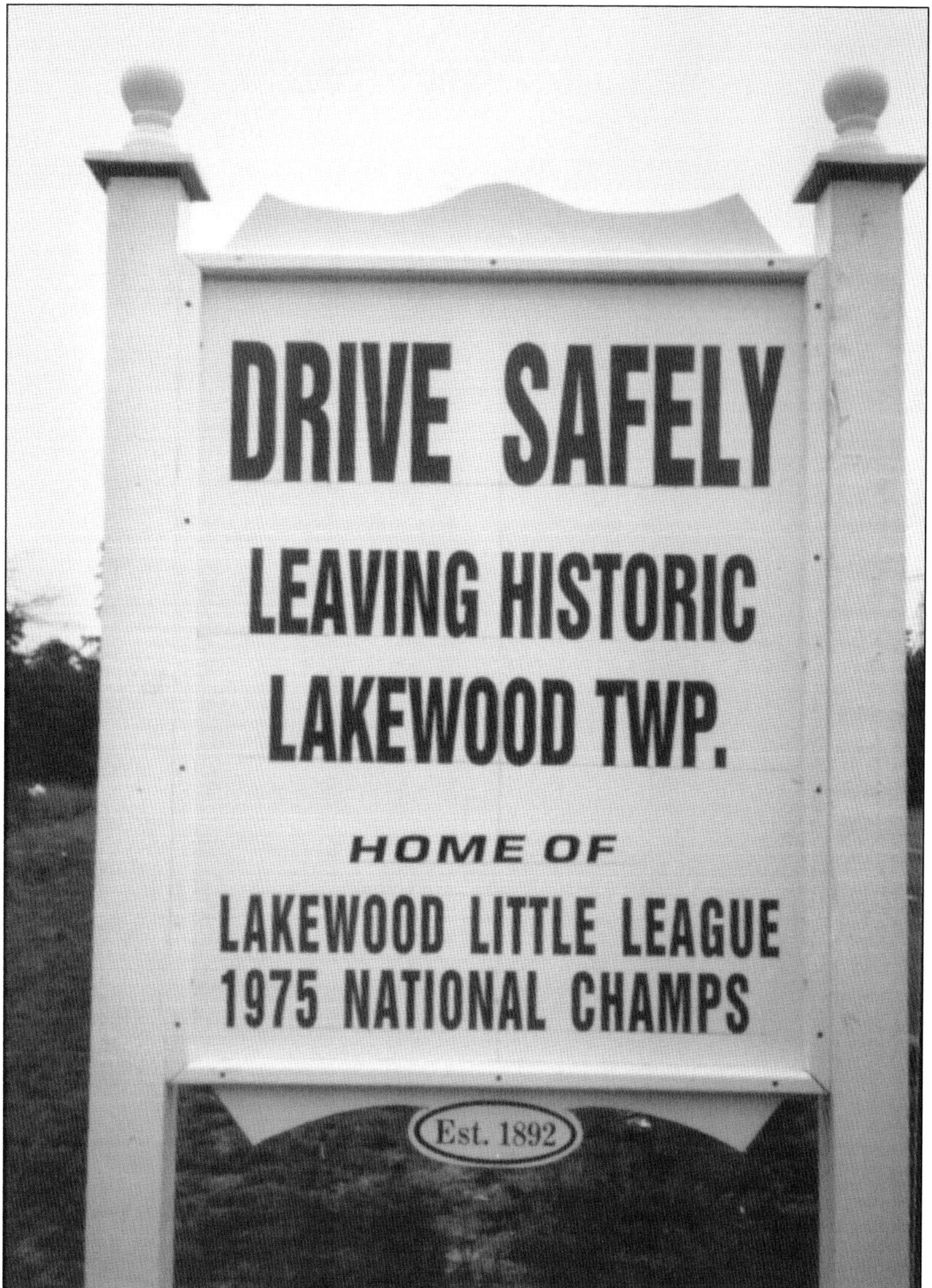

When Leaving Sunny Lakewood, I need no picture art to mind me of her beauties
They're folded in my heart.
Her loveliness hath made me whole—her peace hath filled my very soul.

—Selection from an advertisement brochure for the Laurel-in-the-Pines Hotel, c. 1900.

ACKNOWLEDGMENTS

I would first like to recognize Barbara Rivolta, Kathy Parente, and the Ocean County Historical Society (OCHS) for their outstanding efforts in the preservation of the historic photographs that you have just viewed. A majority of these images come from the photographic collection of Richard Steele and the negative collection of Fred W. Tupper. The Tupper collection came to the OCHS courtesy of Mary Hulbert. I would like to mention the following people for their selfless contributions to this work: Jill Katus, Betty Grant, Betsy Dudas, Leisa Clayton, Jack Van Etten, Pat Halpin, Dan Kozelnik, Al Platt, Irene Kozelnik, Matthew Bedell, and Richard Strickler. I would also like to commend the Lakewood Heritage Commission on its tireless effort to preserve one of the most historical and wonderful places in the state of New Jersey.